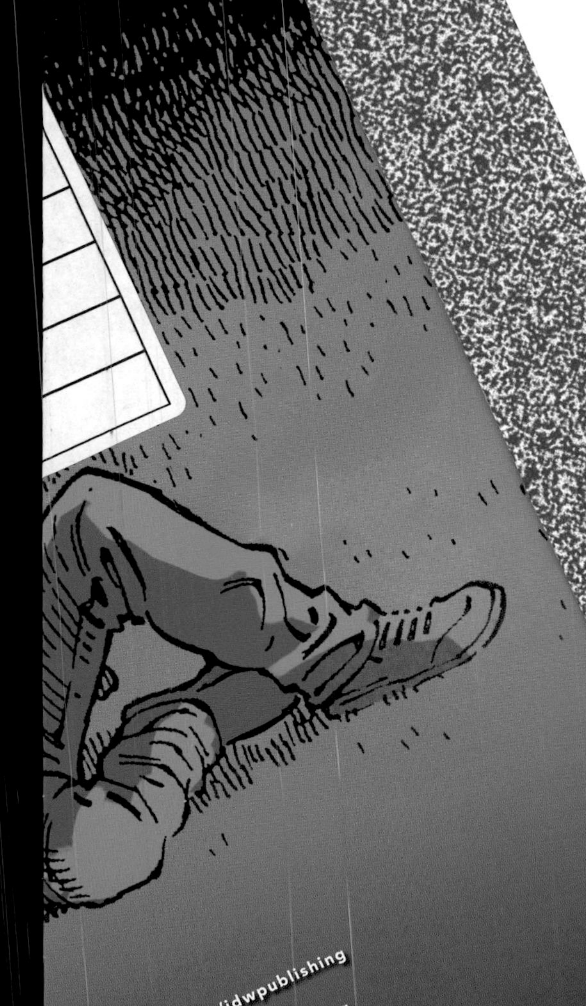

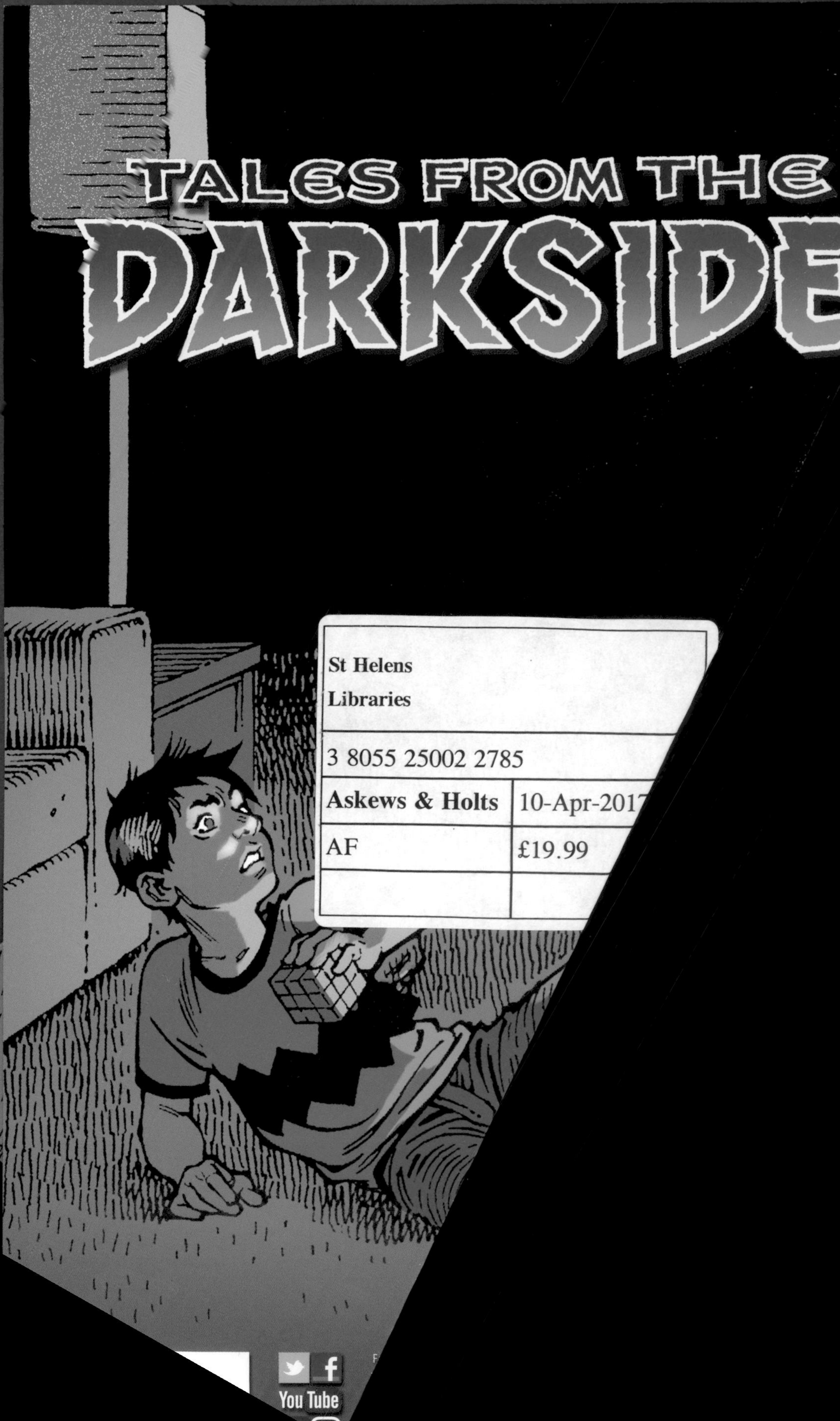
TALES FROM THE
DARKSIDE

Script by
Joe Hill

Adaptation by
Michael Benedetto

Art by
Gabriel Rodriguez

Colors by
Ryan Hill

Letters by
Robbie Robbins & Chris Mowry

Series Edits by
Chris Ryall

Tales from the Darkside created by
George Romero

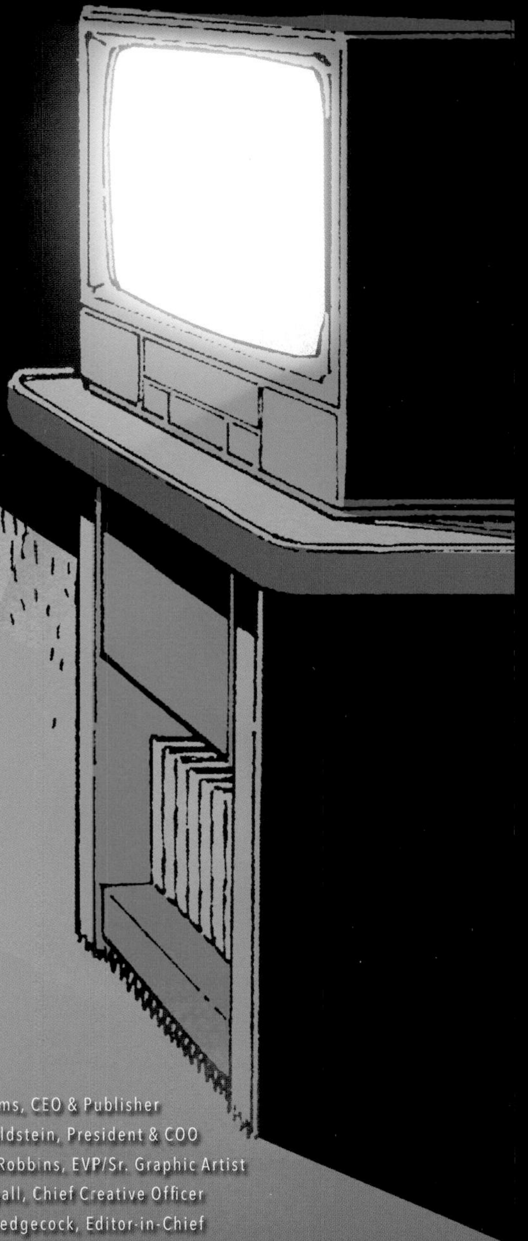

COVER ARTIST GABRIEL RODRIGUEZ

COLLECTION EDITORS JUSTIN EISINGER AND ALONZO SIMON

COLLECTION DESIGNER TOM B. LONG

PUBLISHER TED ADAMS

ISBN: 978-1-63140-819-9 20 19 18 17 1 2 3 4

TALES FROM THE DARKSIDE. JANUARY 2017. FIRST PRINTING.

Originally published as TALES FROM THE DARKSIDE issues #1–4.

Special Thanks to Risa Kessler, John Van Citters, and Sean Dailey for their invaluable assistance.

SLEEPWALKER

ART BY GABRIEL RODRIGUEZ
COLORS BY RYAN HILL

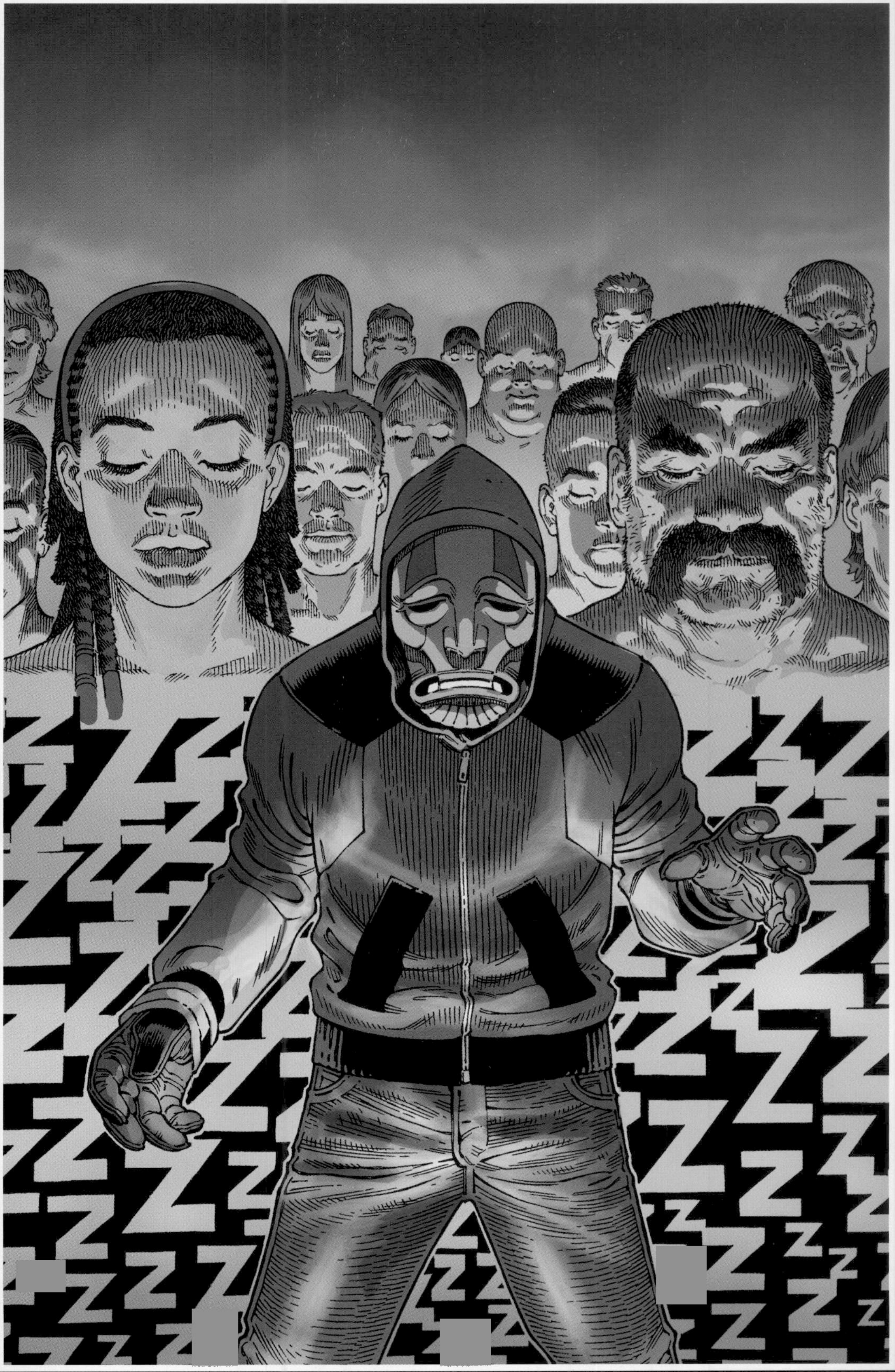

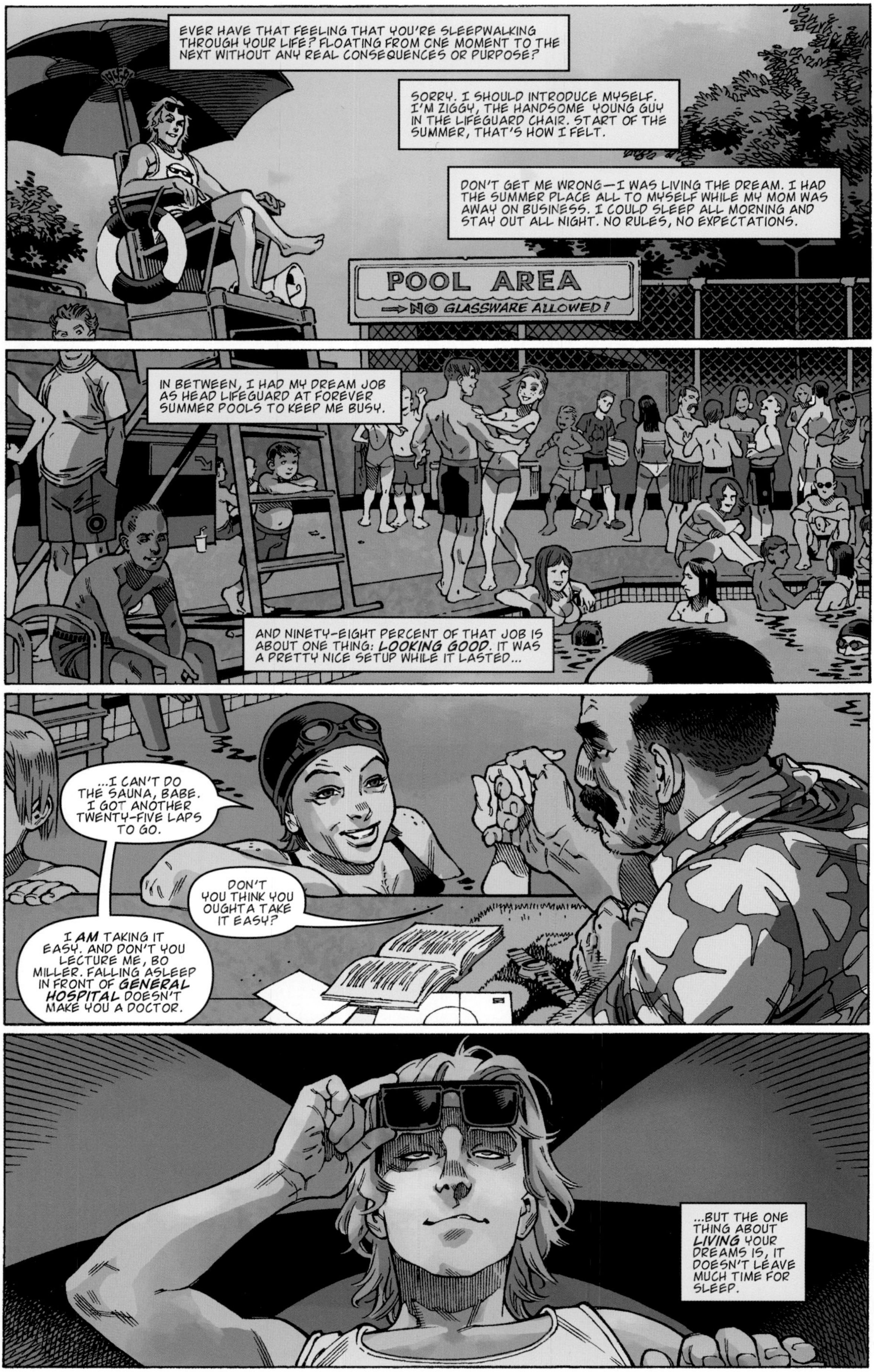

EVER HAVE THAT FEELING THAT YOU'RE SLEEPWALKING THROUGH YOUR LIFE? FLOATING FROM ONE MOMENT TO THE NEXT WITHOUT ANY REAL CONSEQUENCES OR PURPOSE?
SORRY. I SHOULD INTRODUCE MYSELF. I'M ZIGGY, THE HANDSOME YOUNG GUY IN THE LIFEGUARD CHAIR. START OF THE SUMMER, THAT'S HOW I FELT.
DON'T GET ME WRONG—I WAS LIVING THE DREAM. I HAD THE SUMMER PLACE ALL TO MYSELF WHILE MY MOM WAS AWAY ON BUSINESS. I COULD SLEEP ALL MORNING AND STAY OUT ALL NIGHT. NO RULES, NO EXPECTATIONS.
POOL AREA
NO GLASSWARE ALLOWED!
IN BETWEEN, I HAD MY DREAM JOB AS HEAD LIFEGUARD AT FOREVER SUMMER POOLS TO KEEP ME BUSY.
AND NINETY-EIGHT PERCENT OF THAT JOB IS ABOUT ONE THING: LOOKING GOOD. IT WAS A PRETTY NICE SETUP WHILE IT LASTED...
...I CAN'T DO THE SAUNA, BABE. I GOT ANOTHER TWENTY-FIVE LAPS TO GO.
DON'T YOU THINK YOU OUGHTA TAKE IT EASY?
I AM TAKING IT EASY. AND DON'T YOU LECTURE ME, BO MILLER. FALLING ASLEEP IN FRONT OF GENERAL HOSPITAL DOESN'T MAKE YOU A DOCTOR.
...BUT THE ONE THING ABOUT LIVING YOUR DREAMS IS, IT DOESN'T LEAVE MUCH TIME FOR SLEEP.

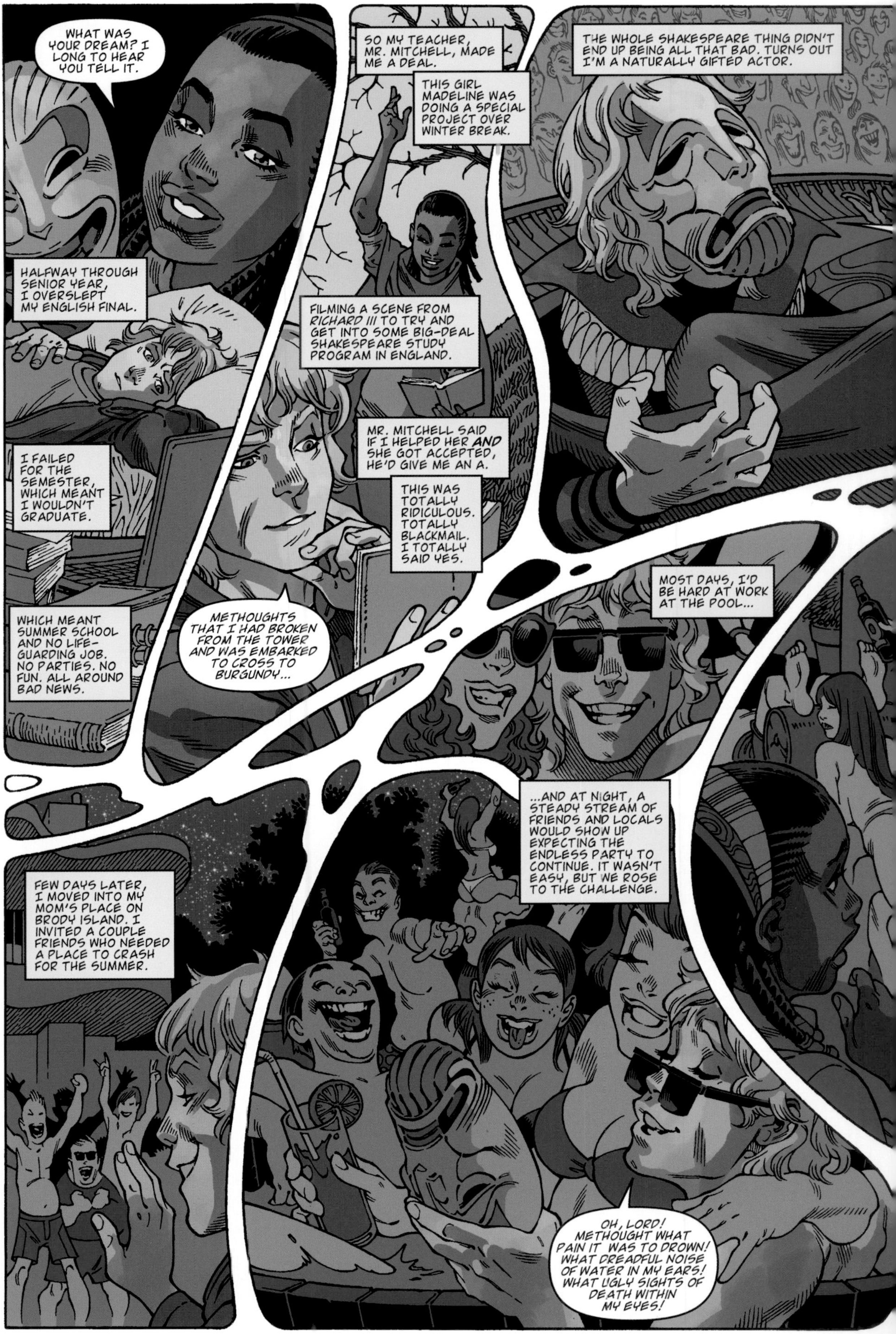
WHAT WAS YOUR DREAM? I LONG TO HEAR YOU TELL IT.
HALFWAY THROUGH SENIOR YEAR, I OVERSLEPT MY ENGLISH FINAL.
I FAILED FOR THE SEMESTER, WHICH MEANT I WOULDN'T GRADUATE.
WHICH MEANT SUMMER SCHOOL AND NO LIFE-GUARDING JOB. NO PARTIES. NO FUN. ALL AROUND BAD NEWS.
SO MY TEACHER, MR. MITCHELL, MADE ME A DEAL.
THIS GIRL MADELINE WAS DOING A SPECIAL PROJECT OVER WINTER BREAK.
FILMING A SCENE FROM *RICHARD III* TO TRY AND GET INTO SOME BIG-DEAL SHAKESPEARE STUDY PROGRAM IN ENGLAND.
MR. MITCHELL SAID IF I HELPED HER ***AND*** SHE GOT ACCEPTED, HE'D GIVE ME AN A.
THIS WAS TOTALLY RIDICULOUS. TOTALLY BLACKMAIL. I TOTALLY SAID YES.
METHOUGHTS THAT I HAD BROKEN FROM THE TOWER AND WAS EMBARKED TO CROSS TO BURGUNDY...
THE WHOLE SHAKESPEARE THING DIDN'T END UP BEING ALL THAT BAD. TURNS OUT I'M A NATURALLY GIFTED ACTOR.
MOST DAYS, I'D BE HARD AT WORK AT THE POOL...
FEW DAYS LATER, I MOVED INTO MY MOM'S PLACE ON BRODY ISLAND. I INVITED A COUPLE FRIENDS WHO NEEDED A PLACE TO CRASH FOR THE SUMMER.
...AND AT NIGHT, A STEADY STREAM OF FRIENDS AND LOCALS WOULD SHOW UP EXPECTING THE ENDLESS PARTY TO CONTINUE. IT WASN'T EASY, BUT WE ROSE TO THE CHALLENGE.
OH, LORD! METHOUGHT WHAT PAIN IT WAS TO DROWN! WHAT DREADFUL NOISE OF WATER IN MY EARS! WHAT UGLY SIGHTS OF DEATH WITHIN MY EYES!

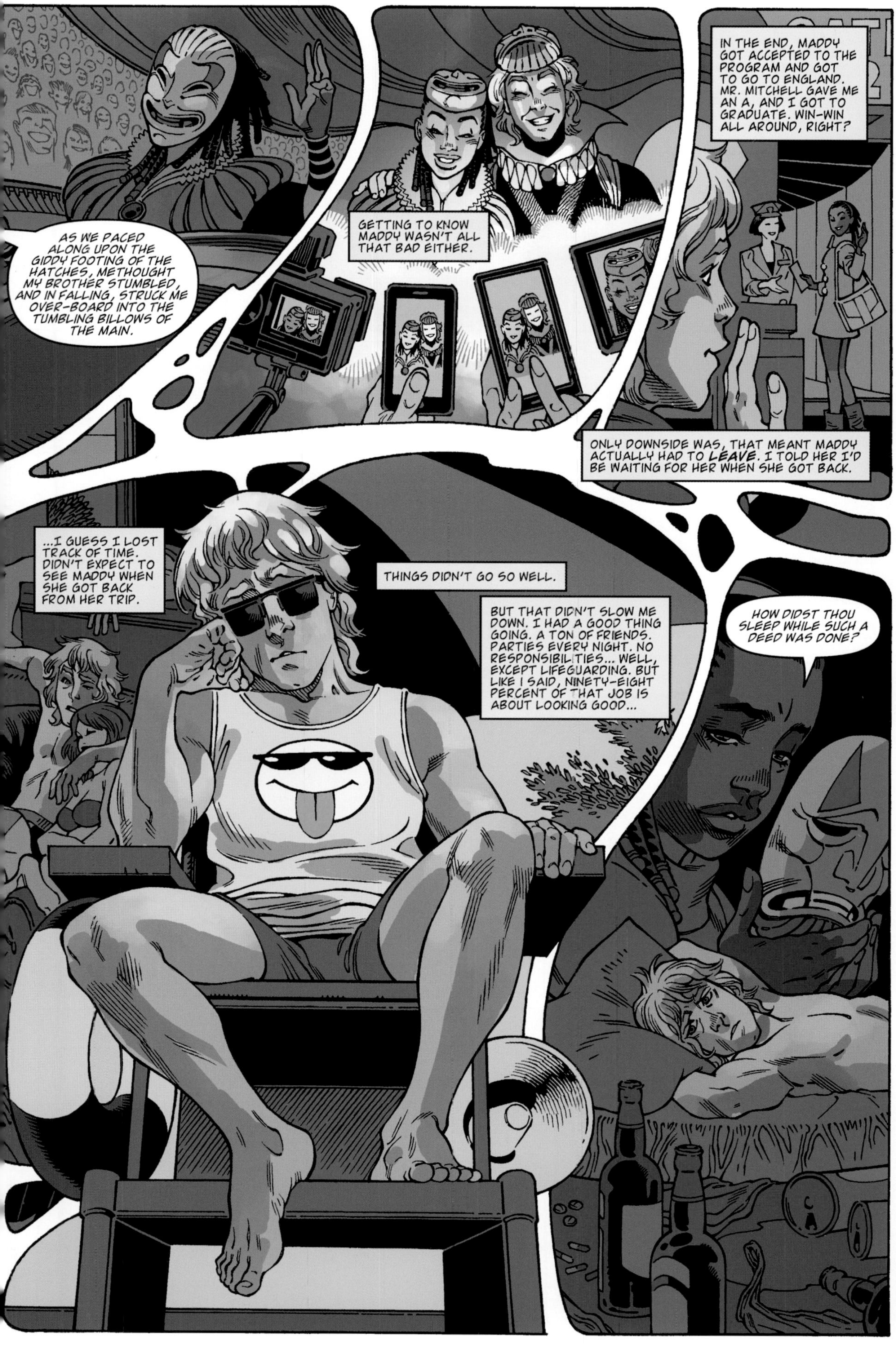

AS WE PACED ALONG UPON THE GIDDY FOOTING OF THE HATCHES, METHOUGHT MY BROTHER STUMBLED, AND IN FALLING, STRUCK ME OVER-BOARD INTO THE TUMBLING BILLOWS OF THE MAIN.
GETTING TO KNOW MADDY WASN'T ALL THAT BAD EITHER.
IN THE END, MADDY GOT ACCEPTED TO THE PROGRAM AND GOT TO GO TO ENGLAND. MR. MITCHELL GAVE ME AN A, AND I GOT TO GRADUATE. WIN-WIN ALL AROUND, RIGHT?
ONLY DOWNSIDE WAS, THAT MEANT MADDY ACTUALLY HAD TO LEAVE. I TOLD HER I'D BE WAITING FOR HER WHEN SHE GOT BACK.
THINGS DIDN'T GO SO WELL.
BUT THAT DIDN'T SLOW ME DOWN. I HAD A GOOD THING GOING. A TON OF FRIENDS. PARTIES EVERY NIGHT. NO RESPONSIBILITIES... WELL, EXCEPT LIFEGUARDING. BUT LIKE I SAID, NINETY-EIGHT PERCENT OF THAT JOB IS ABOUT LOOKING GOOD...
...I GUESS I LOST TRACK OF TIME. DIDN'T EXPECT TO SEE MADDY WHEN SHE GOT BACK FROM HER TRIP.
HOW DIDST THOU SLEEP WHILE SUCH A DEED WAS DONE?

...THE OTHER TWO PERCENT IS MAKING SURE NO ONE DROWNS.

WHA...?

HELP! SOMEBODY HELP!

OH NO.

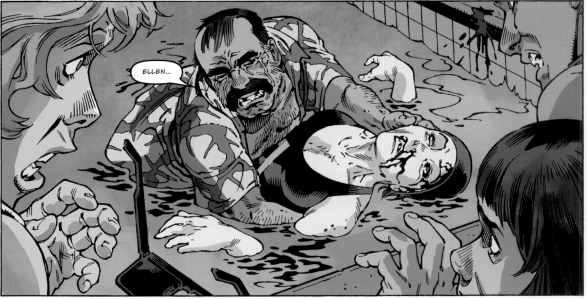

ELLEN...

NO ONE KNEW. NO ONE HAD ANY IDEA I WAS ASLEEP WHEN SHE WENT UNDER. AS FAR AS THE WORLD WAS CONCERNED, I WAS ON DUTY THE WHOLE TIME.

THE CORONER SAID SHE PROBABLY COULDN'T HAVE BEEN SAVED EVEN IF I'D GOTTEN TO HER IN TIME. SOMETHING ABOUT A WEAKNESS IN THE WALL OF HER HEART.

MY MOM HAD TO CUT HER BUSINESS TRIP SHORT TO COME BACK FOR THE TRIAL. SHE GOT ONE OF HER HIGH-POWERED LAWYER CO-WORKERS TO REPRESENT ME.

THE HEARING WAS OVER IN AN HOUR. THE JUDGE EVEN TOLD ME NOT TO BLAME MYSELF.

HEY, YOU! HEY!

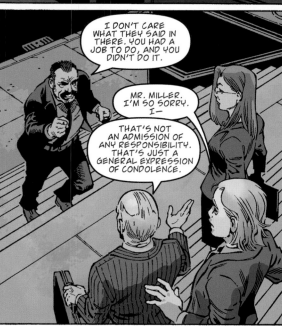

I DON'T CARE WHAT THEY SAID IN THERE. YOU HAD A JOB TO DO, AND YOU DIDN'T DO IT.

MR. MILLER. I'M SO SORRY. I—

THAT'S NOT AN ADMISSION OF ANY RESPONSIBILITY. THAT'S JUST A GENERAL EXPRESSION OF CONDOLENCE.

YOU MIGHT AS WELL HAVE NOT BEEN THERE AT ALL. YOU WERE ASLEEP ON THE JOB AND NOW MY WIFE'S DEAD.

MR. MILLER, I KNOW I... LET YOUR WIFE DOWN... BUT I DON'T THINK I WAS... IT'S HARD TO REMEMBER...

STEP BACK, SIR. I WON'T HAVE YOU HARASSING MY CLIENT.

JESUS CHRIST. SHUT UP, ZIGGY. YOU'VE CAUSED ENOUGH TROUBLE ALREADY, SO JUST KEEP YOUR MOUTH SHUT.

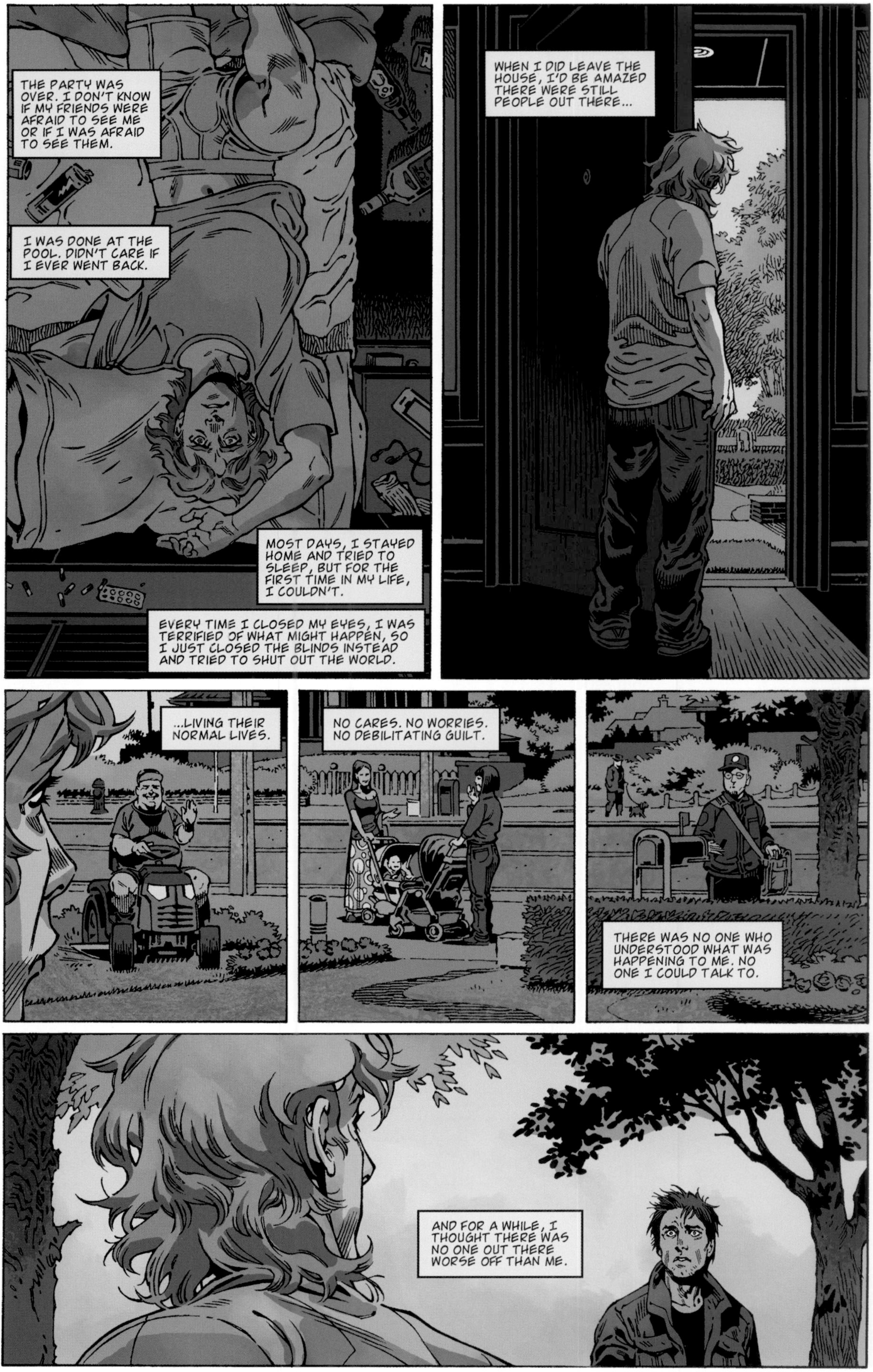
THE PARTY WAS OVER. I DON'T KNOW IF MY FRIENDS WERE AFRAID TO SEE ME OR IF I WAS AFRAID TO SEE THEM.
I WAS DONE AT THE POOL. DIDN'T CARE IF I EVER WENT BACK.
MOST DAYS, I STAYED HOME AND TRIED TO SLEEP, BUT FOR THE FIRST TIME IN MY LIFE, I COULDN'T.
EVERY TIME I CLOSED MY EYES, I WAS TERRIFIED OF WHAT MIGHT HAPPEN, SO I JUST CLOSED THE BLINDS INSTEAD AND TRIED TO SHUT OUT THE WORLD.
WHEN I DID LEAVE THE HOUSE, I'D BE AMAZED THERE WERE STILL PEOPLE OUT THERE...
...LIVING THEIR NORMAL LIVES.
NO CARES. NO WORRIES. NO DEBILITATING GUILT.
THERE WAS NO ONE WHO UNDERSTOOD WHAT WAS HAPPENING TO ME. NO ONE I COULD TALK TO.
AND FOR A WHILE, I THOUGHT THERE WAS NO ONE OUT THERE WORSE OFF THAN ME.

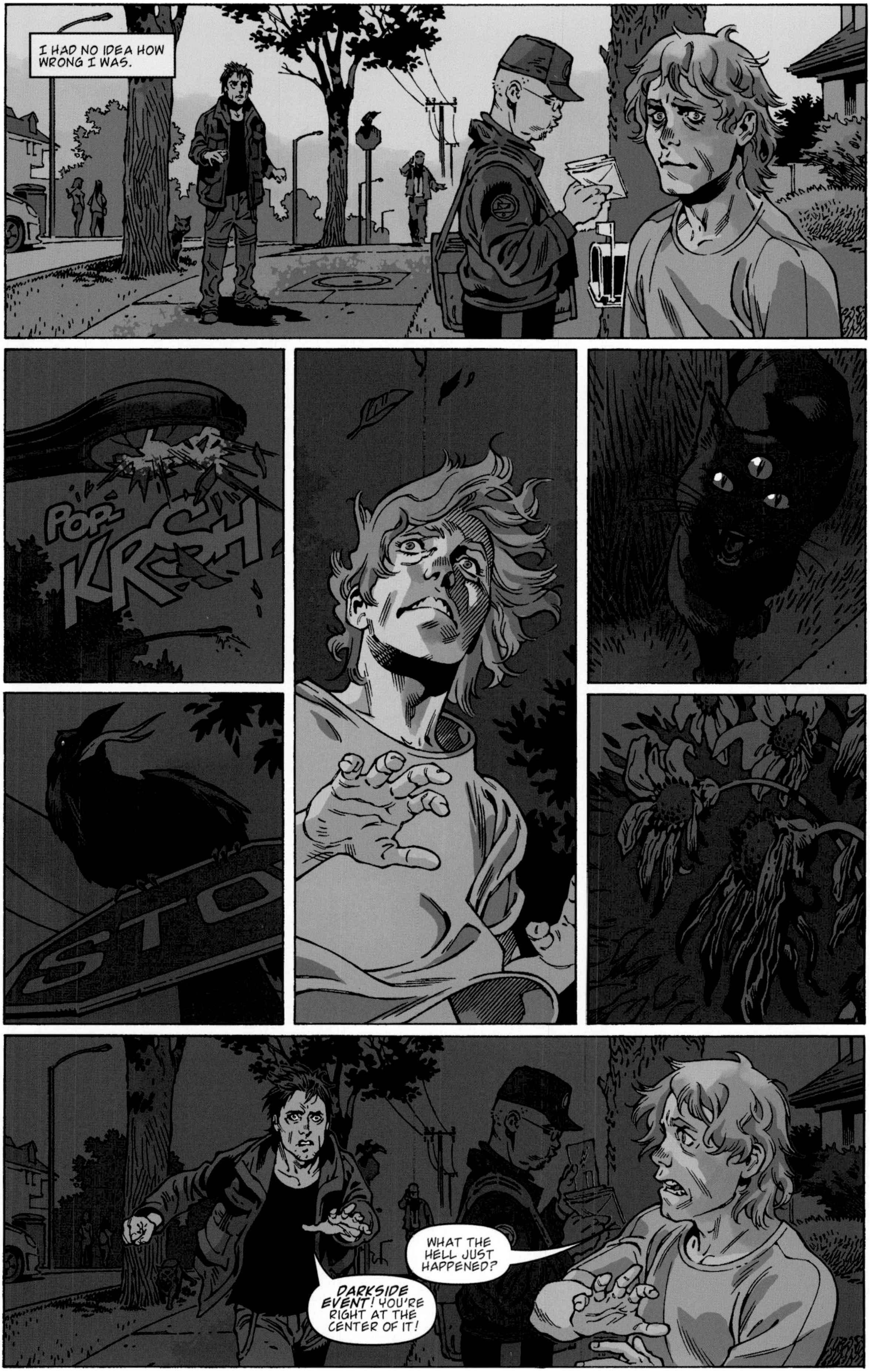
I HAD NO IDEA HOW WRONG I WAS.
POP
KRSH
STO
WHAT THE HELL JUST HAPPENED?
DARKSIDE EVENT! YOU'RE RIGHT AT THE CENTER OF IT!

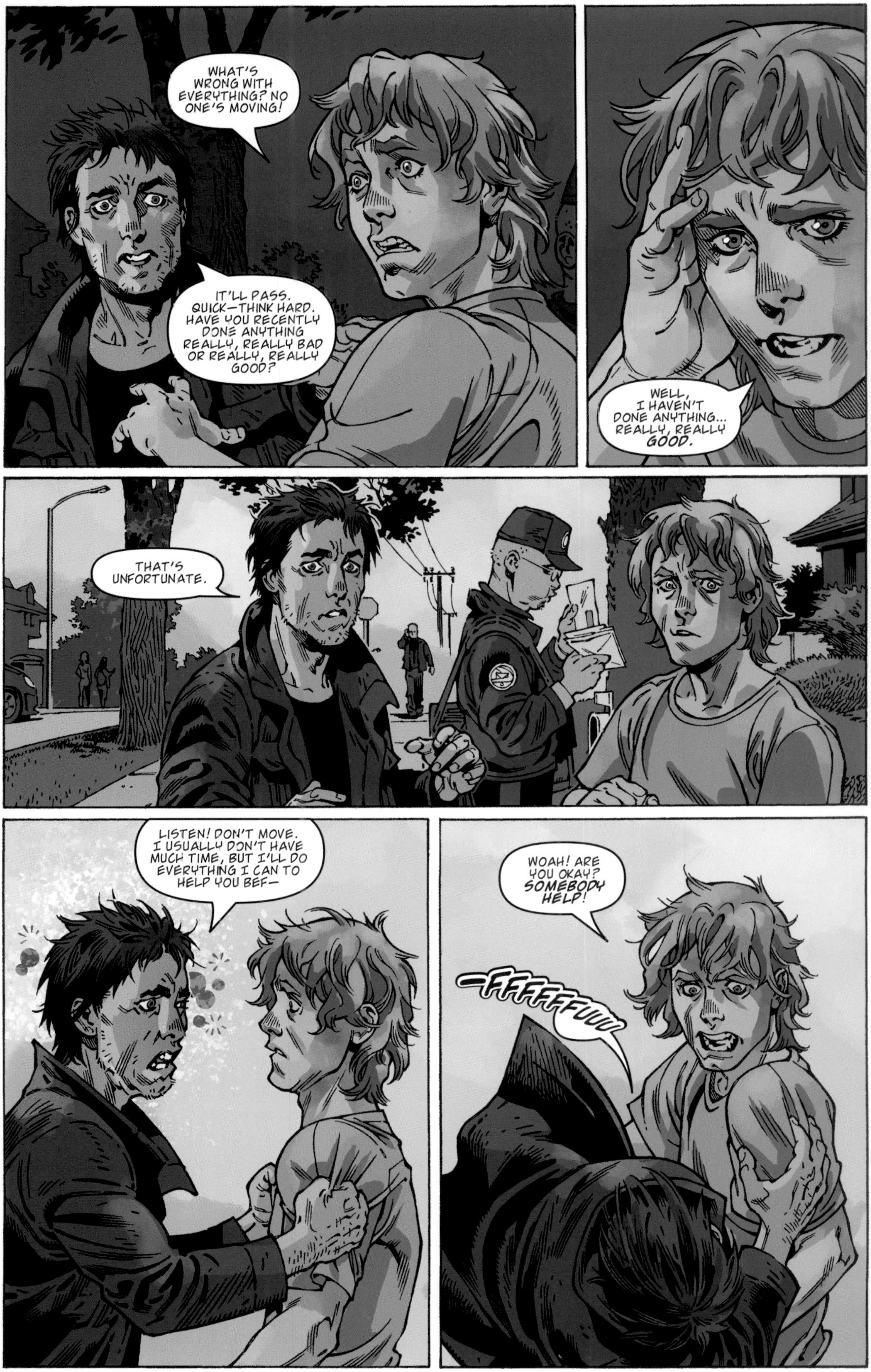
WHAT'S WRONG WITH EVERYTHING? NO ONE'S MOVING!
IT'LL PASS. QUICK—THINK HARD. HAVE YOU RECENTLY DONE ANYTHING REALLY, REALLY BAD OR REALLY, REALLY GOOD?
WELL, I HAVEN'T DONE ANYTHING... REALLY, REALLY GOOD.
THAT'S UNFORTUNATE.
LISTEN! DON'T MOVE. I USUALLY DON'T HAVE MUCH TIME, BUT I'LL DO EVERYTHING I CAN TO HELP YOU BEF—
WOAH! ARE YOU OKAY? SOMEBODY HELP!
—FFFFFFUUU

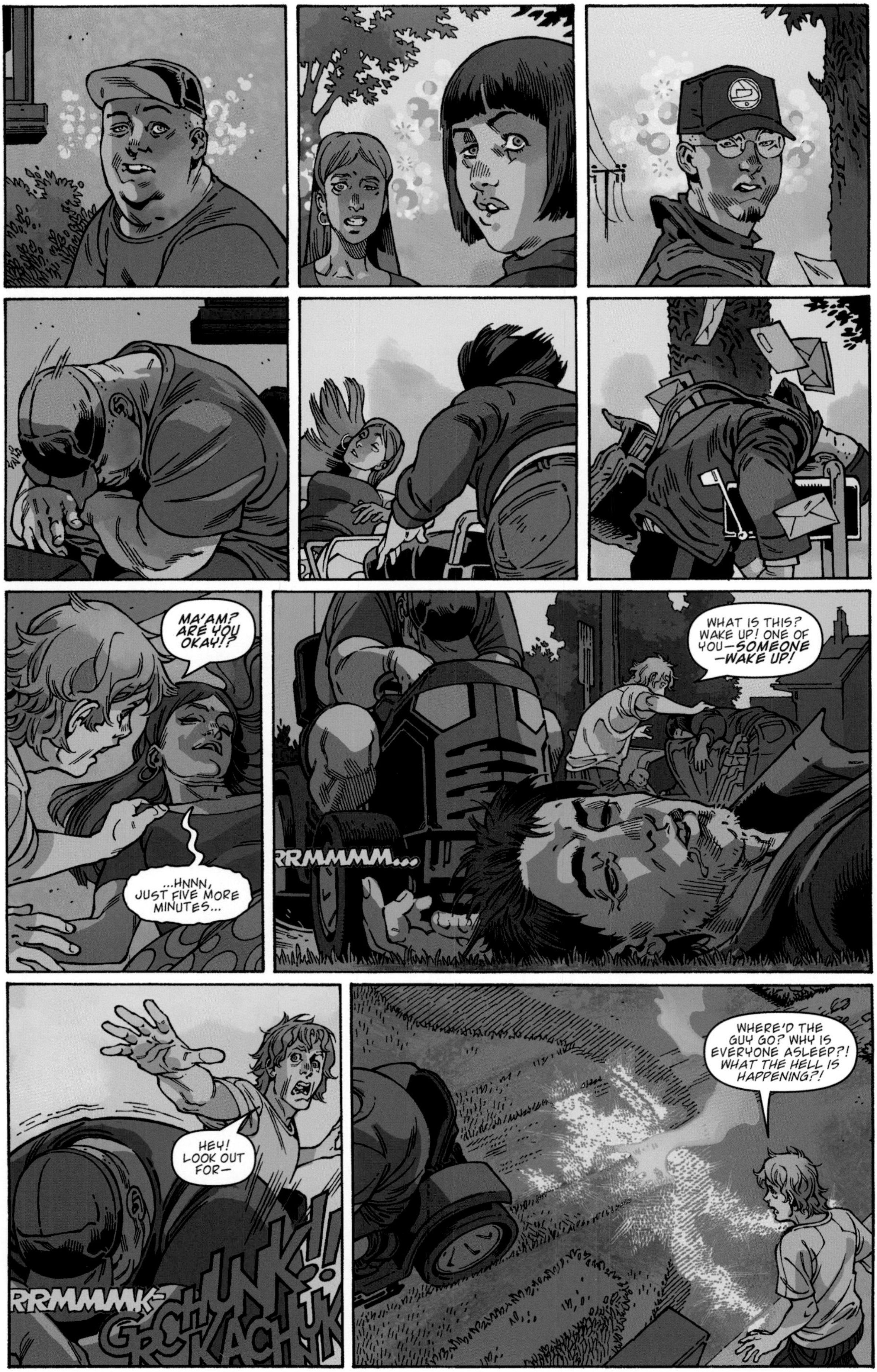
MA'AM? ARE YOU OKAY!?
...HNNN, JUST FIVE MORE MINUTES...
WHAT IS THIS? WAKE UP! ONE OF YOU—SOMEONE—WAKE UP!
RRMMMM...
HEY! LOOK OUT FOR—
RRMMMK-
GRCHUNK!
KACHUK
WHERE'D THE GUY GO? WHY IS EVERYONE ASLEEP?! WHAT THE HELL IS HAPPENING?!

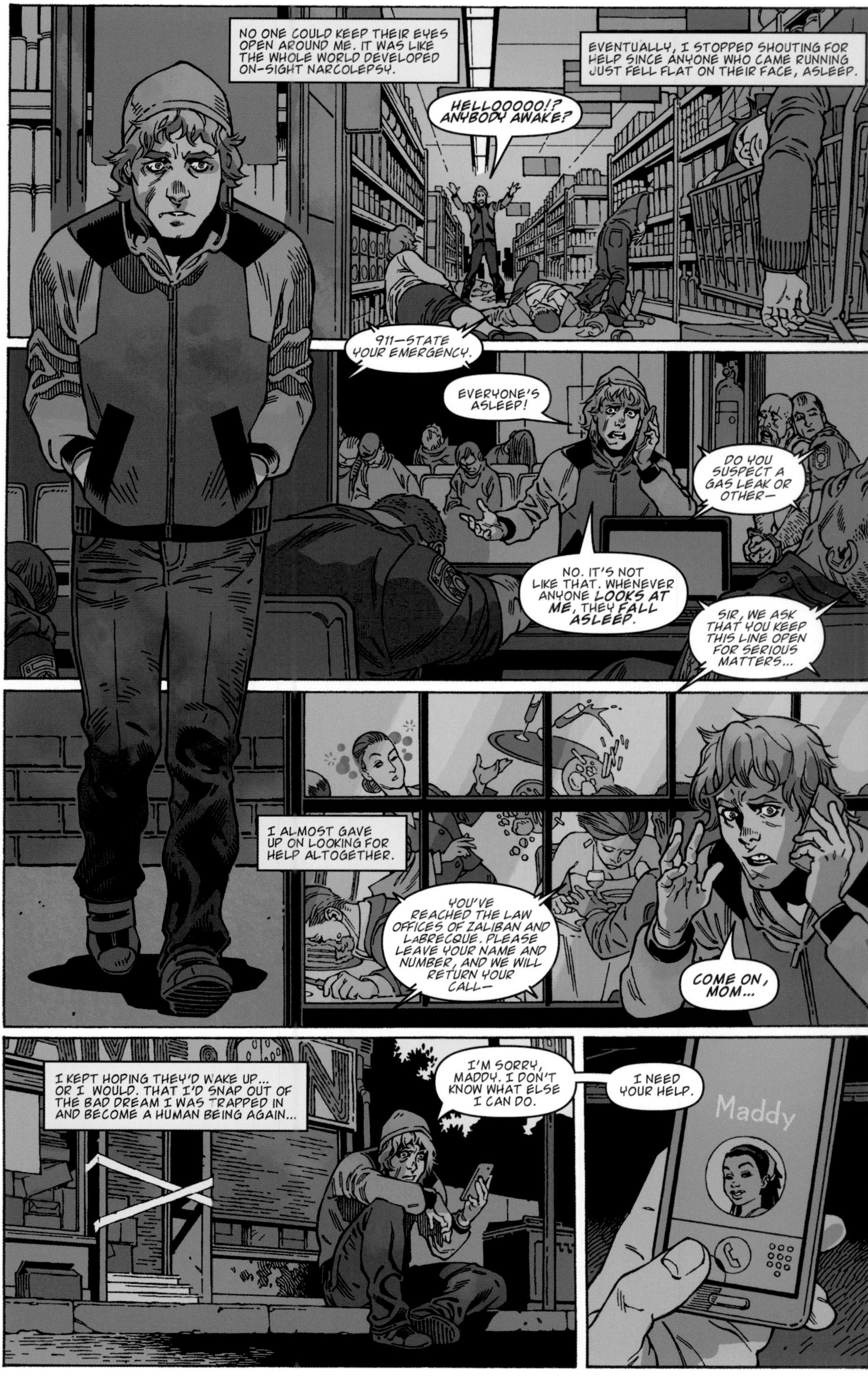
NO ONE COULD KEEP THEIR EYES OPEN AROUND ME. IT WAS LIKE THE WHOLE WORLD DEVELOPED ON-SIGHT NARCOLEPSY.
EVENTUALLY, I STOPPED SHOUTING FOR HELP SINCE ANYONE WHO CAME RUNNING JUST FELL FLAT ON THEIR FACE, ASLEEP.
HELLOOOOO!? ANYBODY AWAKE?
911—STATE YOUR EMERGENCY.
EVERYONE'S ASLEEP!
DO YOU SUSPECT A GAS LEAK OR OTHER—
NO. IT'S NOT LIKE THAT. WHENEVER ANYONE LOOKS AT ME, THEY FALL ASLEEP.
SIR, WE ASK THAT YOU KEEP THIS LINE OPEN FOR SERIOUS MATTERS...
I ALMOST GAVE UP ON LOOKING FOR HELP ALTOGETHER.
YOU'VE REACHED THE LAW OFFICES OF ZALIBAN AND LABRECQUE. PLEASE LEAVE YOUR NAME AND NUMBER, AND WE WILL RETURN YOUR CALL—
COME ON, MOM...
I KEPT HOPING THEY'D WAKE UP... OR I WOULD. THAT I'D SNAP OUT OF THE BAD DREAM I WAS TRAPPED IN AND BECOME A HUMAN BEING AGAIN...
I'M SORRY, MADDY. I DON'T KNOW WHAT ELSE I CAN DO.
I NEED YOUR HELP.
Maddy

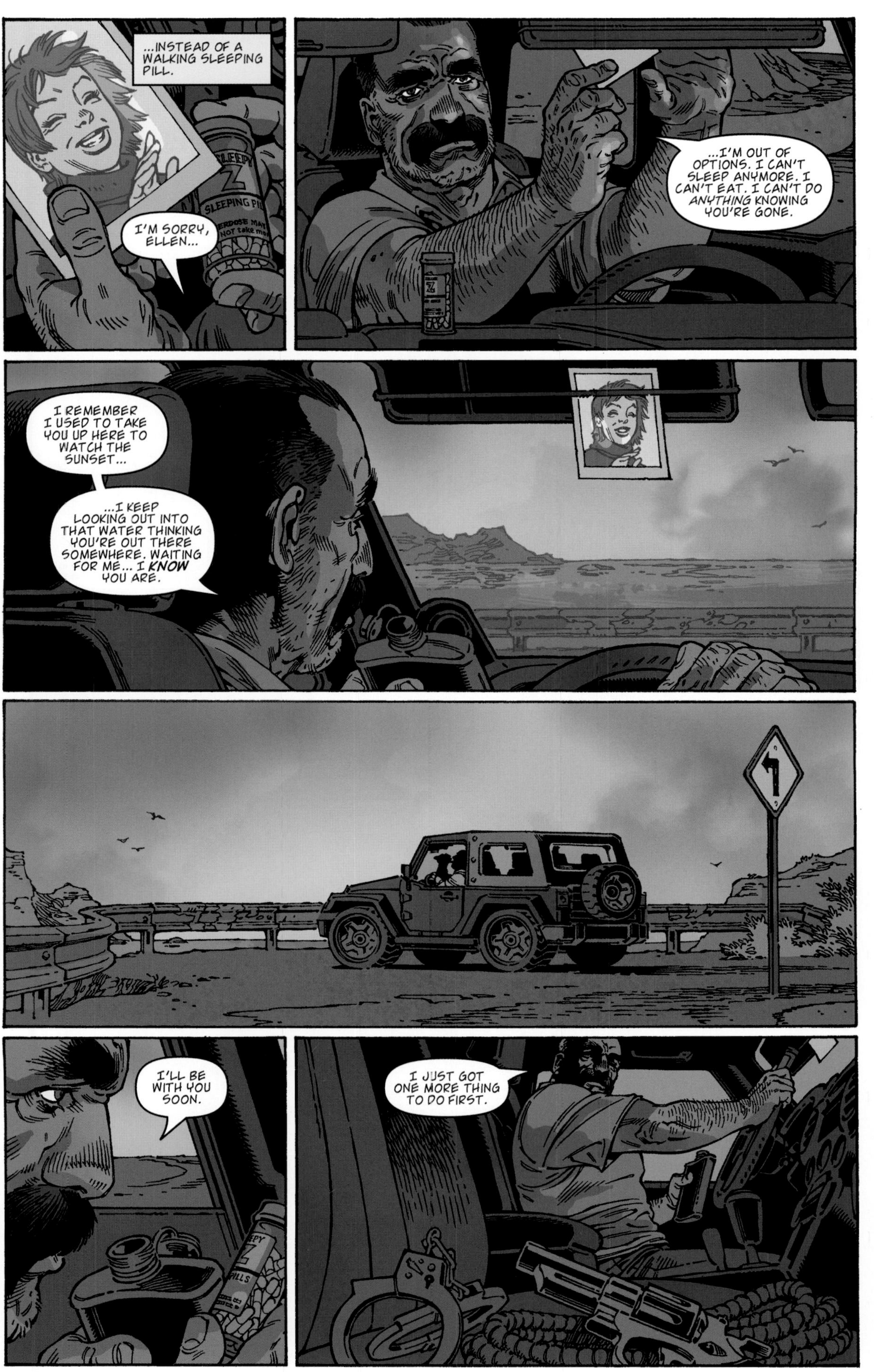
...INSTEAD OF A WALKING SLEEPING PILL.
I'M SORRY, ELLEN...
...I'M OUT OF OPTIONS. I CAN'T SLEEP ANYMORE. I CAN'T EAT. I CAN'T DO *ANYTHING* KNOWING YOU'RE GONE.
I REMEMBER I USED TO TAKE YOU UP HERE TO WATCH THE SUNSET...
...I KEEP LOOKING OUT INTO THAT WATER THINKING YOU'RE OUT THERE SOMEWHERE. WAITING FOR ME... I ***KNOW*** YOU ARE.
I'LL BE WITH YOU SOON.
I JUST GOT ONE MORE THING TO DO FIRST.

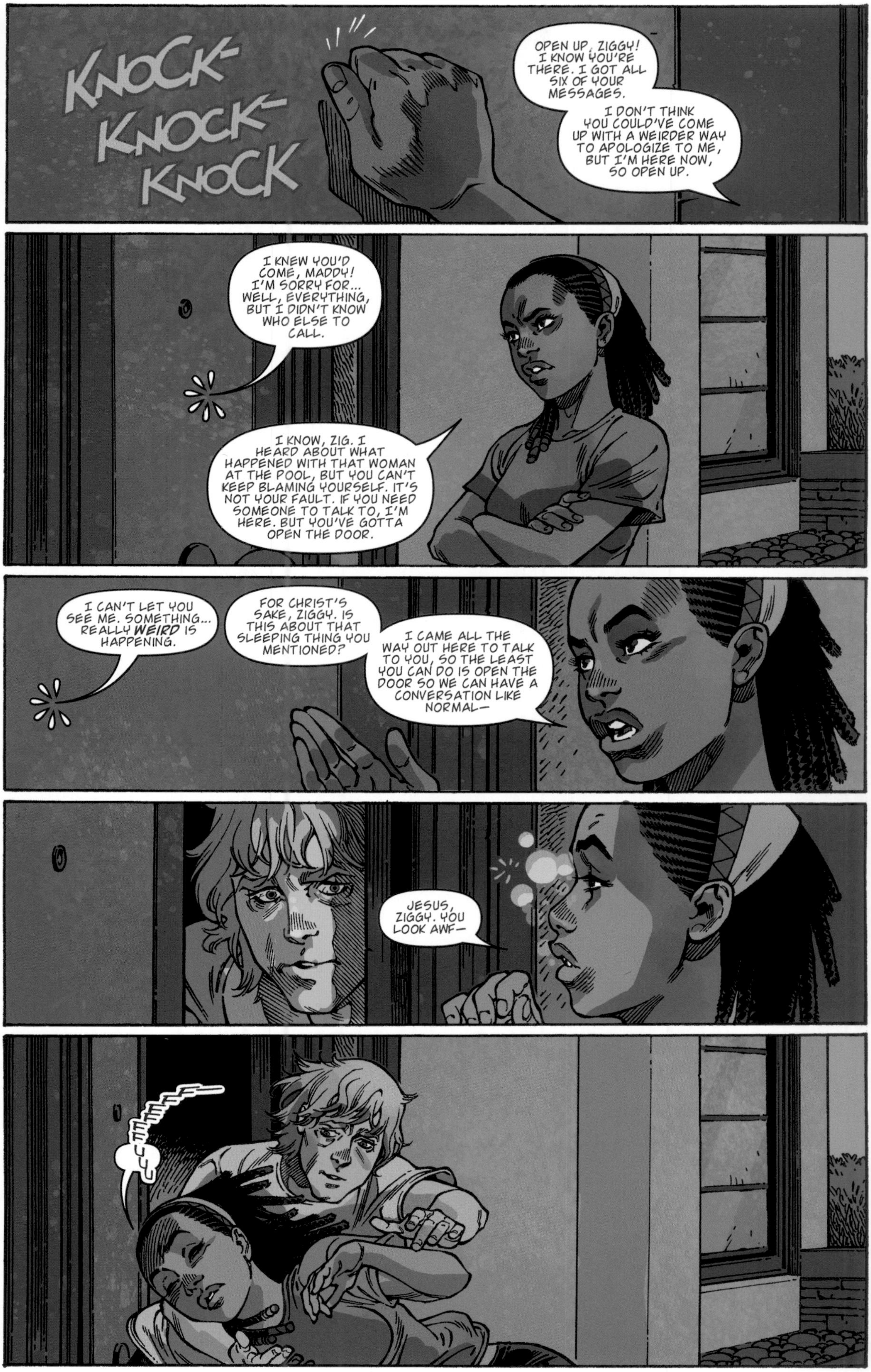
KNOCK-KNOCK-KNOCK
OPEN UP, ZIGGY! I KNOW YOU'RE THERE. I GOT ALL SIX OF YOUR MESSAGES.
I DON'T THINK YOU COULD'VE COME UP WITH A WEIRDER WAY TO APOLOGIZE TO ME, BUT I'M HERE NOW, SO OPEN UP.
I KNEW YOU'D COME, MADDY! I'M SORRY FOR... WELL, EVERYTHING, BUT I DIDN'T KNOW WHO ELSE TO CALL.
I KNOW, ZIG. I HEARD ABOUT WHAT HAPPENED WITH THAT WOMAN AT THE POOL, BUT YOU CAN'T KEEP BLAMING YOURSELF. IT'S NOT YOUR FAULT. IF YOU NEED SOMEONE TO TALK TO, I'M HERE. BUT YOU'VE GOTTA OPEN THE DOOR.
I CAN'T LET YOU SEE ME. SOMETHING... REALLY WEIRD IS HAPPENING.
FOR CHRIST'S SAKE, ZIGGY. IS THIS ABOUT THAT SLEEPING THING YOU MENTIONED?
I CAME ALL THE WAY OUT HERE TO TALK TO YOU, SO THE LEAST YOU CAN DO IS OPEN THE DOOR SO WE CAN HAVE A CONVERSATION LIKE NORMAL—
JESUS, ZIGGY. YOU LOOK AWF—
EEEEFFUU

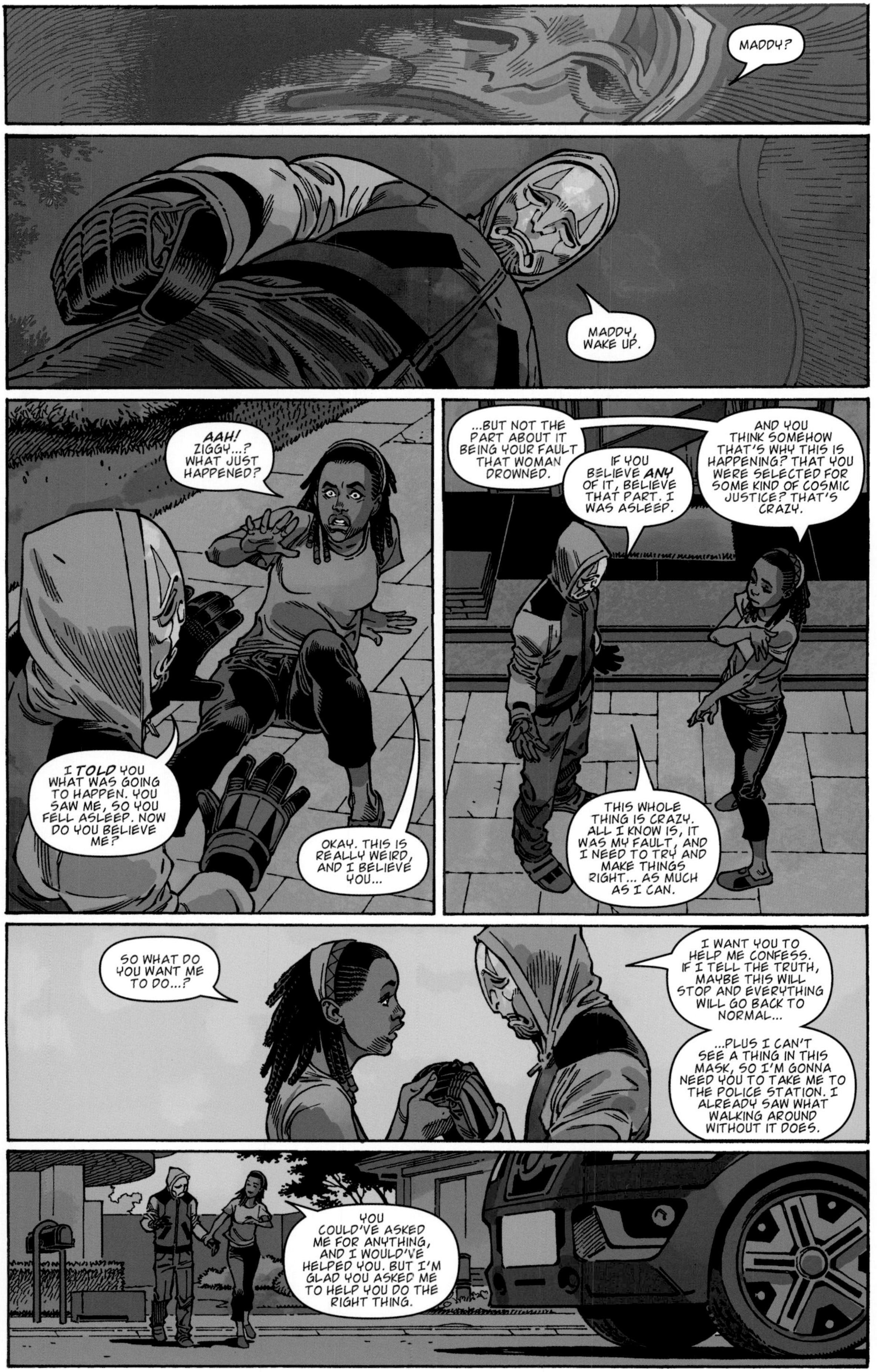
MADDY?
MADDY, WAKE UP.
AAH! ZIGGY...? WHAT JUST HAPPENED?
I TOLD YOU WHAT WAS GOING TO HAPPEN. YOU SAW ME, SO YOU FELL ASLEEP. NOW DO YOU BELIEVE ME?
OKAY. THIS IS REALLY WEIRD, AND I BELIEVE YOU...
...BUT NOT THE PART ABOUT IT BEING YOUR FAULT THAT WOMAN DROWNED.
IF YOU BELIEVE ANY OF IT, BELIEVE THAT PART. I WAS ASLEEP.
AND YOU THINK SOMEHOW THAT'S WHY THIS IS HAPPENING? THAT YOU WERE SELECTED FOR SOME KIND OF COSMIC JUSTICE? THAT'S CRAZY.
THIS WHOLE THING IS CRAZY. ALL I KNOW IS, IT WAS MY FAULT, AND I NEED TO TRY AND MAKE THINGS RIGHT... AS MUCH AS I CAN.
SO WHAT DO YOU WANT ME TO DO...?
I WANT YOU TO HELP ME CONFESS. IF I TELL THE TRUTH, MAYBE THIS WILL STOP AND EVERYTHING WILL GO BACK TO NORMAL...
...PLUS I CAN'T SEE A THING IN THIS MASK, SO I'M GONNA NEED YOU TO TAKE ME TO THE POLICE STATION. I ALREADY SAW WHAT WALKING AROUND WITHOUT IT DOES.
YOU COULD'VE ASKED ME FOR ANYTHING, AND I WOULD'VE HELPED YOU. BUT I'M GLAD YOU ASKED ME TO HELP YOU DO THE RIGHT THING.

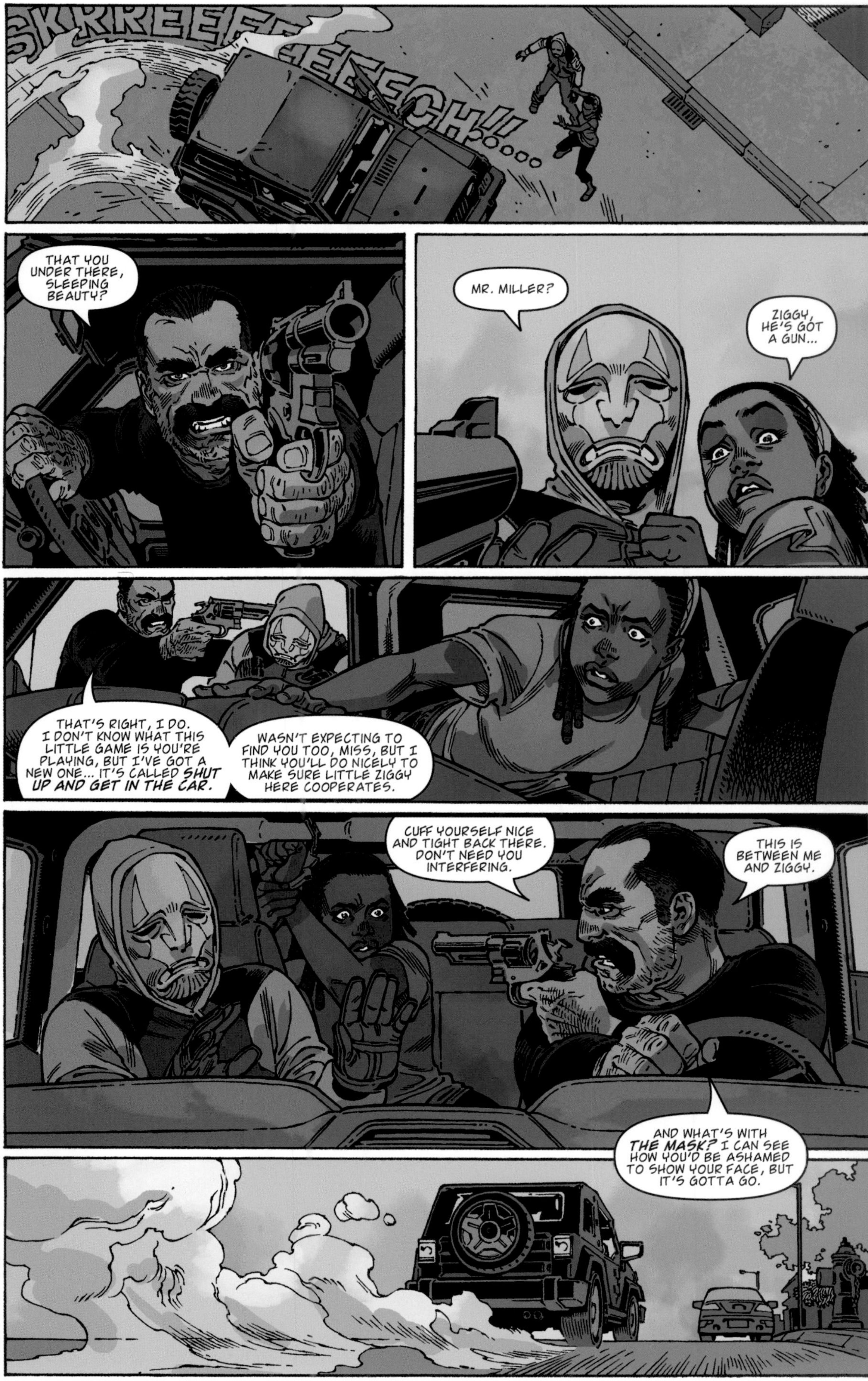
SKRREEEEEEEEECH!! OOOO
THAT YOU UNDER THERE, SLEEPING BEAUTY?
MR. MILLER?
ZIGGY, HE'S GOT A GUN...
THAT'S RIGHT, I DO. I DON'T KNOW WHAT THIS LITTLE GAME IS YOU'RE PLAYING, BUT I'VE GOT A NEW ONE... IT'S CALLED SHUT UP AND GET IN THE CAR.
WASN'T EXPECTING TO FIND YOU TOO, MISS, BUT I THINK YOU'LL DO NICELY TO MAKE SURE LITTLE ZIGGY HERE COOPERATES.
CUFF YOURSELF NICE AND TIGHT BACK THERE. DON'T NEED YOU INTERFERING.
THIS IS BETWEEN ME AND ZIGGY.
AND WHAT'S WITH THE MASK? I CAN SEE HOW YOU'D BE ASHAMED TO SHOW YOUR FACE, BUT IT'S GOTTA GO.

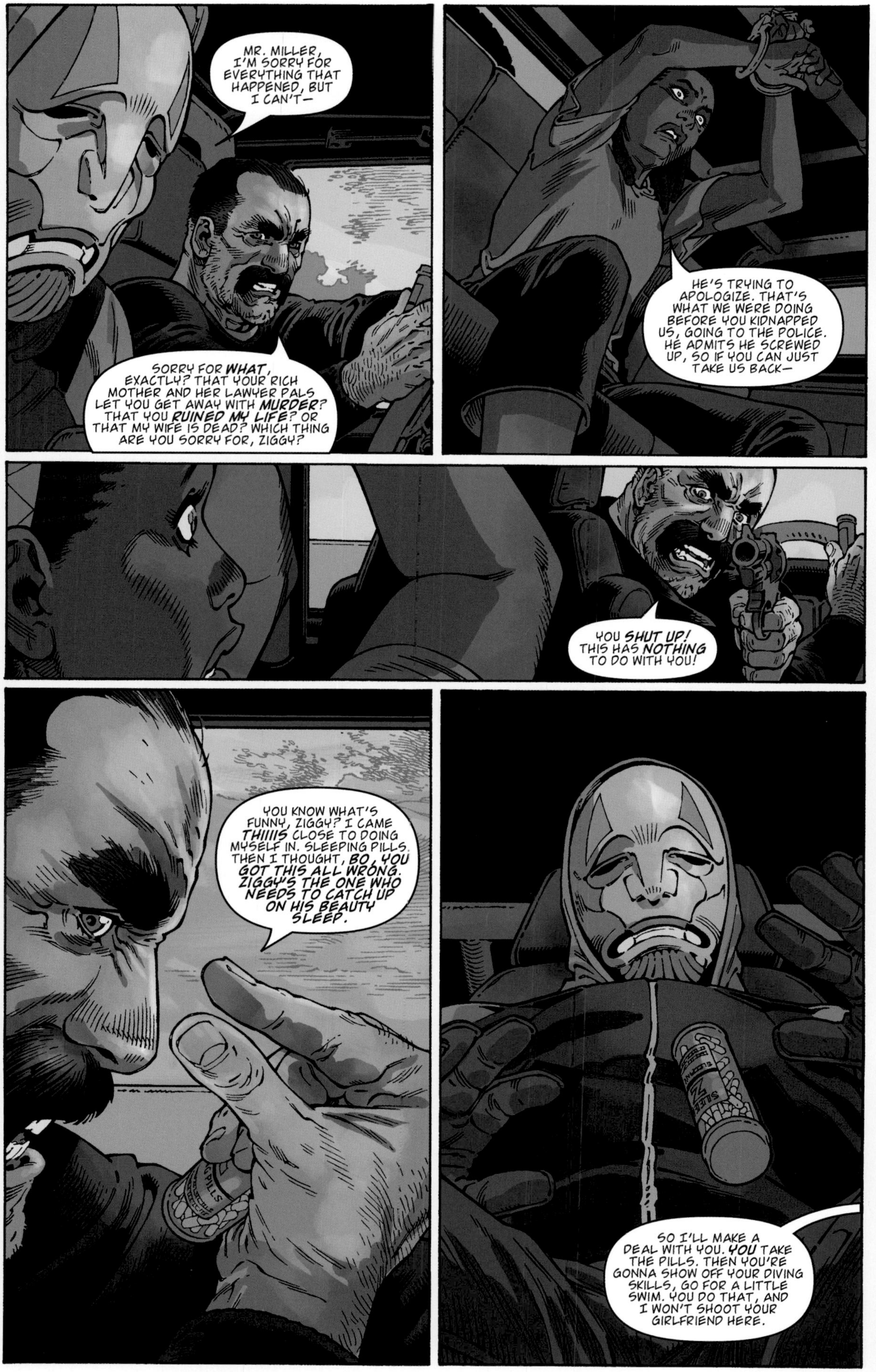
MR. MILLER, I'M SORRY FOR EVERYTHING THAT HAPPENED, BUT I CAN'T—
SORRY FOR **WHAT**, EXACTLY? THAT YOUR RICH MOTHER AND HER LAWYER PALS LET YOU GET AWAY WITH **MURDER**? THAT YOU **RUINED MY LIFE**? OR THAT MY WIFE IS DEAD? WHICH THING ARE YOU SORRY FOR, ZIGGY?
HE'S TRYING TO APOLOGIZE. THAT'S WHAT WE WERE DOING BEFORE YOU KIDNAPPED US, GOING TO THE POLICE. HE ADMITS HE SCREWED UP, SO IF YOU CAN JUST TAKE US BACK—
YOU **SHUT UP!** THIS HAS **NOTHING** TO DO WITH YOU!
YOU KNOW WHAT'S FUNNY, ZIGGY? I CAME **THIIIIS** CLOSE TO DOING MYSELF IN. SLEEPING PILLS. THEN I THOUGHT, **BO, YOU GOT THIS ALL WRONG. ZIGGY'S THE ONE WHO NEEDS TO CATCH UP ON HIS BEAUTY SLEEP.**
SO I'LL MAKE A DEAL WITH YOU. **YOU** TAKE THE PILLS. THEN YOU'RE GONNA SHOW OFF YOUR DIVING SKILLS, GO FOR A LITTLE SWIM. YOU DO THAT, AND I WON'T SHOOT YOUR GIRLFRIEND HERE.

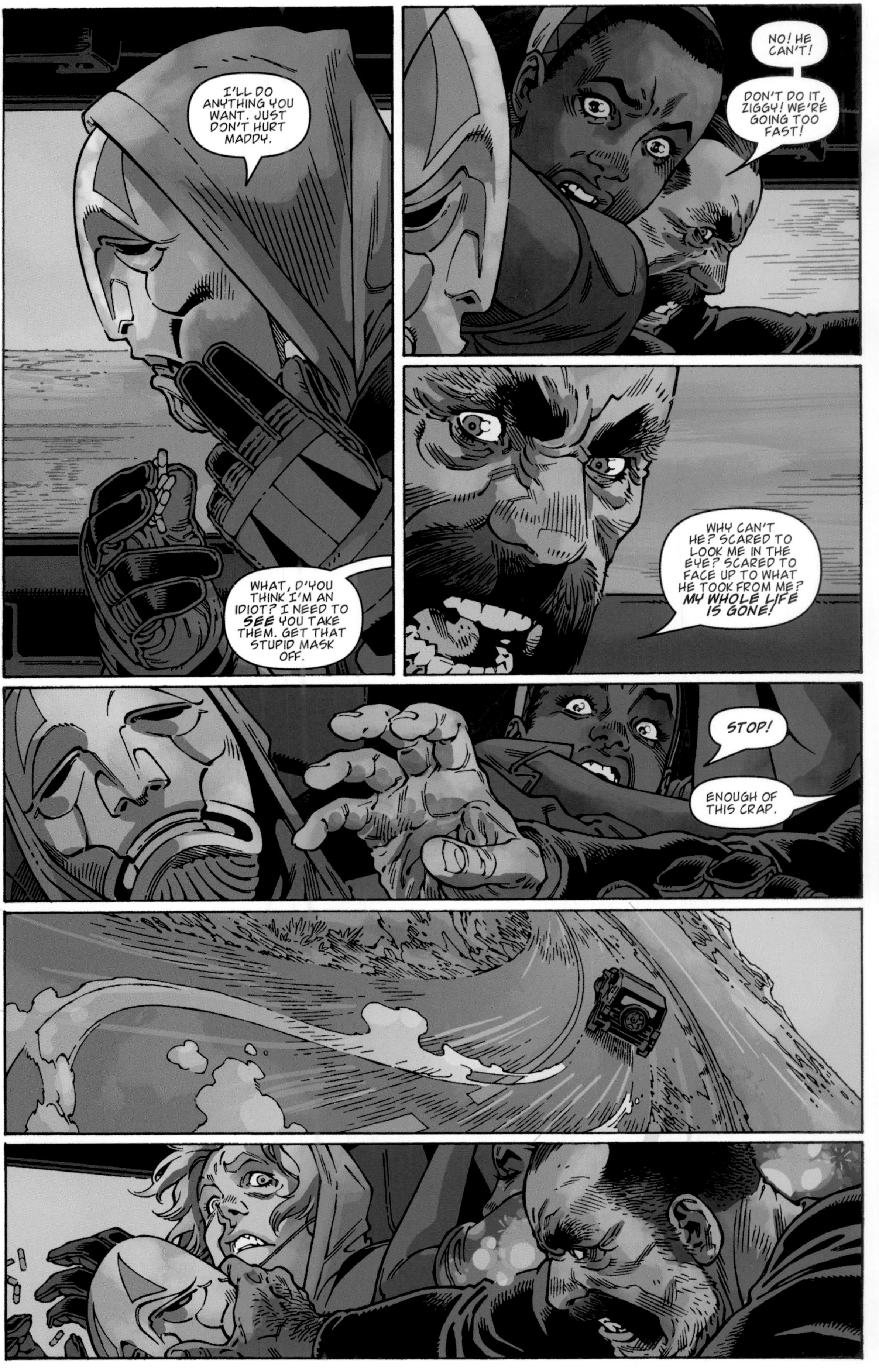
I'LL DO ANYTHING YOU WANT. JUST DON'T HURT MADDY.
WHAT, D'YOU THINK I'M AN IDIOT? I NEED TO SEE YOU TAKE THEM. GET THAT STUPID MASK OFF.
NO! HE CAN'T!
DON'T DO IT, ZIGGY! WE'RE GOING TOO FAST!
WHY CAN'T HE? SCARED TO LOOK ME IN THE EYE? SCARED TO FACE UP TO WHAT HE TOOK FROM ME? MY WHOLE LIFE IS GONE!
STOP!
ENOUGH OF THIS CRAP.

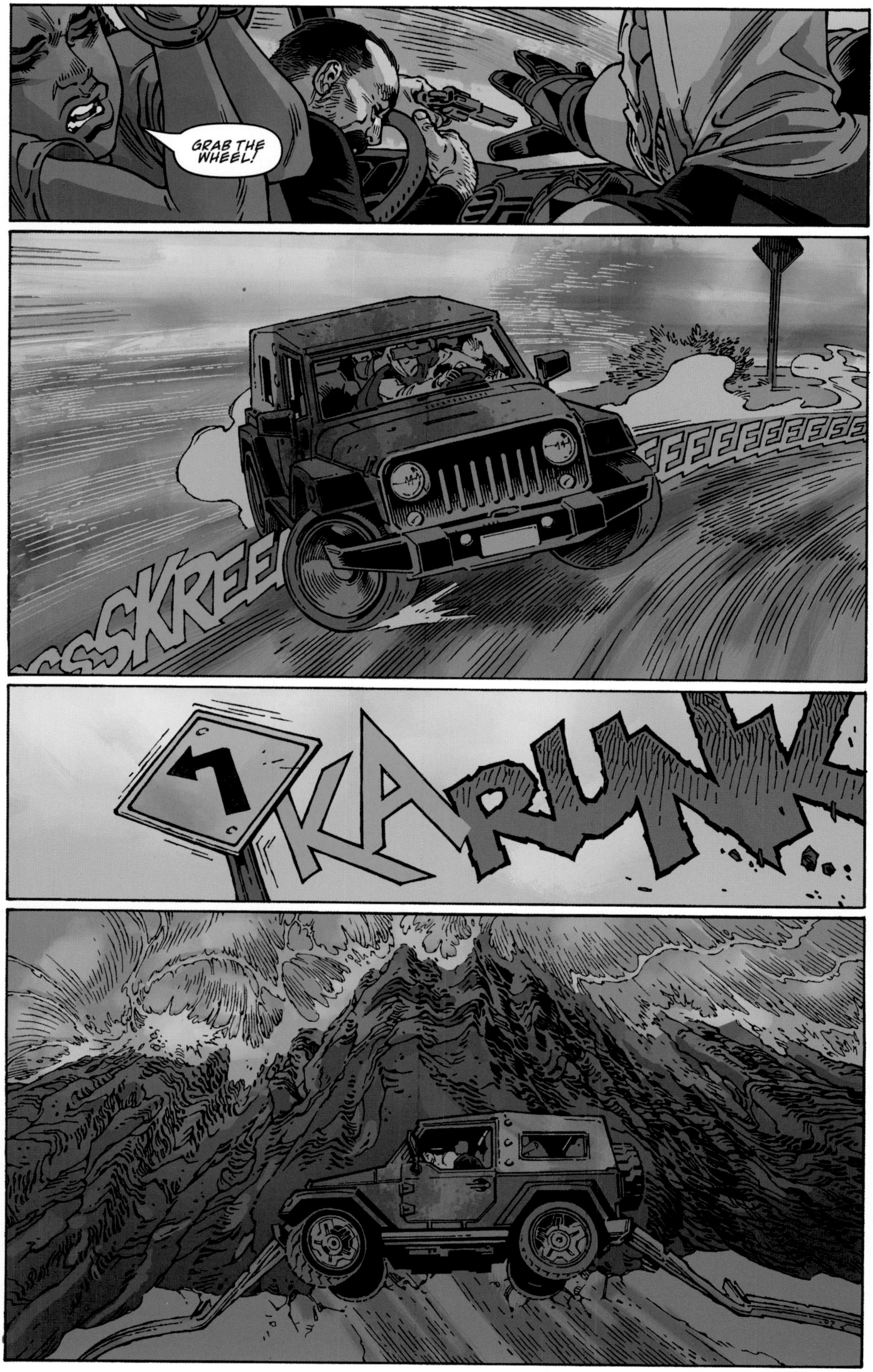
GRAB THE WHEEL!
SSKREE
EEEEEEEEEE
KARUNK

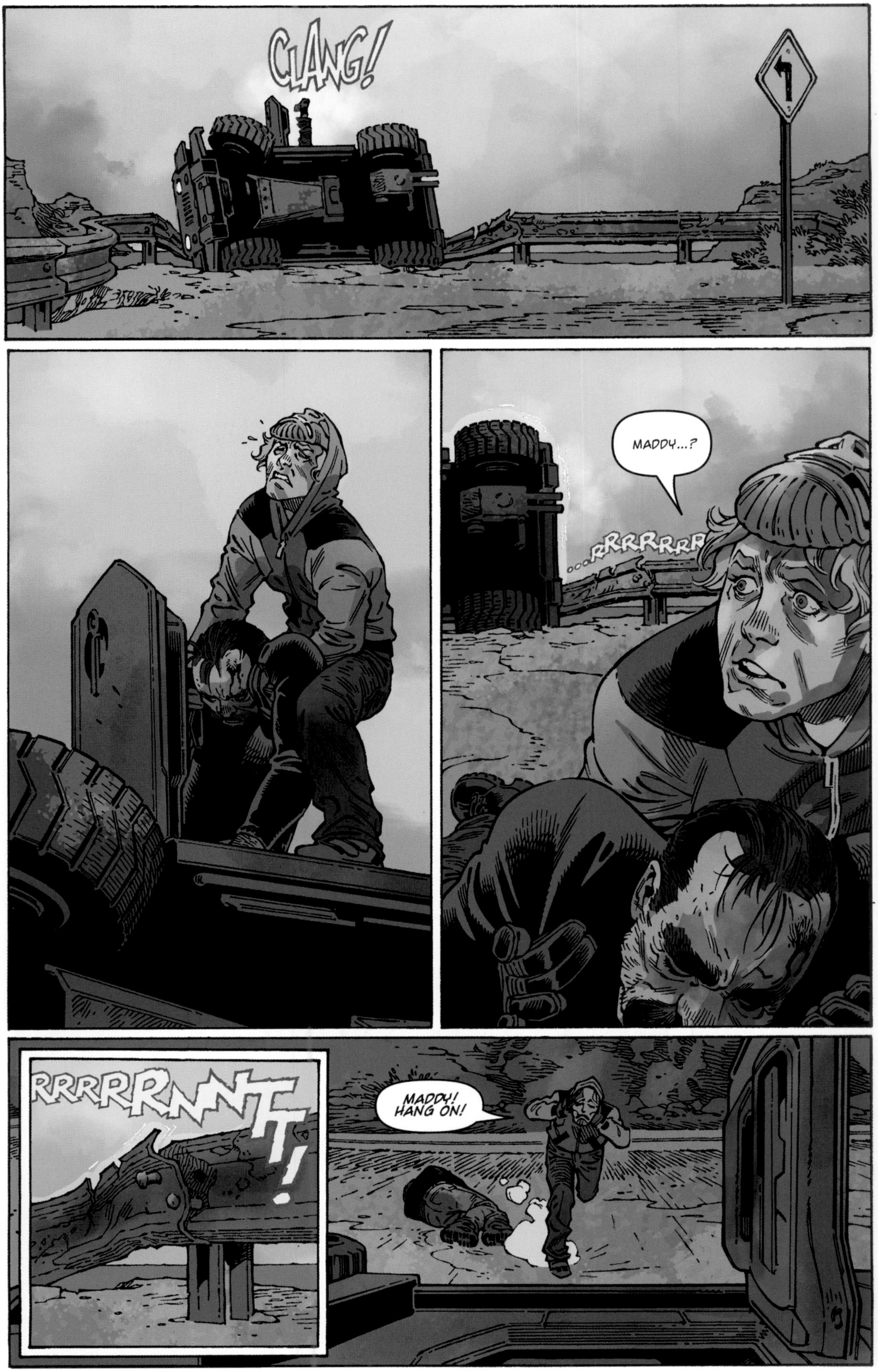
CLANG!
MADDY...?
...RRRRRRR
RRRRRNNNT!
MADDY! HANG ON!

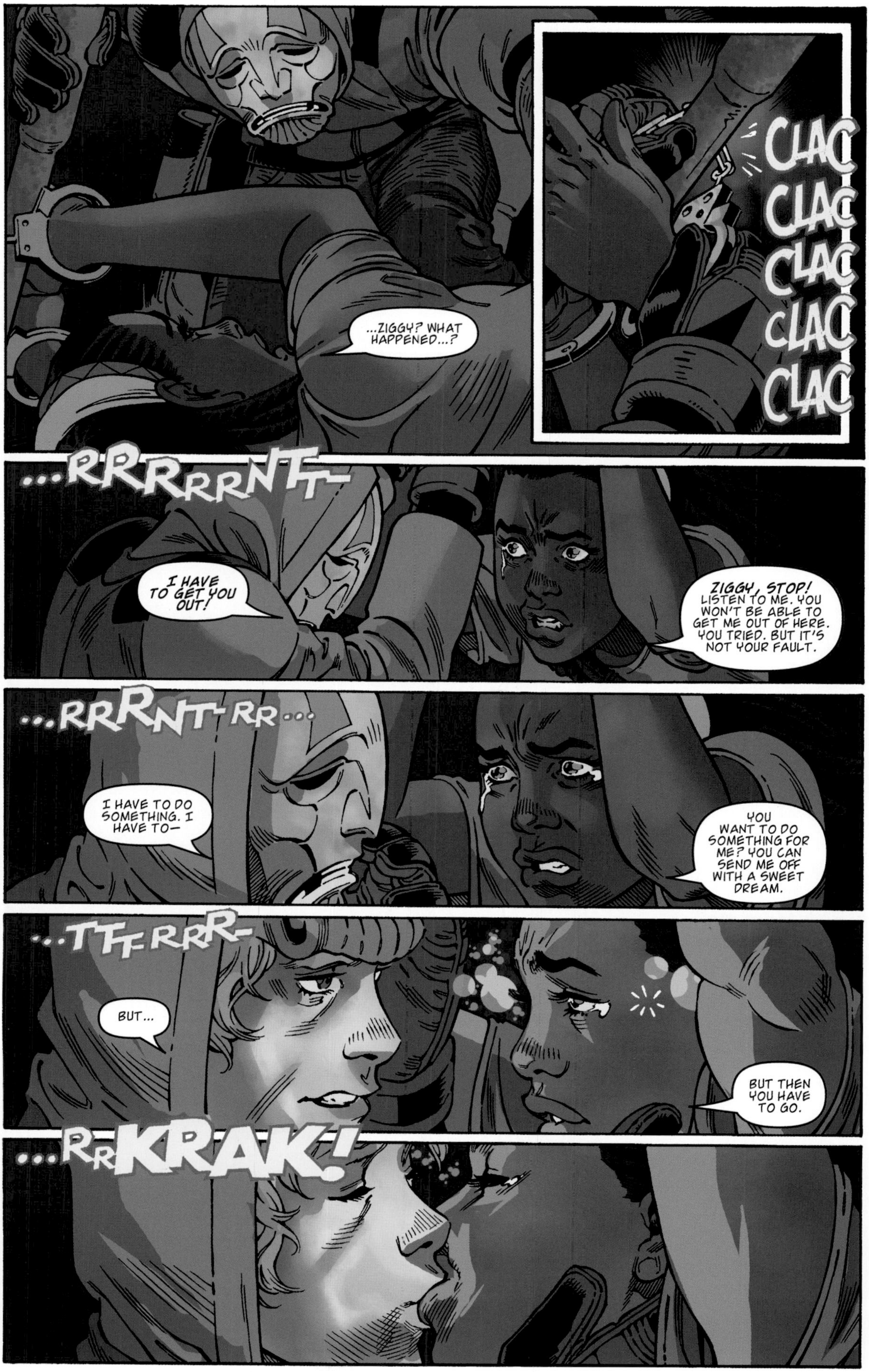

...ZIGGY? WHAT HAPPENED...?
CLAC
CLAC
CLAC
CLAC
CLAC
...RRRRRRNTT-
I HAVE TO GET YOU OUT!
ZIGGY, STOP! LISTEN TO ME. YOU WON'T BE ABLE TO GET ME OUT OF HERE. YOU TRIED. BUT IT'S NOT YOUR FAULT.
...RRRNT-RR...
I HAVE TO DO SOMETHING. I HAVE TO—
YOU WANT TO DO SOMETHING FOR ME? YOU CAN SEND ME OFF WITH A SWEET DREAM.
...TTFRRR-
BUT...
BUT THEN YOU HAVE TO GO.
...RRKRAK!

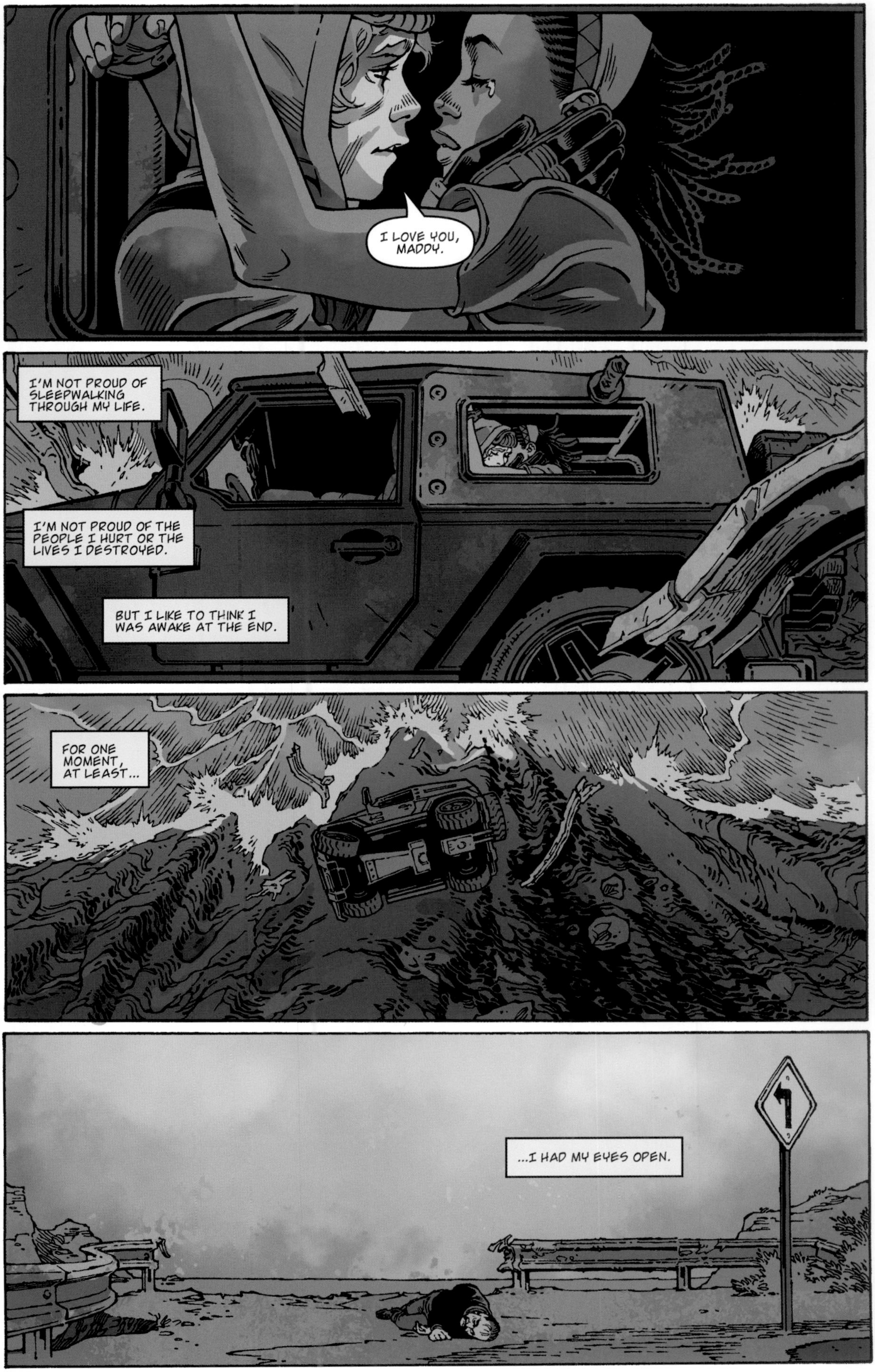
I LOVE YOU, MADDY.
I'M NOT PROUD OF SLEEPWALKING THROUGH MY LIFE.
I'M NOT PROUD OF THE PEOPLE I HURT OR THE LIVES I DESTROYED.
BUT I LIKE TO THINK I WAS AWAKE AT THE END.
FOR ONE MOMENT, AT LEAST...
...I HAD MY EYES OPEN.

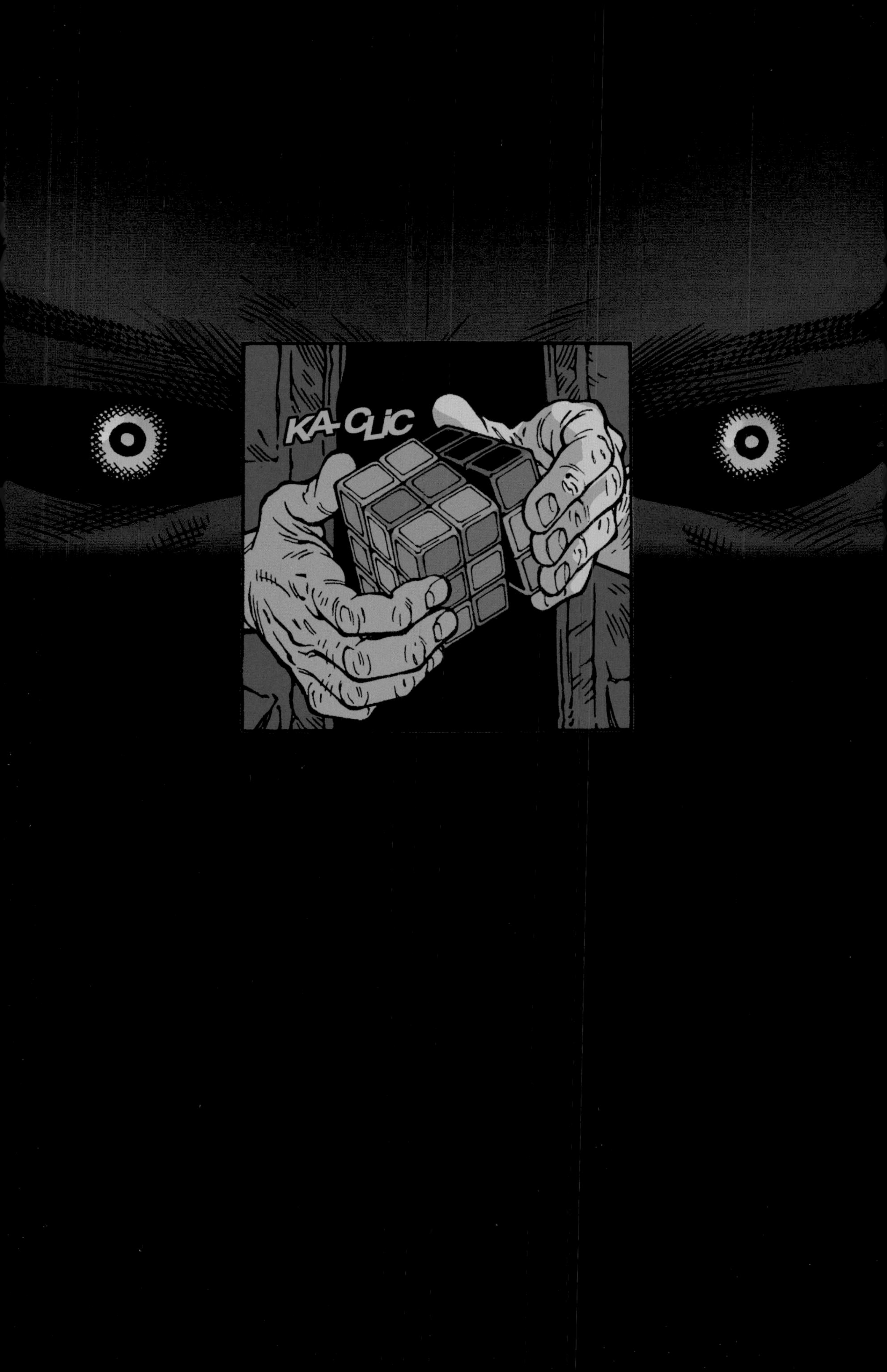
KA-CLIC

BLACK BOX

ART BY GABRIEL RODRIGUEZ
COLORS BY RYAN HILL

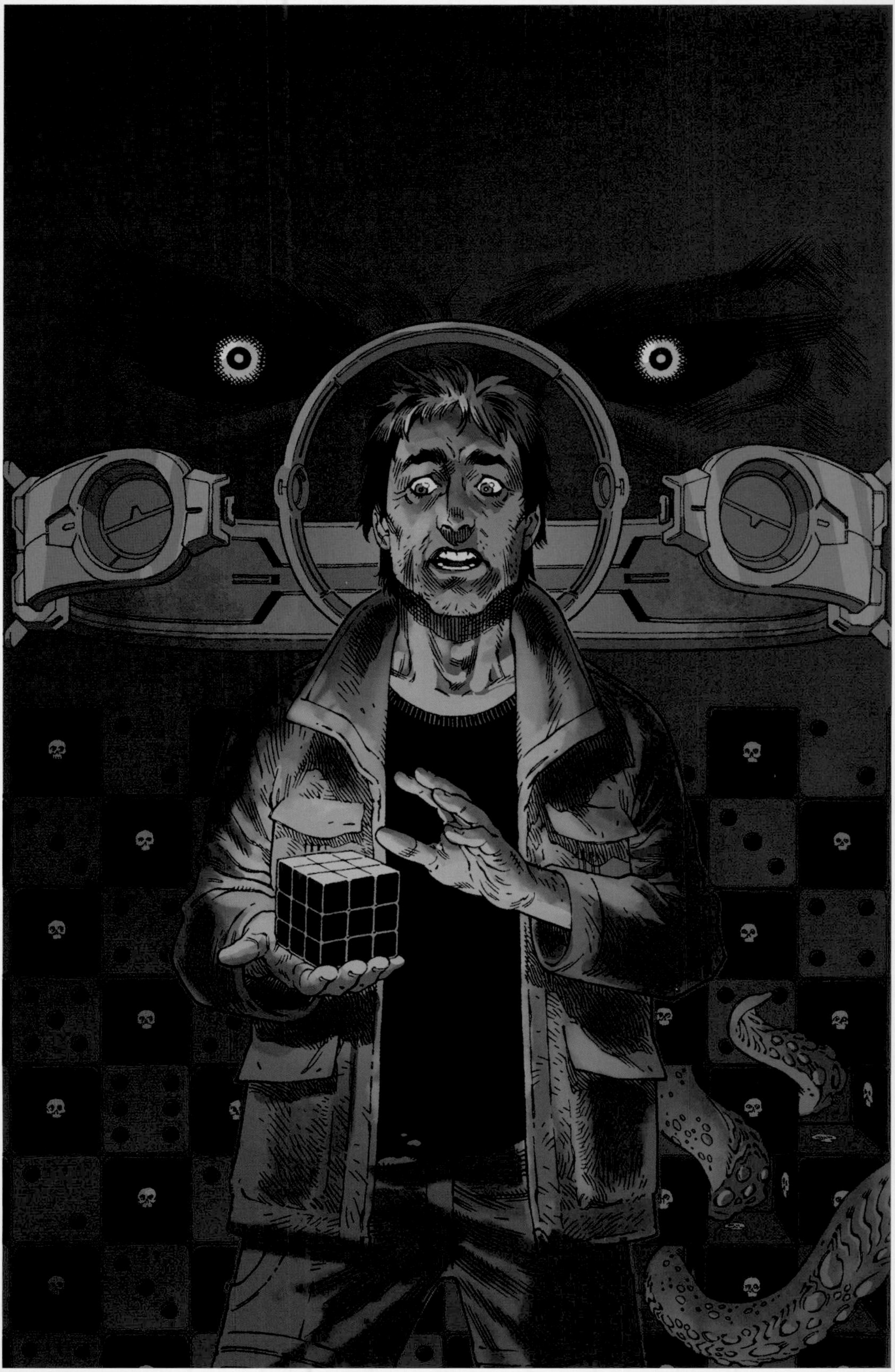

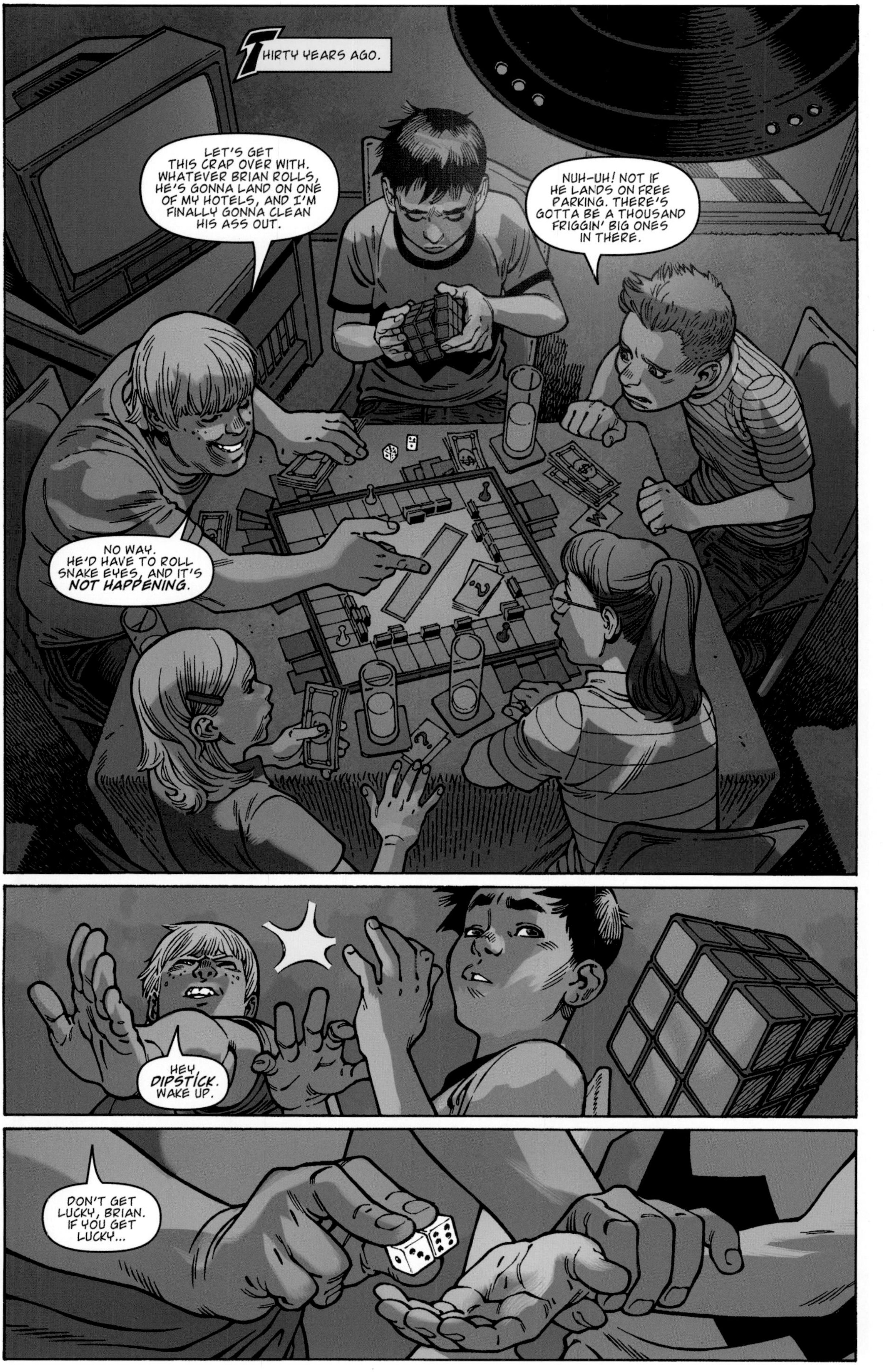
THIRTY YEARS AGO.
LET'S GET THIS CRAP OVER WITH. WHATEVER BRIAN ROLLS, HE'S GONNA LAND ON ONE OF MY HOTELS, AND I'M FINALLY GONNA CLEAN HIS ASS OUT.
NUH-UH! NOT IF HE LANDS ON FREE PARKING. THERE'S GOTTA BE A THOUSAND FRIGGIN' BIG ONES IN THERE.
NO WAY. HE'D HAVE TO ROLL SNAKE EYES, AND IT'S NOT HAPPENING.
HEY DIPSTICK. WAKE UP.
DON'T GET LUCKY, BRIAN. IF YOU GET LUCKY...

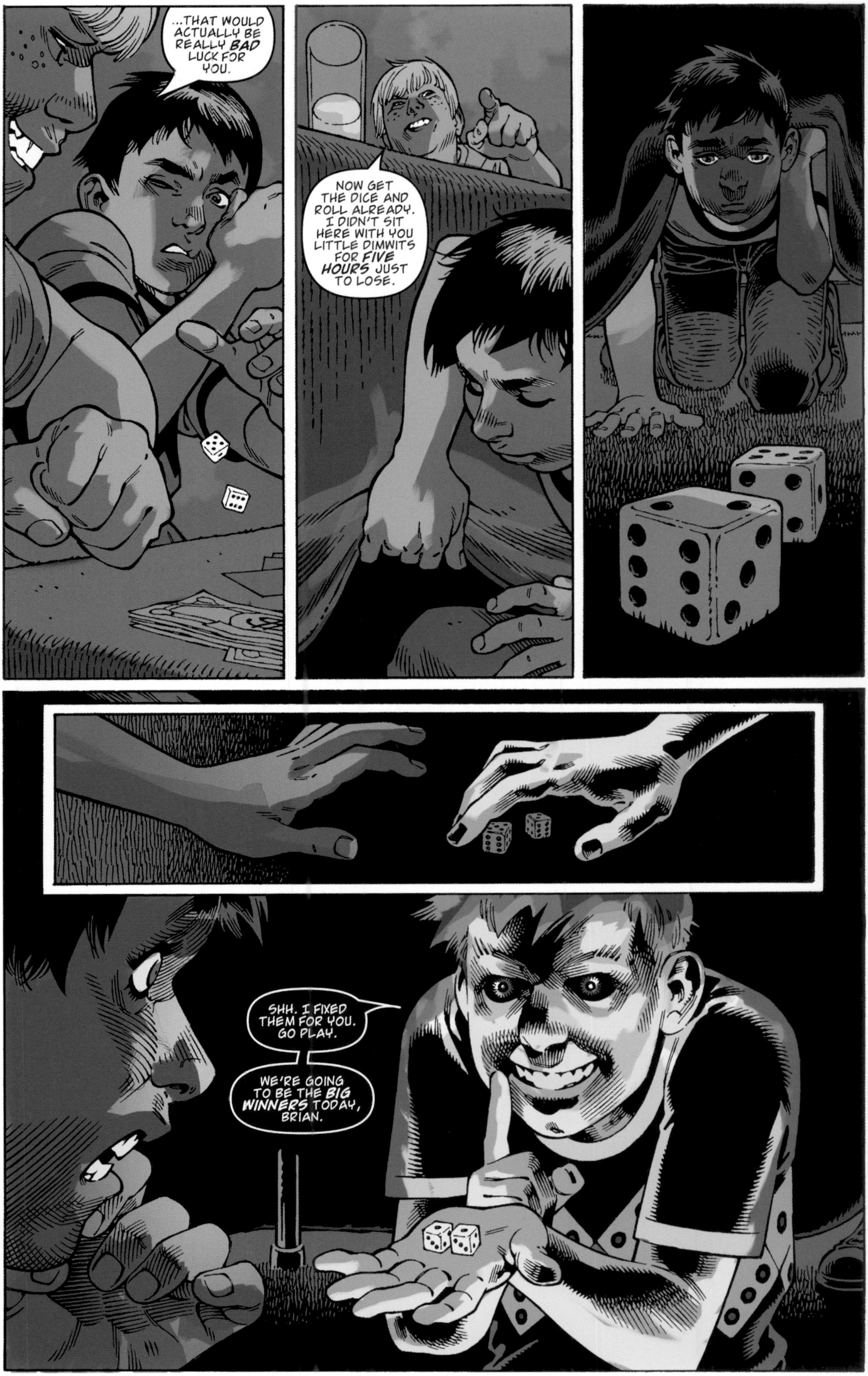
...THAT WOULD ACTUALLY BE REALLY BAD LUCK FOR YOU.
NOW GET THE DICE AND ROLL ALREADY. I DIDN'T SIT HERE WITH YOU LITTLE DIMWITS FOR FIVE HOURS JUST TO LOSE.
SHH. I FIXED THEM FOR YOU. GO PLAY.
WE'RE GOING TO BE THE BIG WINNERS TODAY, BRIAN.

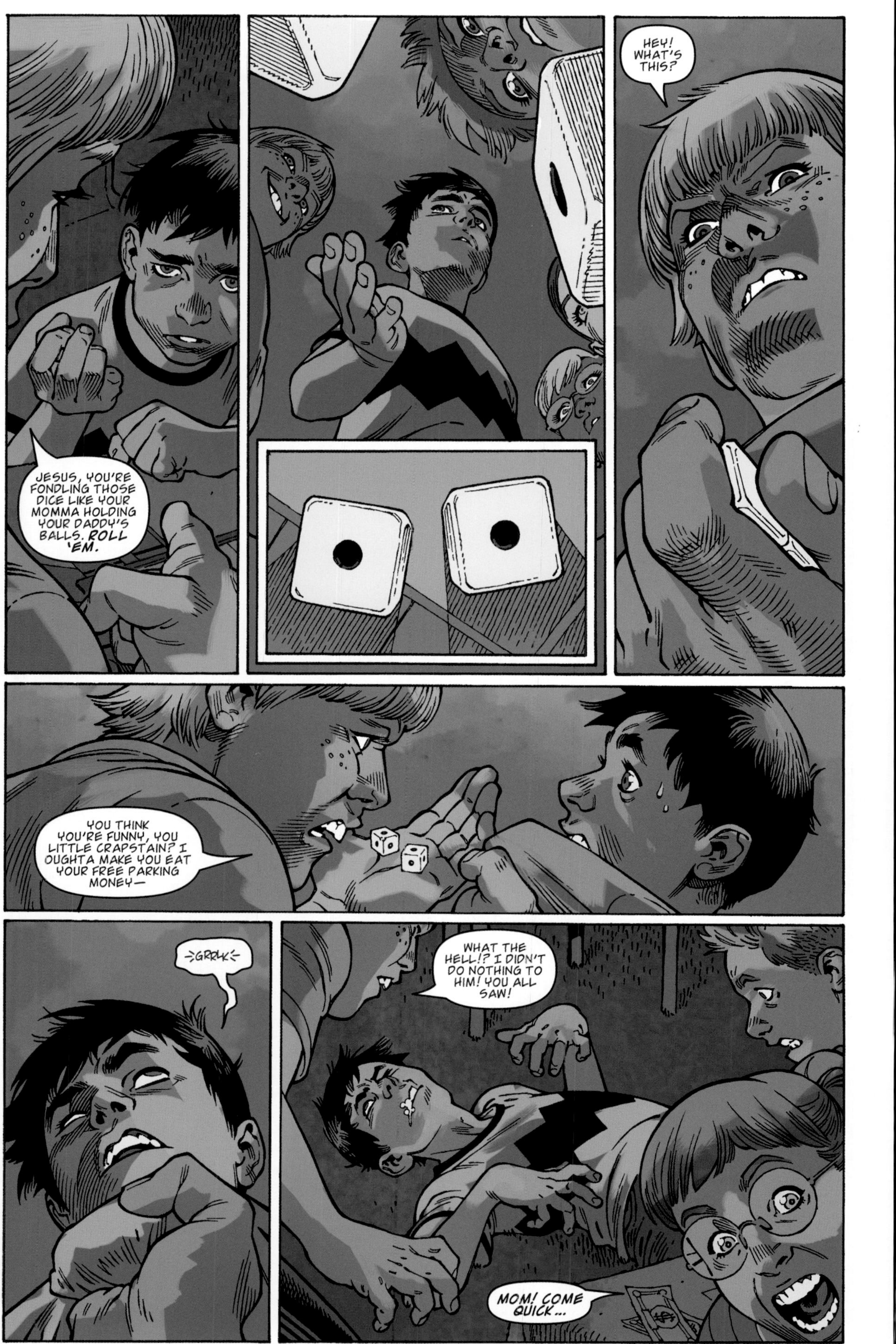
JESUS, YOU'RE FONDLING THOSE DICE LIKE YOUR MOMMA HOLDING YOUR DADDY'S BALLS. ROLL 'EM.
HEY! WHAT'S THIS?
YOU THINK YOU'RE FUNNY, YOU LITTLE CRAPSTAIN? I OUGHTA MAKE YOU EAT YOUR FREE PARKING MONEY—
-GRRLK-
WHAT THE HELL!? I DIDN'T DO NOTHING TO HIM! YOU ALL SAW!
MOM! COME QUICK...

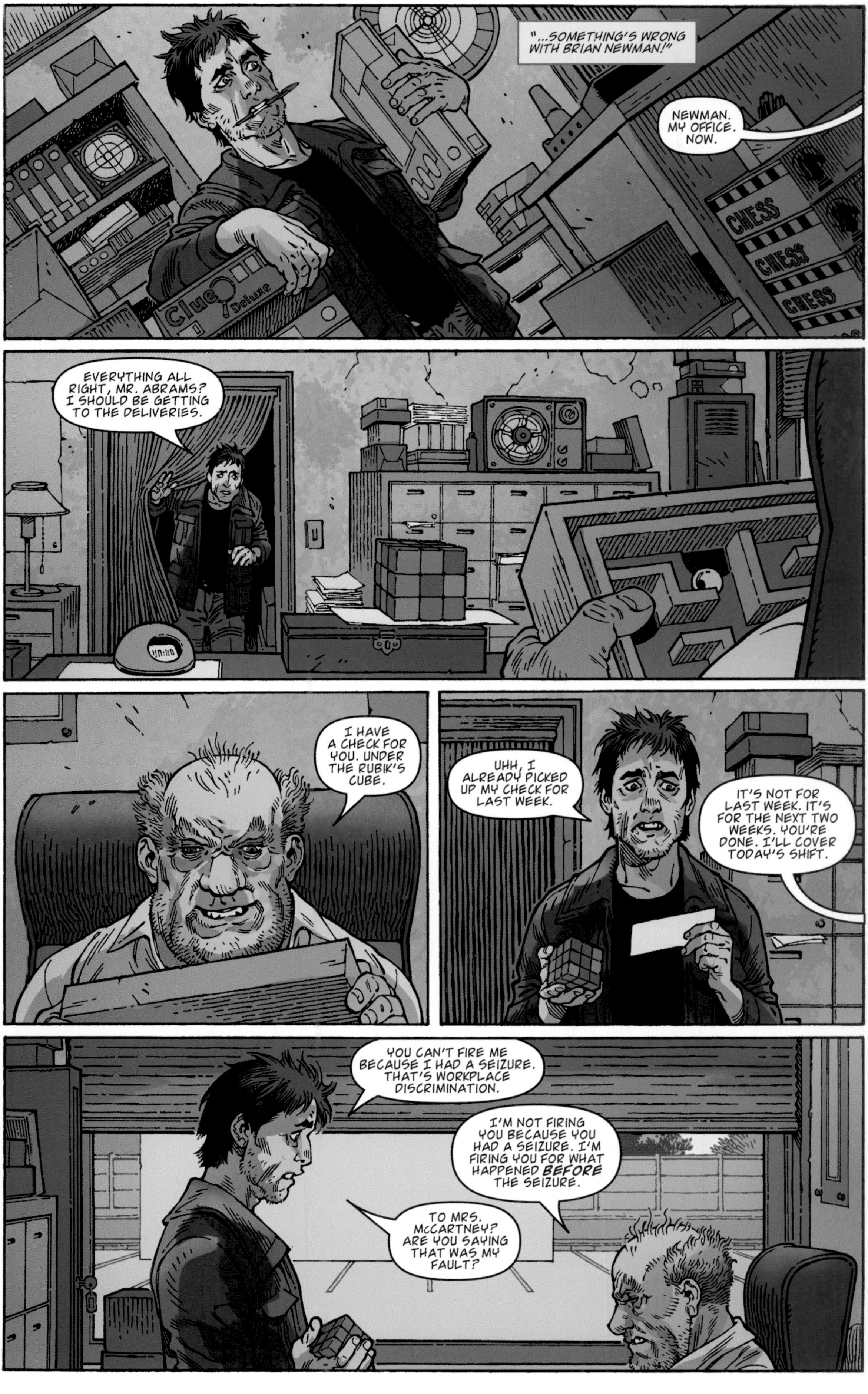
"...SOMETHING'S WRONG WITH BRIAN NEWMAN!"
NEWMAN. MY OFFICE. NOW.
CHESS
CHESS
CHESS
Clue Deluxe
EVERYTHING ALL RIGHT, MR. ABRAMS? I SHOULD BE GETTING TO THE DELIVERIES.
I HAVE A CHECK FOR YOU. UNDER THE RUBIK'S CUBE.
UHH, I ALREADY PICKED UP MY CHECK FOR LAST WEEK.
IT'S NOT FOR LAST WEEK. IT'S FOR THE NEXT TWO WEEKS. YOU'RE DONE. I'LL COVER TODAY'S SHIFT.
YOU CAN'T FIRE ME BECAUSE I HAD A SEIZURE. THAT'S WORKPLACE DISCRIMINATION.
I'M NOT FIRING YOU BECAUSE YOU HAD A SEIZURE. I'M FIRING YOU FOR WHAT HAPPENED BEFORE THE SEIZURE.
TO MRS. McCARTNEY? ARE YOU SAYING THAT WAS MY FAULT?

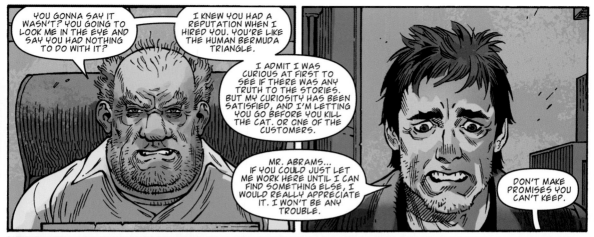

YOU GONNA SAY IT WASN'T? YOU GOING TO LOOK ME IN THE EYE AND SAY YOU HAD NOTHING TO DO WITH IT?

I KNEW YOU HAD A REPUTATION WHEN I HIRED YOU. YOU'RE LIKE THE HUMAN BERMUDA TRIANGLE.

I ADMIT I WAS CURIOUS AT FIRST TO SEE IF THERE WAS ANY TRUTH TO THE STORIES. BUT MY CURIOSITY HAS BEEN SATISFIED, AND I'M LETTING YOU GO BEFORE YOU KILL THE CAT. OR ONE OF THE CUSTOMERS.

MR. ABRAMS... IF YOU COULD JUST LET ME WORK HERE UNTIL I CAN FIND SOMETHING ELSE, I WOULD REALLY APPRECIATE IT. I WON'T BE ANY TROUBLE.

DON'T MAKE PROMISES YOU CAN'T KEEP.

I DON'T THINK YOU UNDERSTAND HOW IMPORTANT IT IS TO ME TO KEEP WORKING. TO AT LEAST HAVE THAT.

I UNDERSTAND. I JUST DON'T *CARE*. YOU WANT A JOB, GET YOURSELF A REALITY SHOW OR SOMETHING. THEY LOVE PASTY FREAKS LIKE YOU ON TV.

AND I WANT THAT RUBIK'S CUBE BACK, NEWMAN.

NEWMAN!

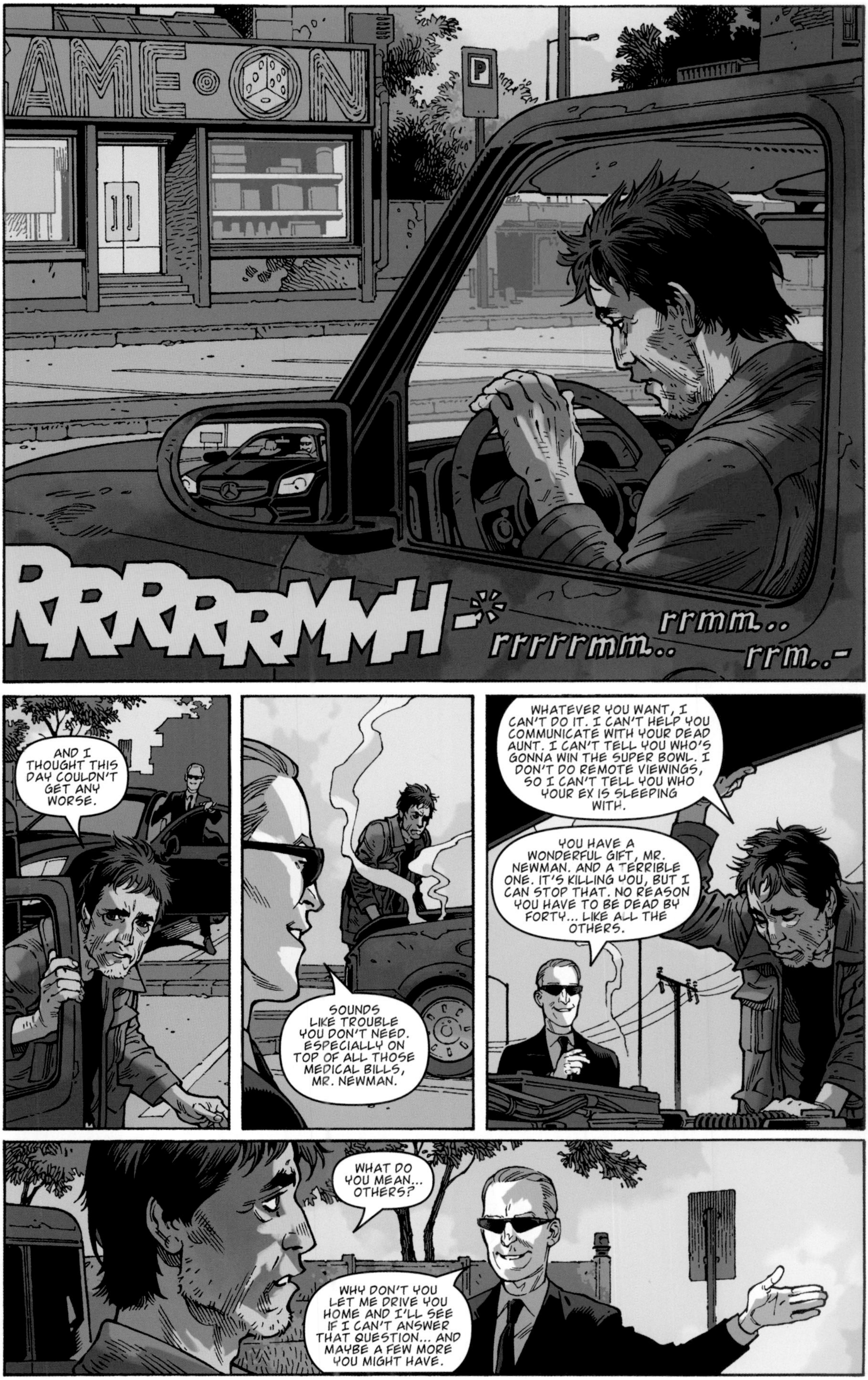
AME ON
P
RRRRRRMMH-
rrrrrmm..
rrmm..
rrm..-
AND I THOUGHT THIS DAY COULDN'T GET ANY WORSE.
SOUNDS LIKE TROUBLE YOU DON'T NEED. ESPECIALLY ON TOP OF ALL THOSE MEDICAL BILLS, MR. NEWMAN.
WHATEVER YOU WANT, I CAN'T DO IT. I CAN'T HELP YOU COMMUNICATE WITH YOUR DEAD AUNT. I CAN'T TELL YOU WHO'S GONNA WIN THE SUPER BOWL. I DON'T DO REMOTE VIEWINGS, SO I CAN'T TELL YOU WHO YOUR EX IS SLEEPING WITH.
YOU HAVE A WONDERFUL GIFT, MR. NEWMAN. AND A TERRIBLE ONE. IT'S KILLING YOU, BUT I CAN STOP THAT. NO REASON YOU HAVE TO BE DEAD BY FORTY... LIKE ALL THE OTHERS.
WHAT DO YOU MEAN... OTHERS?
WHY DON'T YOU LET ME DRIVE YOU HOME AND I'LL SEE IF I CAN'T ANSWER THAT QUESTION... AND MAYBE A FEW MORE YOU MIGHT HAVE.

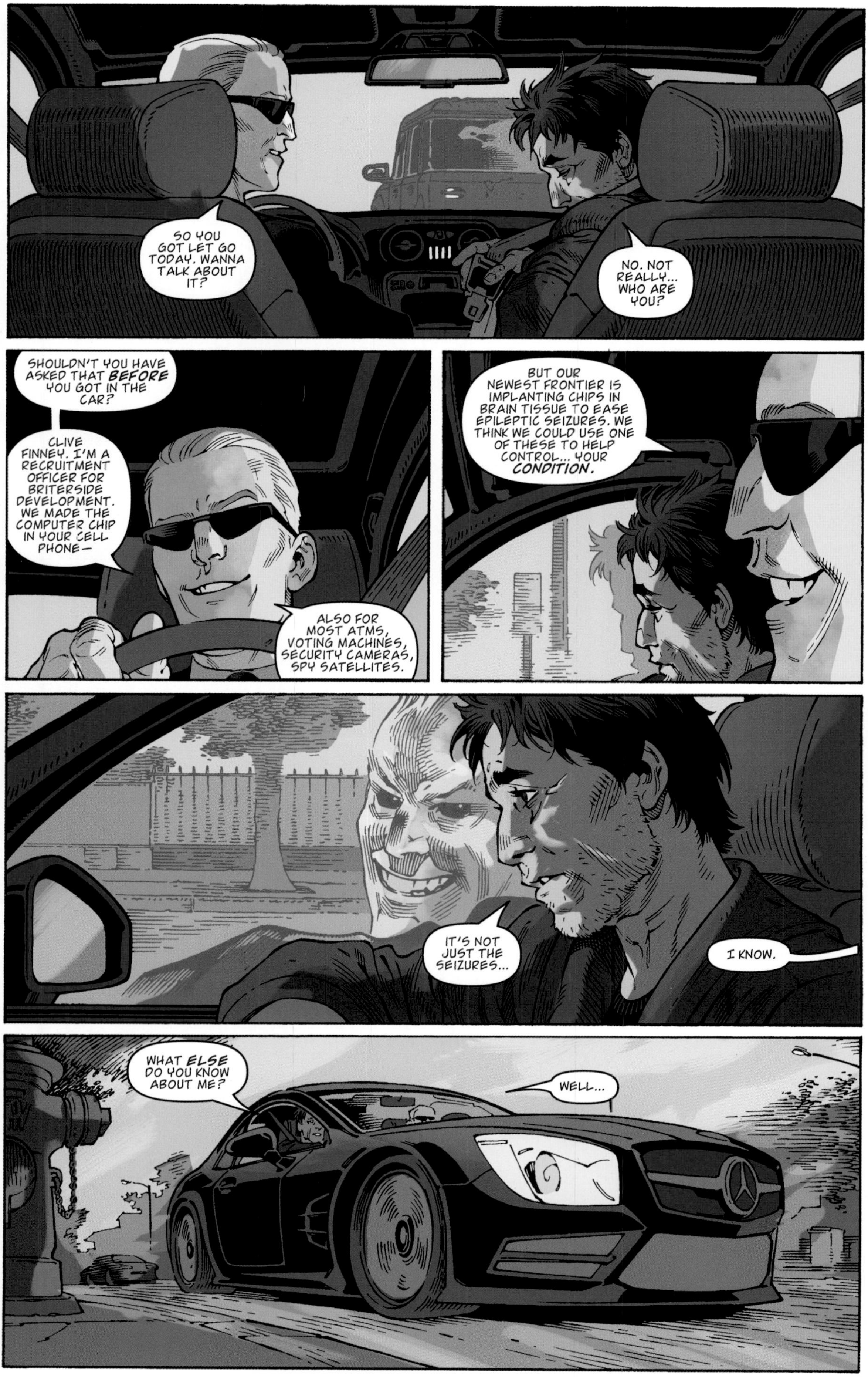
SO YOU GOT LET GO TODAY. WANNA TALK ABOUT IT?
NO. NOT REALLY... WHO ARE YOU?
SHOULDN'T YOU HAVE ASKED THAT BEFORE YOU GOT IN THE CAR?
CLIVE FINNEY. I'M A RECRUITMENT OFFICER FOR BRITERSIDE DEVELOPMENT. WE MADE THE COMPUTER CHIP IN YOUR CELL PHONE—
ALSO FOR MOST ATMS, VOTING MACHINES, SECURITY CAMERAS, SPY SATELLITES.
BUT OUR NEWEST FRONTIER IS IMPLANTING CHIPS IN BRAIN TISSUE TO EASE EPILEPTIC SEIZURES. WE THINK WE COULD USE ONE OF THESE TO HELP CONTROL... YOUR CONDITION.
IT'S NOT JUST THE SEIZURES...
I KNOW.
WHAT ELSE DO YOU KNOW ABOUT ME?
WELL...

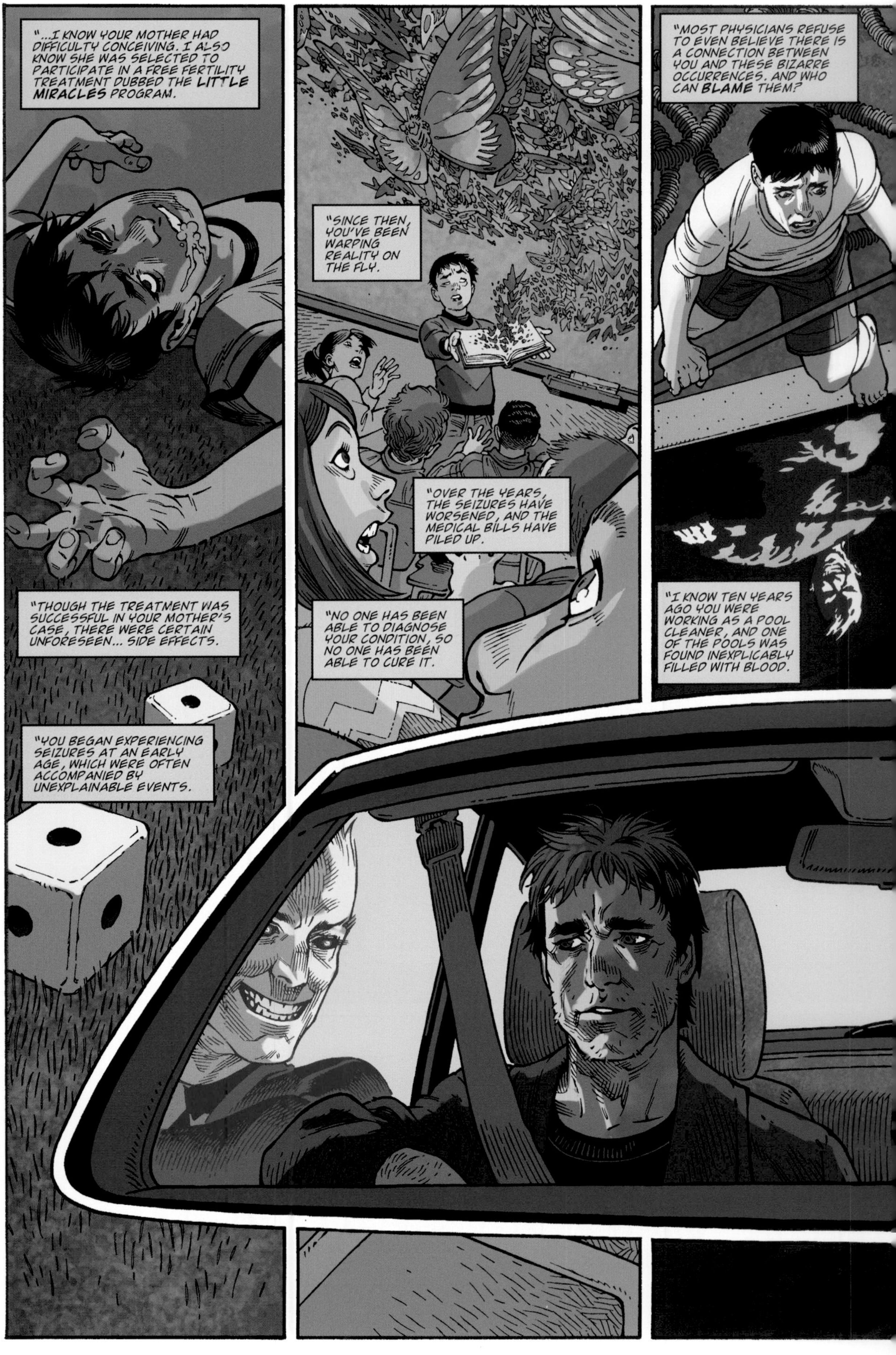
"...I KNOW YOUR MOTHER HAD DIFFICULTY CONCEIVING. I ALSO KNOW SHE WAS SELECTED TO PARTICIPATE IN A FREE FERTILITY TREATMENT DUBBED THE LITTLE MIRACLES PROGRAM.
"THOUGH THE TREATMENT WAS SUCCESSFUL IN YOUR MOTHER'S CASE, THERE WERE CERTAIN UNFORESEEN... SIDE EFFECTS.
"YOU BEGAN EXPERIENCING SEIZURES AT AN EARLY AGE, WHICH WERE OFTEN ACCOMPANIED BY UNEXPLAINABLE EVENTS.
"SINCE THEN, YOU'VE BEEN WARPING REALITY ON THE FLY.
"OVER THE YEARS, THE SEIZURES HAVE WORSENED, AND THE MEDICAL BILLS HAVE PILED UP.
"NO ONE HAS BEEN ABLE TO DIAGNOSE YOUR CONDITION, SO NO ONE HAS BEEN ABLE TO CURE IT.
"MOST PHYSICIANS REFUSE TO EVEN BELIEVE THERE IS A CONNECTION BETWEEN YOU AND THESE BIZARRE OCCURRENCES. AND WHO CAN BLAME THEM?
"I KNOW TEN YEARS AGO YOU WERE WORKING AS A POOL CLEANER, AND ONE OF THE POOLS WAS FOUND INEXPLICABLY FILLED WITH BLOOD.

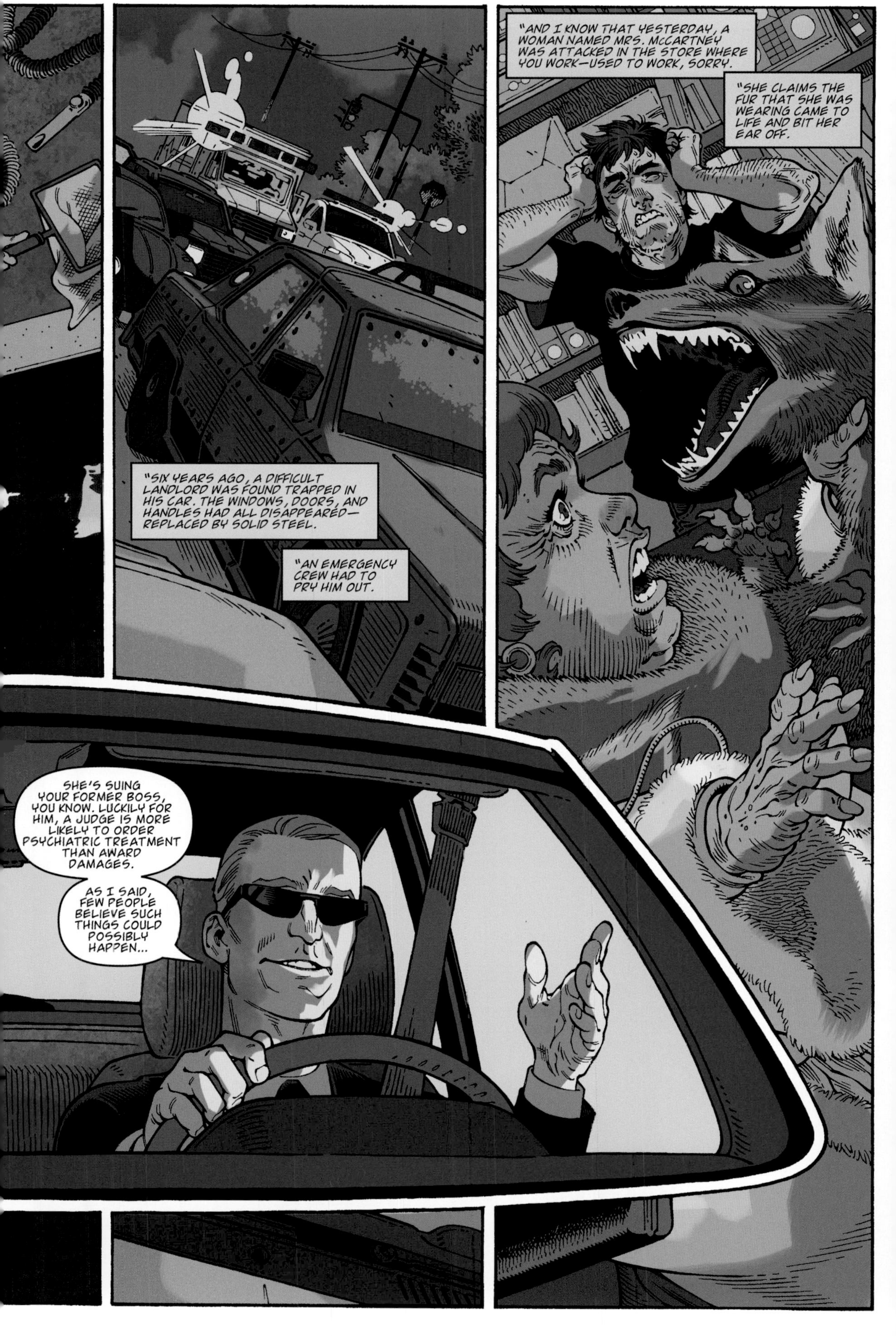
"SIX YEARS AGO, A DIFFICULT LANDLORD WAS FOUND TRAPPED IN HIS CAR. THE WINDOWS, DOORS, AND HANDLES HAD ALL DISAPPEARED—REPLACED BY SOLID STEEL.
"AN EMERGENCY CREW HAD TO PRY HIM OUT.
"AND I KNOW THAT YESTERDAY, A WOMAN NAMED MRS. McCARTNEY WAS ATTACKED IN THE STORE WHERE YOU WORK—USED TO WORK, SORRY.
"SHE CLAIMS THE FUR THAT SHE WAS WEARING CAME TO LIFE AND BIT HER EAR OFF.
SHE'S SUING YOUR FORMER BOSS, YOU KNOW. LUCKILY FOR HIM, A JUDGE IS MORE LIKELY TO ORDER PSYCHIATRIC TREATMENT THAN AWARD DAMAGES.
AS I SAID, FEW PEOPLE BELIEVE SUCH THINGS COULD POSSIBLY HAPPEN...

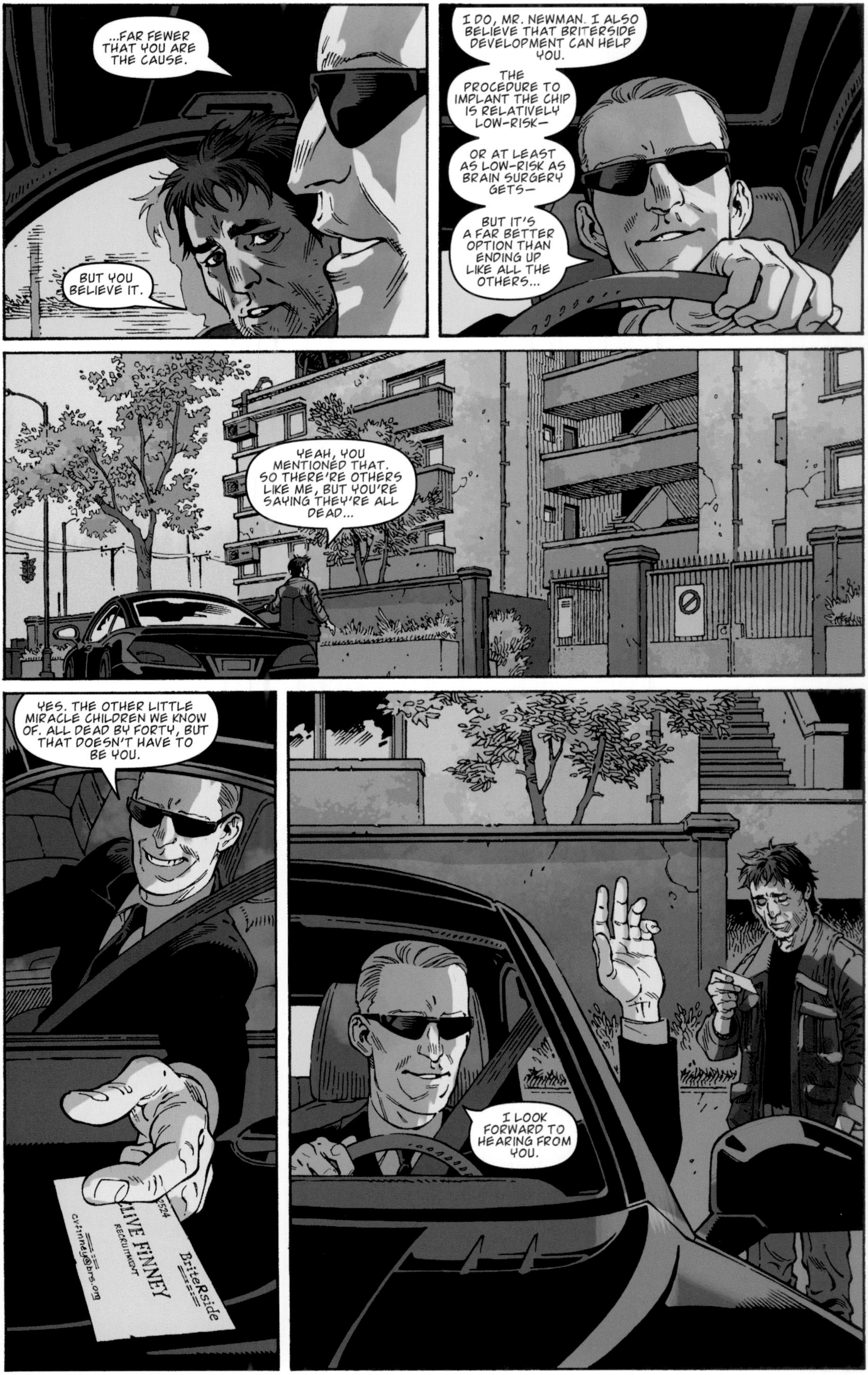
...FAR FEWER THAT YOU ARE THE CAUSE.
BUT YOU BELIEVE IT.
I DO, MR. NEWMAN. I ALSO BELIEVE THAT BRITERSIDE DEVELOPMENT CAN HELP YOU.
THE PROCEDURE TO IMPLANT THE CHIP IS RELATIVELY LOW-RISK—
OR AT LEAST AS LOW-RISK AS BRAIN SURGERY GETS—
BUT IT'S A FAR BETTER OPTION THAN ENDING UP LIKE ALL THE OTHERS...
YEAH, YOU MENTIONED THAT. SO THERE'RE OTHERS LIKE ME, BUT YOU'RE SAYING THEY'RE ALL DEAD...
YES. THE OTHER LITTLE MIRACLE CHILDREN WE KNOW OF. ALL DEAD BY FORTY, BUT THAT DOESN'T HAVE TO BE YOU.
BriteRside
2524
LIVE FINNEY
RECRUITMENT
cvfinney@brs.org
I LOOK FORWARD TO HEARING FROM YOU.

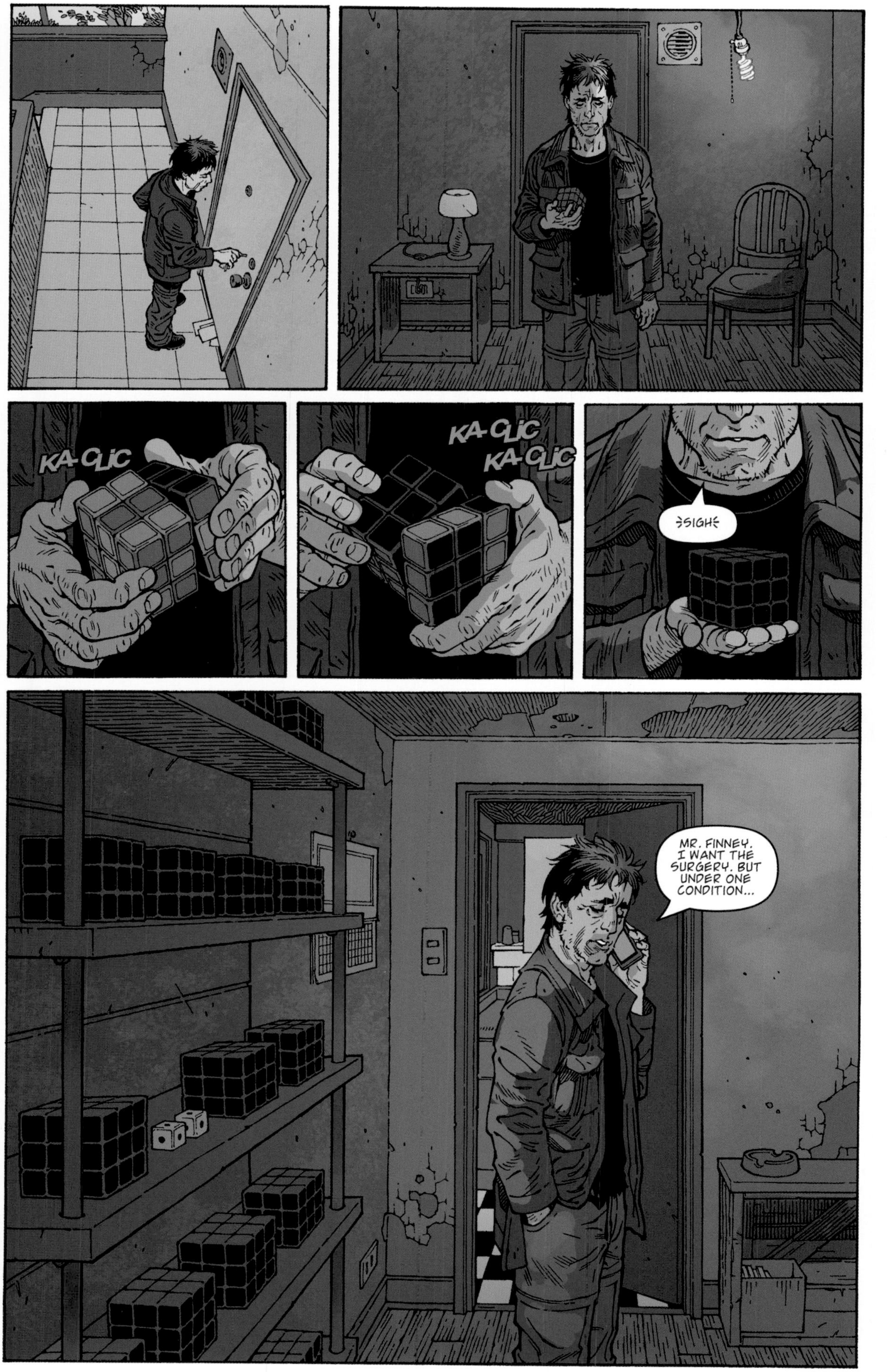

KA-CLIC
KA-CLIC
KA-CLIC
SIGH
MR. FINNEY. I WANT THE SURGERY. BUT UNDER ONE CONDITION...

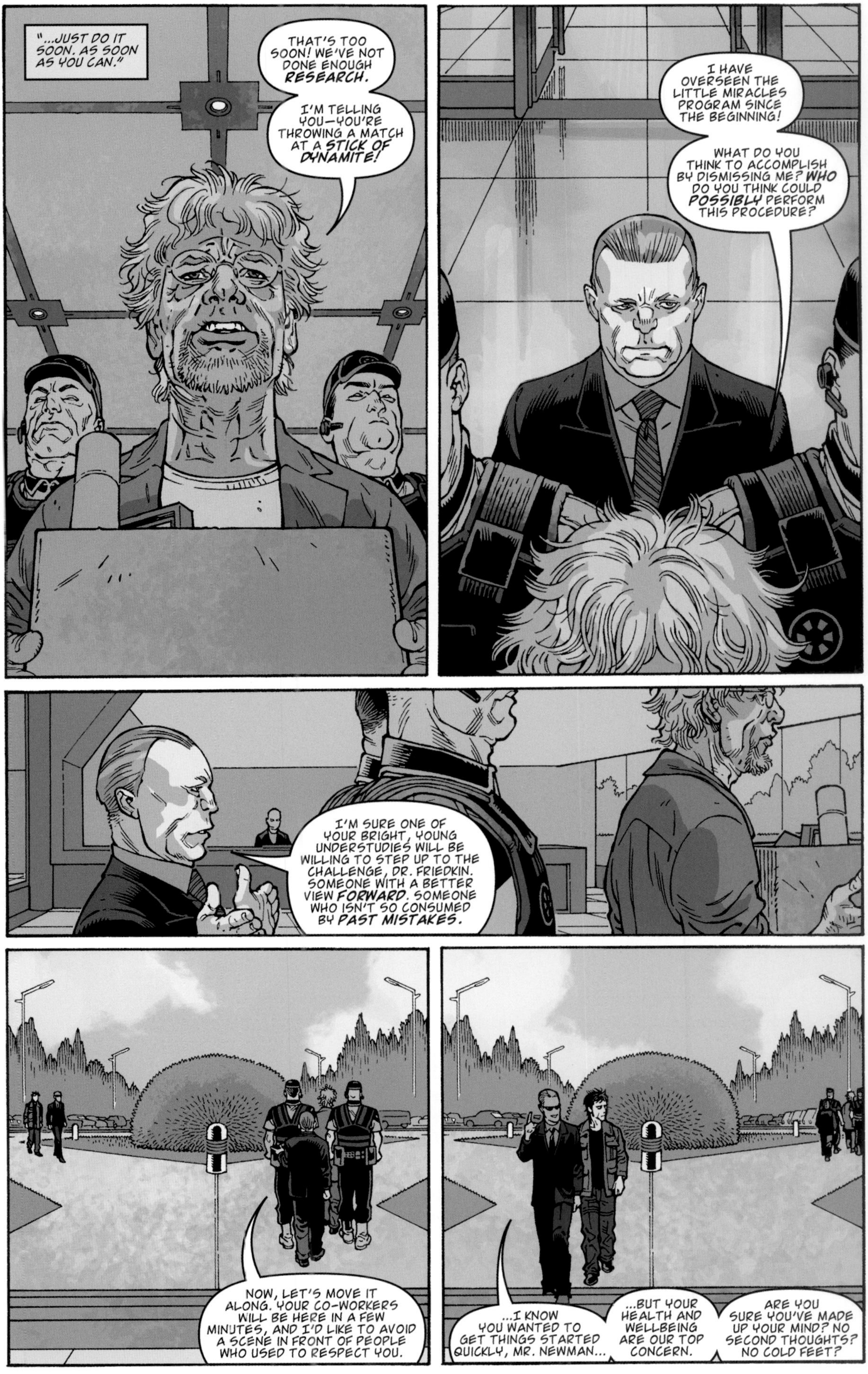
"...JUST DO IT SOON. AS SOON AS YOU CAN."
THAT'S TOO SOON! WE'VE NOT DONE ENOUGH RESEARCH.
I'M TELLING YOU—YOU'RE THROWING A MATCH AT A STICK OF DYNAMITE!
I HAVE OVERSEEN THE LITTLE MIRACLES PROGRAM SINCE THE BEGINNING!
WHAT DO YOU THINK TO ACCOMPLISH BY DISMISSING ME? WHO DO YOU THINK COULD POSSIBLY PERFORM THIS PROCEDURE?
I'M SURE ONE OF YOUR BRIGHT, YOUNG UNDERSTUDIES WILL BE WILLING TO STEP UP TO THE CHALLENGE, DR. FRIEDKIN. SOMEONE WITH A BETTER VIEW FORWARD. SOMEONE WHO ISN'T SO CONSUMED BY PAST MISTAKES.
NOW, LET'S MOVE IT ALONG. YOUR CO-WORKERS WILL BE HERE IN A FEW MINUTES, AND I'D LIKE TO AVOID A SCENE IN FRONT OF PEOPLE WHO USED TO RESPECT YOU.
...I KNOW YOU WANTED TO GET THINGS STARTED QUICKLY, MR. NEWMAN...
...BUT YOUR HEALTH AND WELLBEING ARE OUR TOP CONCERN.
ARE YOU SURE YOU'VE MADE UP YOUR MIND? NO SECOND THOUGHTS? NO COLD FEET?

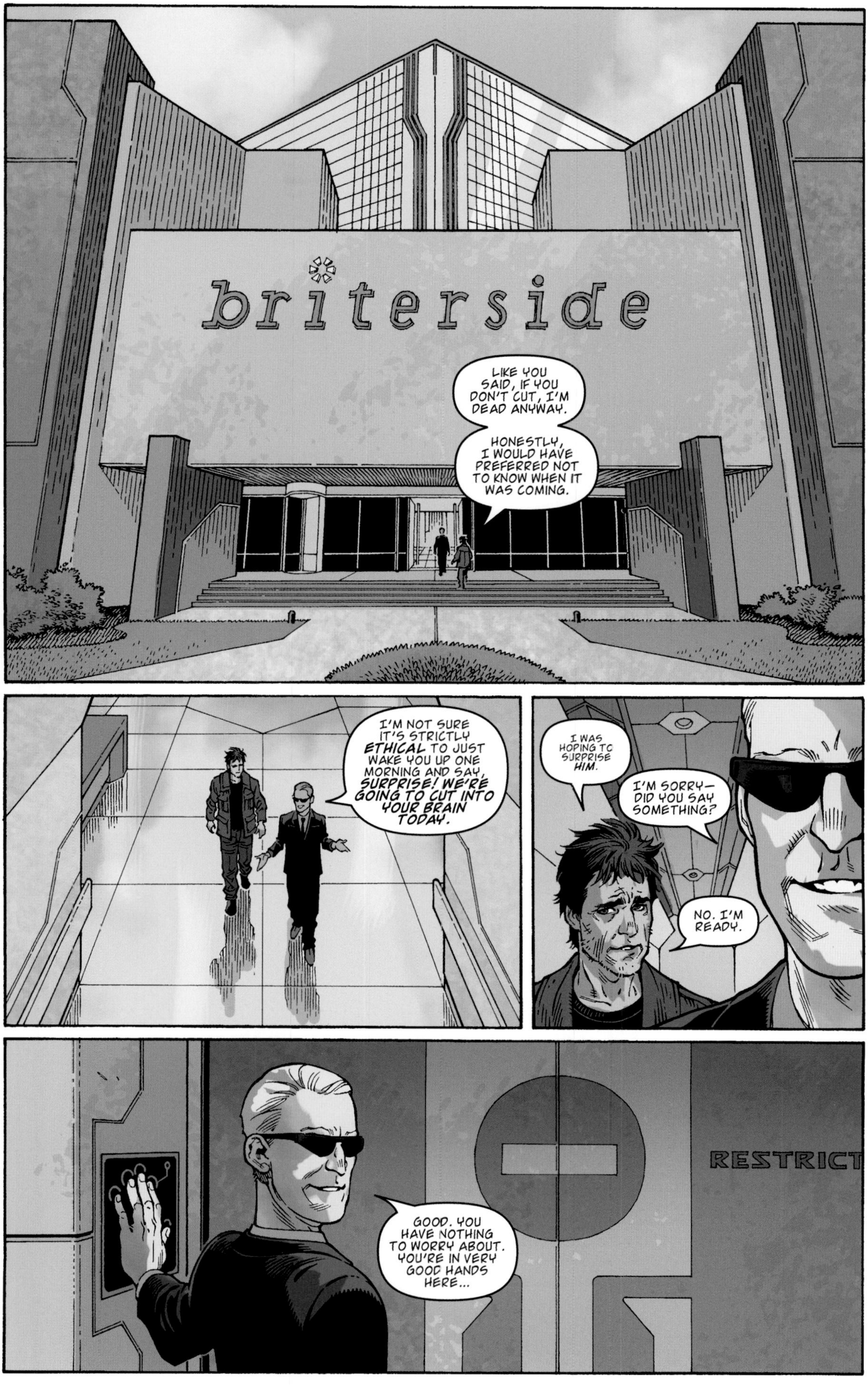
briterside
LIKE YOU SAID, IF YOU DON'T CUT, I'M DEAD ANYWAY.
HONESTLY, I WOULD HAVE PREFERRED NOT TO KNOW WHEN IT WAS COMING.
I'M NOT SURE IT'S STRICTLY ETHICAL TO JUST WAKE YOU UP ONE MORNING AND SAY, SURPRISE! WE'RE GOING TO CUT INTO YOUR BRAIN TODAY.
I WAS HOPING TO SURPRISE HIM.
I'M SORRY— DID YOU SAY SOMETHING?
NO. I'M READY.
RESTRICT
GOOD. YOU HAVE NOTHING TO WORRY ABOUT. YOU'RE IN VERY GOOD HANDS HERE...

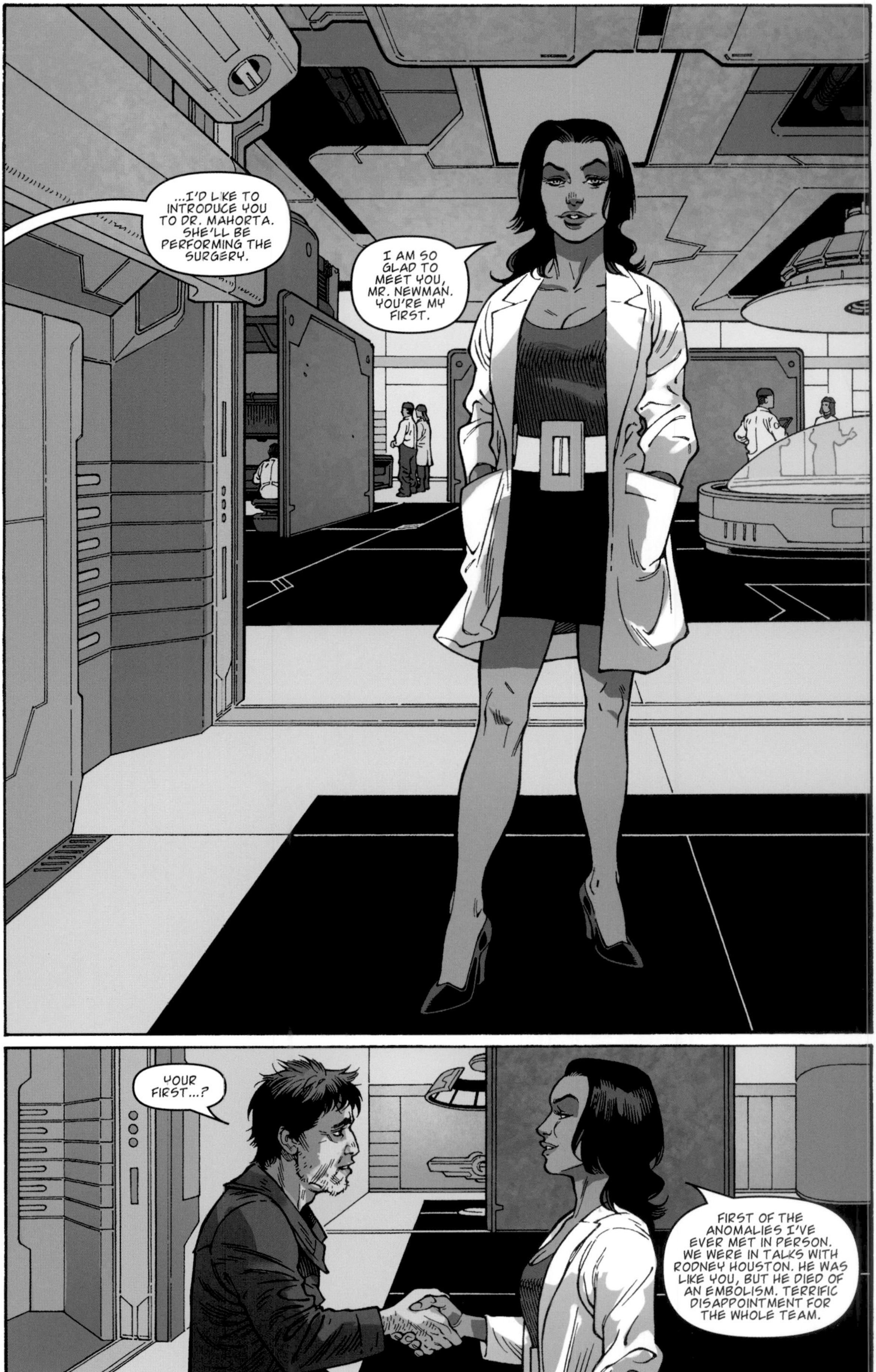
...I'D LIKE TO INTRODUCE YOU TO DR. MAHORTA. SHE'LL BE PERFORMING THE SURGERY.
I AM SO GLAD TO MEET YOU, MR. NEWMAN. YOU'RE MY FIRST.
YOUR FIRST...?
FIRST OF THE ANOMALIES I'VE EVER MET IN PERSON. WE WERE IN TALKS WITH RODNEY HOUSTON. HE WAS LIKE YOU, BUT HE DIED OF AN EMBOLISM. TERRIFIC DISAPPOINTMENT FOR THE WHOLE TEAM.

NOT TO MENTION RODNEY... AND HIS FAMILY...

HE DIDN'T HAVE ANY FAMILY. NOT ALIVE ANYWAY. THEY WERE STRUCK BY LIGHTNING.

THE... WHOLE FAMILY?

YES, THE MOTHER AND FATHER BOTH, AND TWO GRANDPARENTS. NOT ALL AT ONCE. THEY WERE EACH STRUCK AT DIFFERENT TIMES OVER ABOUT A DECADE.

I'M SORRY— I'M GETTING OFF TRACK. I JUST KEEP WONDERING...

...WHAT IT MUST BE LIKE TO BE YOU. WHAT I WOULDN'T GIVE TO HAVE YOUR BRAIN.

YEAH, WELL, DON'T TAKE OFF WITH IT WHILE YOU'VE GOT MY SKULL OPEN. I'M STILL USING IT.

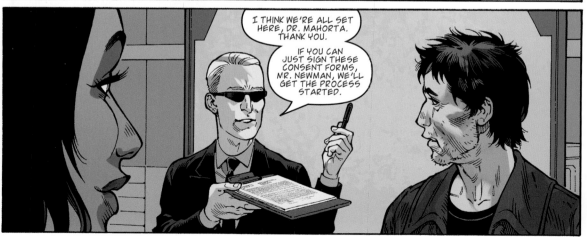

I THINK WE'RE ALL SET HERE, DR. MAHORTA. THANK YOU.

IF YOU CAN JUST SIGN THESE CONSENT FORMS, MR. NEWMAN, WE'LL GET THE PROCESS STARTED.

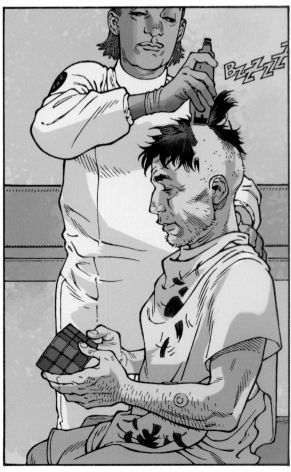

BZZZZZZ

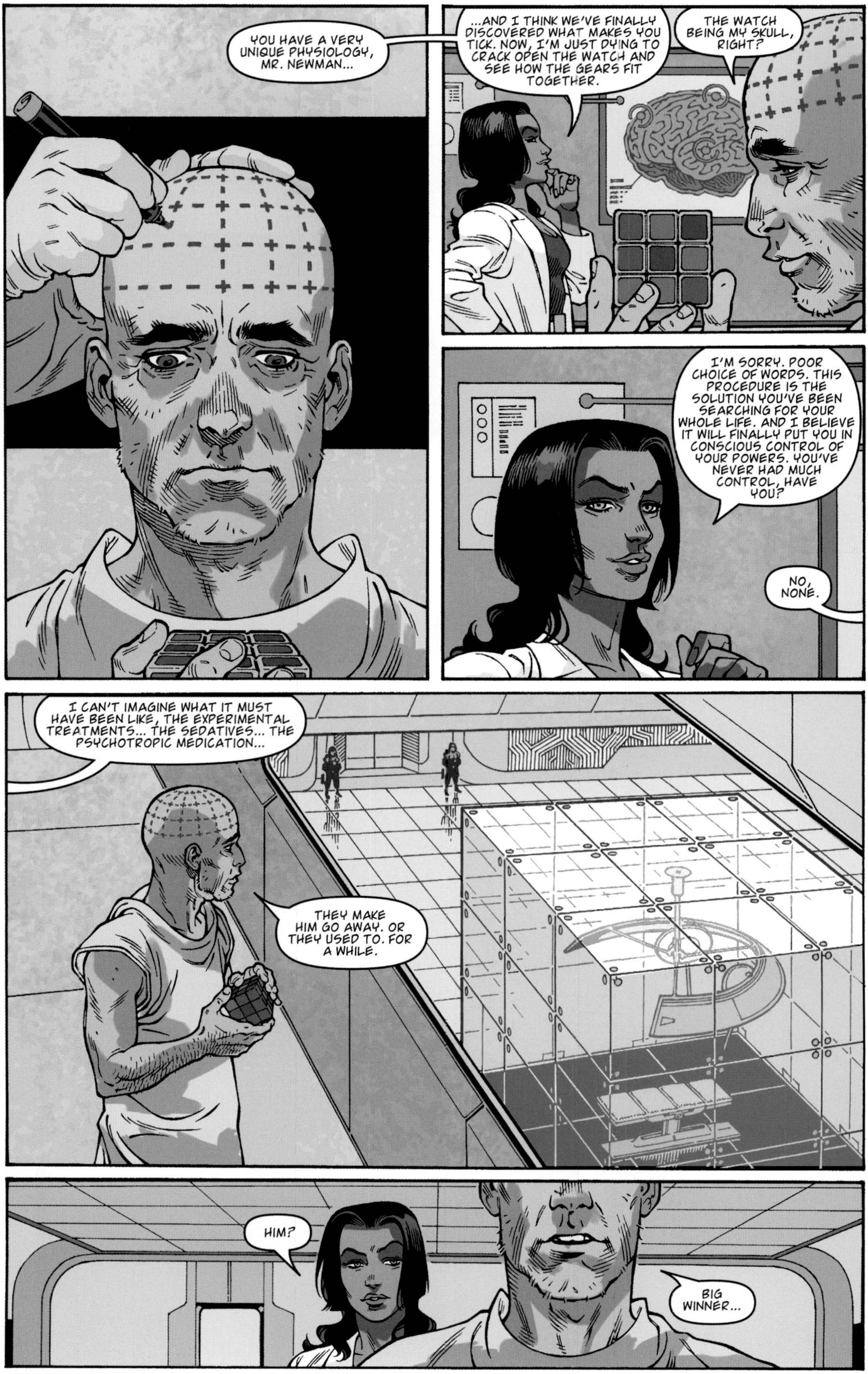
YOU HAVE A VERY UNIQUE PHYSIOLOGY, MR. NEWMAN...
...AND I THINK WE'VE FINALLY DISCOVERED WHAT MAKES YOU TICK. NOW, I'M JUST DYING TO CRACK OPEN THE WATCH AND SEE HOW THE GEARS FIT TOGETHER.
THE WATCH BEING MY SKULL, RIGHT?
I'M SORRY. POOR CHOICE OF WORDS. THIS PROCEDURE IS THE SOLUTION YOU'VE BEEN SEARCHING FOR YOUR WHOLE LIFE. AND I BELIEVE IT WILL FINALLY PUT YOU IN CONSCIOUS CONTROL OF YOUR POWERS. YOU'VE NEVER HAD MUCH CONTROL, HAVE YOU?
NO, NONE.
I CAN'T IMAGINE WHAT IT MUST HAVE BEEN LIKE, THE EXPERIMENTAL TREATMENTS... THE SEDATIVES... THE PSYCHOTROPIC MEDICATION...
THEY MAKE HIM GO AWAY. OR THEY USED TO. FOR A WHILE.
HIM?
BIG WINNER...

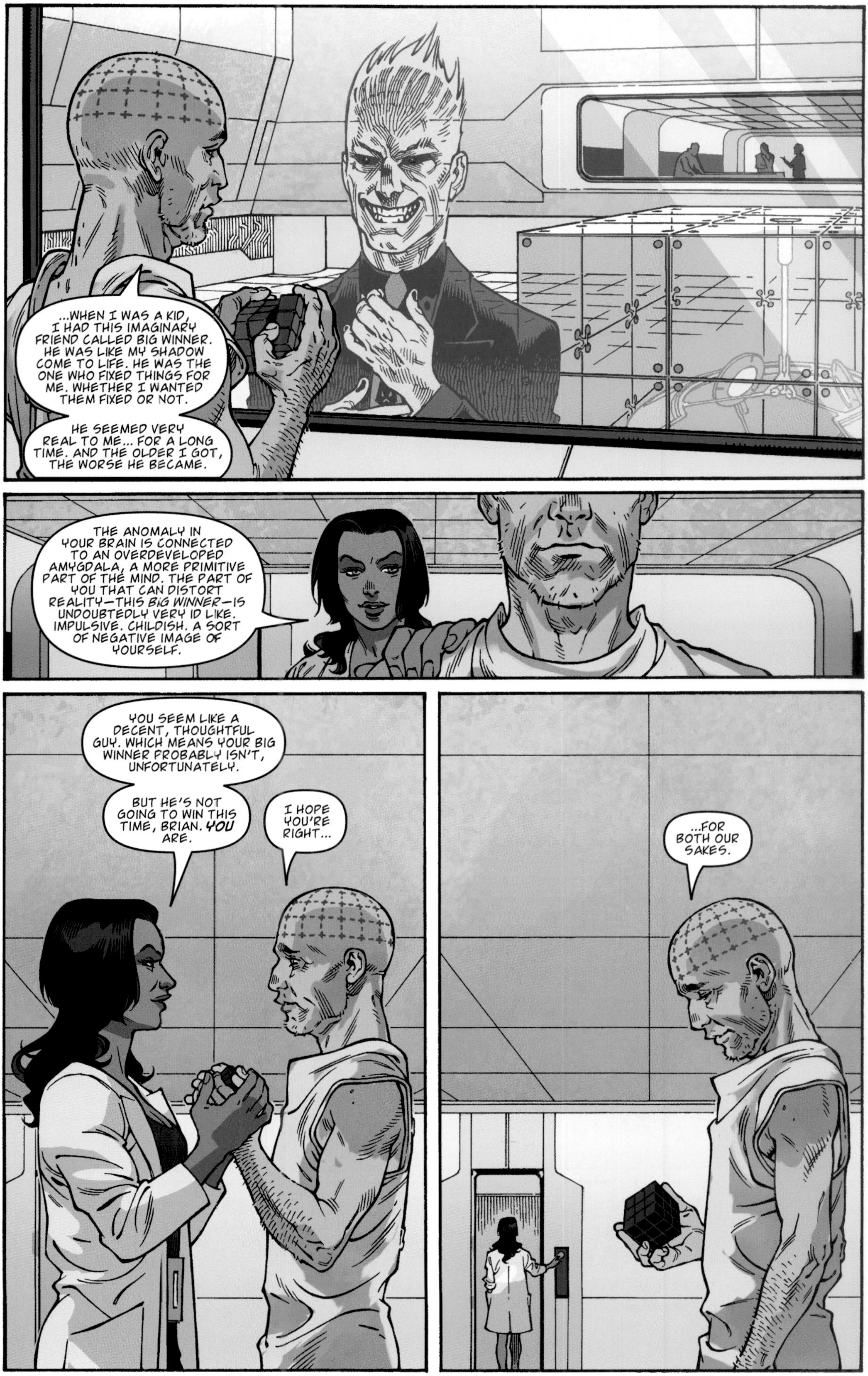
...WHEN I WAS A KID, I HAD THIS IMAGINARY FRIEND CALLED BIG WINNER. HE WAS LIKE MY SHADOW COME TO LIFE. HE WAS THE ONE WHO FIXED THINGS FOR ME. WHETHER I WANTED THEM FIXED OR NOT.
HE SEEMED VERY REAL TO ME... FOR A LONG TIME. AND THE OLDER I GOT, THE WORSE HE BECAME.
THE ANOMALY IN YOUR BRAIN IS CONNECTED TO AN OVERDEVELOPED AMYGDALA, A MORE PRIMITIVE PART OF THE MIND. THE PART OF YOU THAT CAN DISTORT REALITY—THIS *BIG WINNER*—IS UNDOUBTEDLY VERY ID LIKE. IMPULSIVE. CHILDISH. A SORT OF NEGATIVE IMAGE OF YOURSELF.
YOU SEEM LIKE A DECENT, THOUGHTFUL GUY. WHICH MEANS YOUR BIG WINNER PROBABLY ISN'T, UNFORTUNATELY.
BUT HE'S NOT GOING TO WIN THIS TIME, BRIAN. ***YOU*** ARE.
I HOPE YOU'RE RIGHT...
...FOR BOTH OUR SAKES.

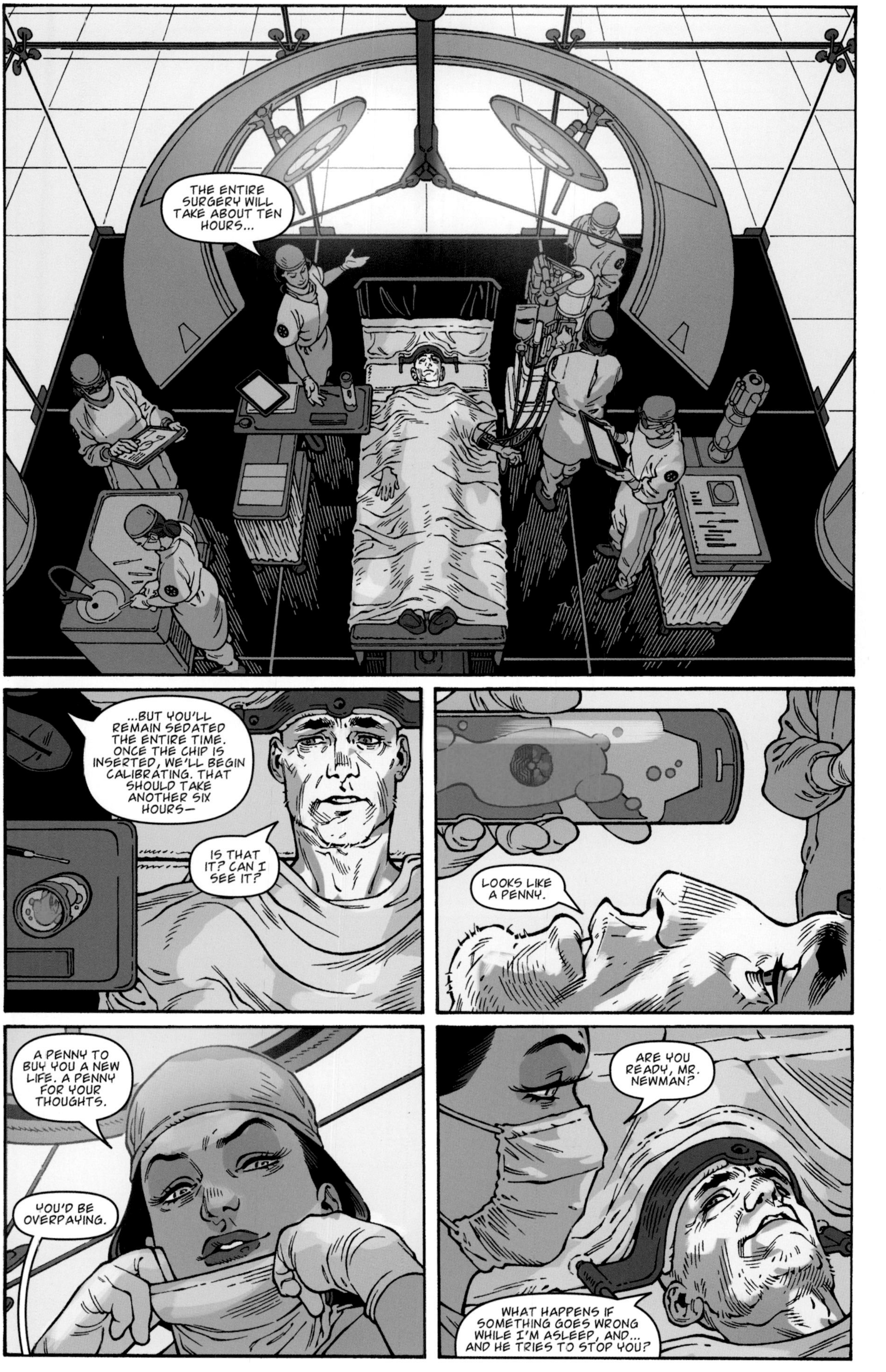
THE ENTIRE SURGERY WILL TAKE ABOUT TEN HOURS...
...BUT YOU'LL REMAIN SEDATED THE ENTIRE TIME. ONCE THE CHIP IS INSERTED, WE'LL BEGIN CALIBRATING. THAT SHOULD TAKE ANOTHER SIX HOURS—
IS THAT IT? CAN I SEE IT?
LOOKS LIKE A PENNY.
A PENNY TO BUY YOU A NEW LIFE. A PENNY FOR YOUR THOUGHTS.
YOU'D BE OVERPAYING.
ARE YOU READY, MR. NEWMAN?
WHAT HAPPENS IF SOMETHING GOES WRONG WHILE I'M ASLEEP, AND... AND HE TRIES TO STOP YOU?

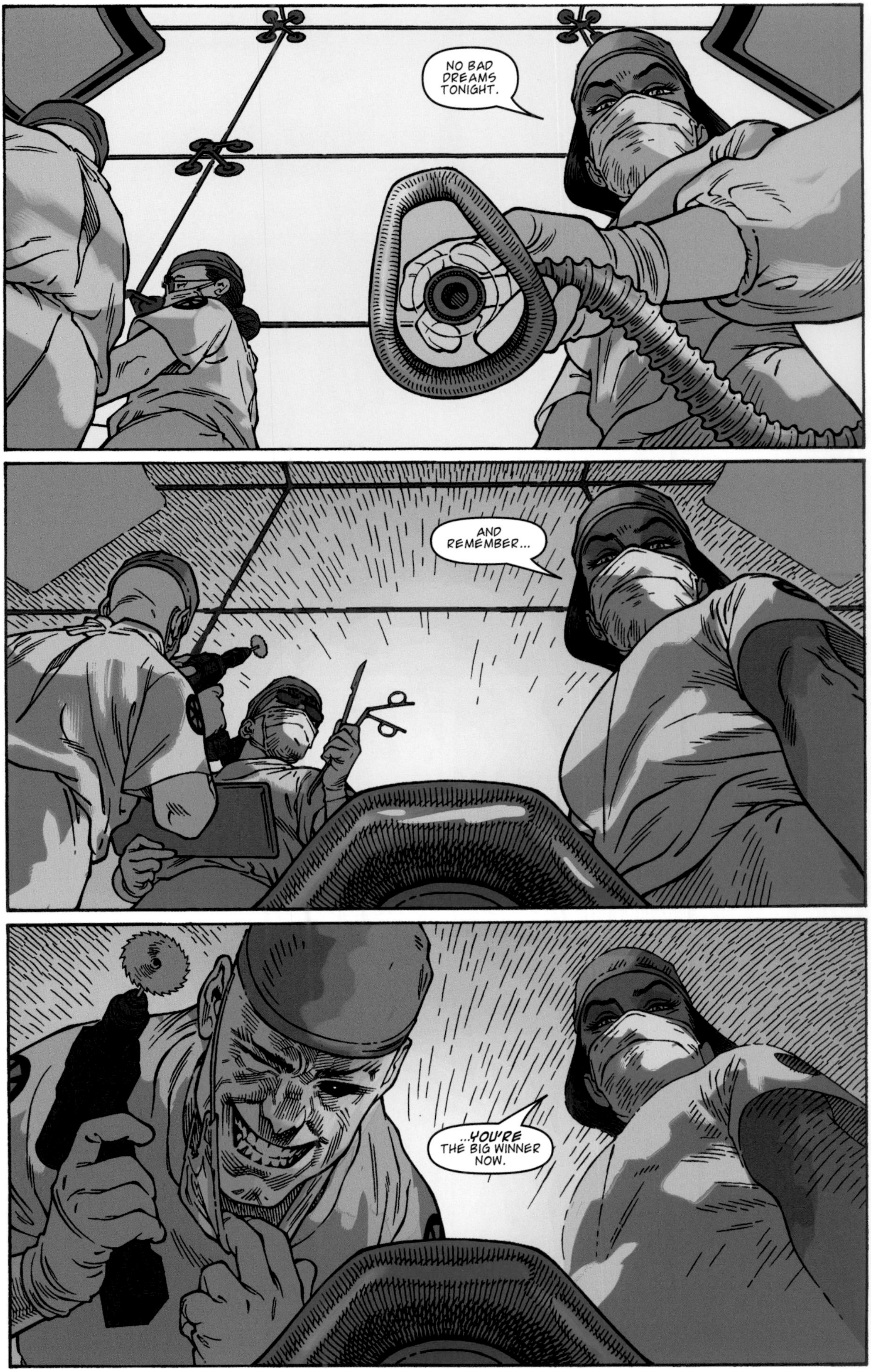
NO BAD DREAMS TONIGHT.
AND REMEMBER...
...YOU'RE THE BIG WINNER NOW.

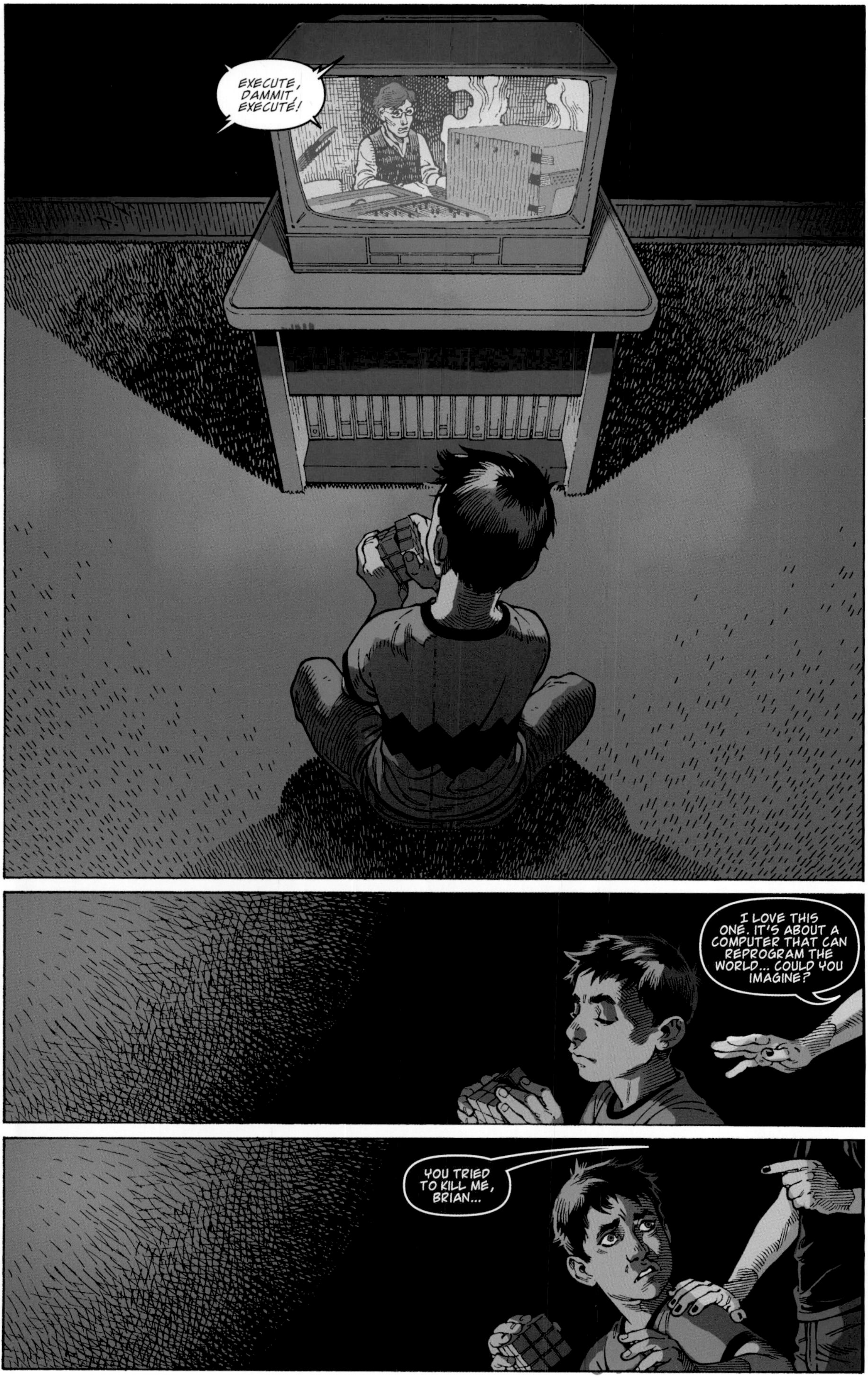
EXECUTE, DAMMIT, EXECUTE!
I LOVE THIS ONE. IT'S ABOUT A COMPUTER THAT CAN REPROGRAM THE WORLD... COULD YOU IMAGINE?
YOU TRIED TO KILL ME, BRIAN...

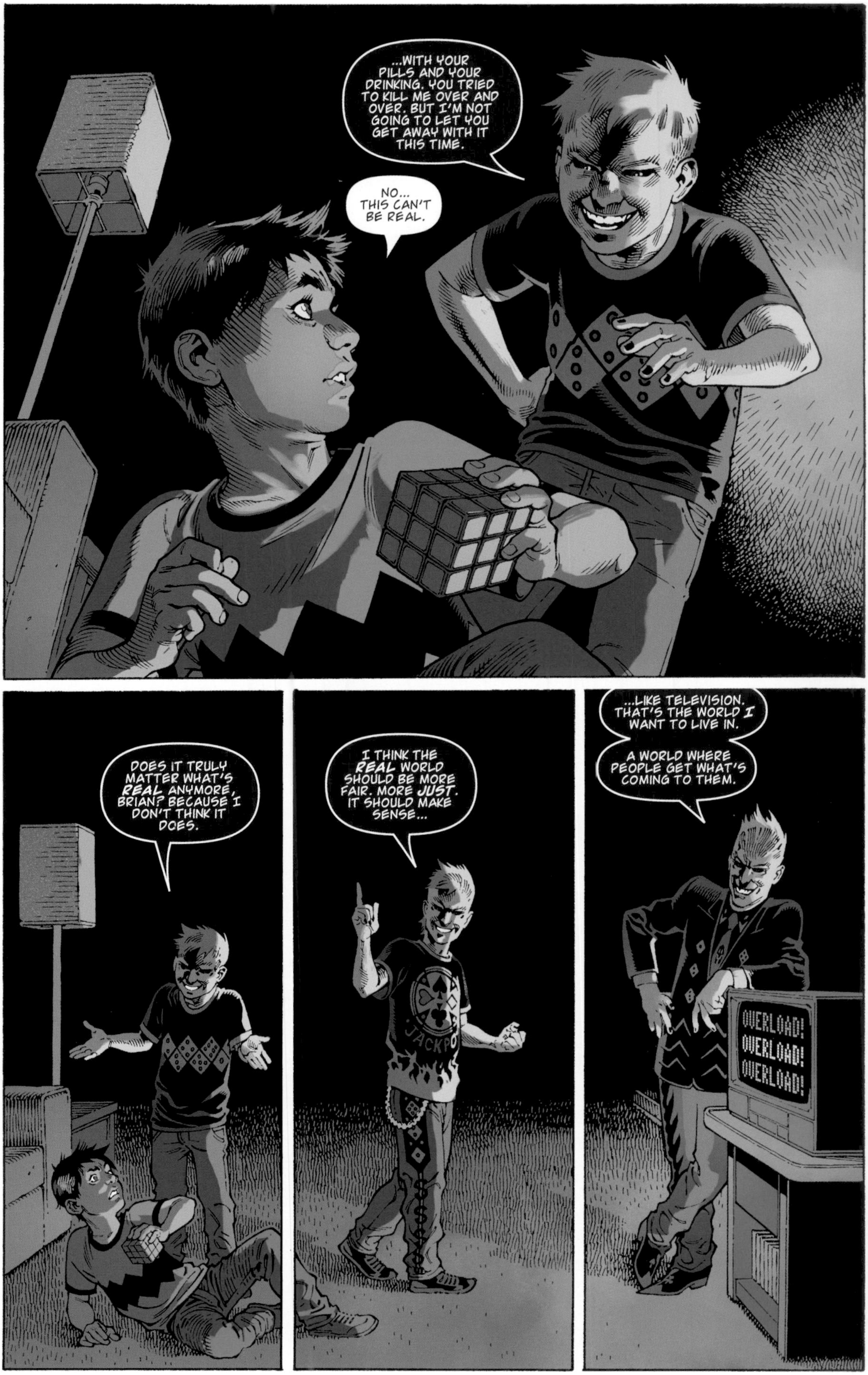
...WITH YOUR PILLS AND YOUR DRINKING. YOU TRIED TO KILL ME OVER AND OVER. BUT I'M NOT GOING TO LET YOU GET AWAY WITH IT THIS TIME.
NO... THIS CAN'T BE REAL.
DOES IT TRULY MATTER WHAT'S REAL ANYMORE, BRIAN? BECAUSE I DON'T THINK IT DOES.
I THINK THE REAL WORLD SHOULD BE MORE FAIR. MORE JUST. IT SHOULD MAKE SENSE...
...LIKE TELEVISION. THAT'S THE WORLD I WANT TO LIVE IN.
A WORLD WHERE PEOPLE GET WHAT'S COMING TO THEM.
OVERLOAD!
OVERLOAD!
OVERLOAD!

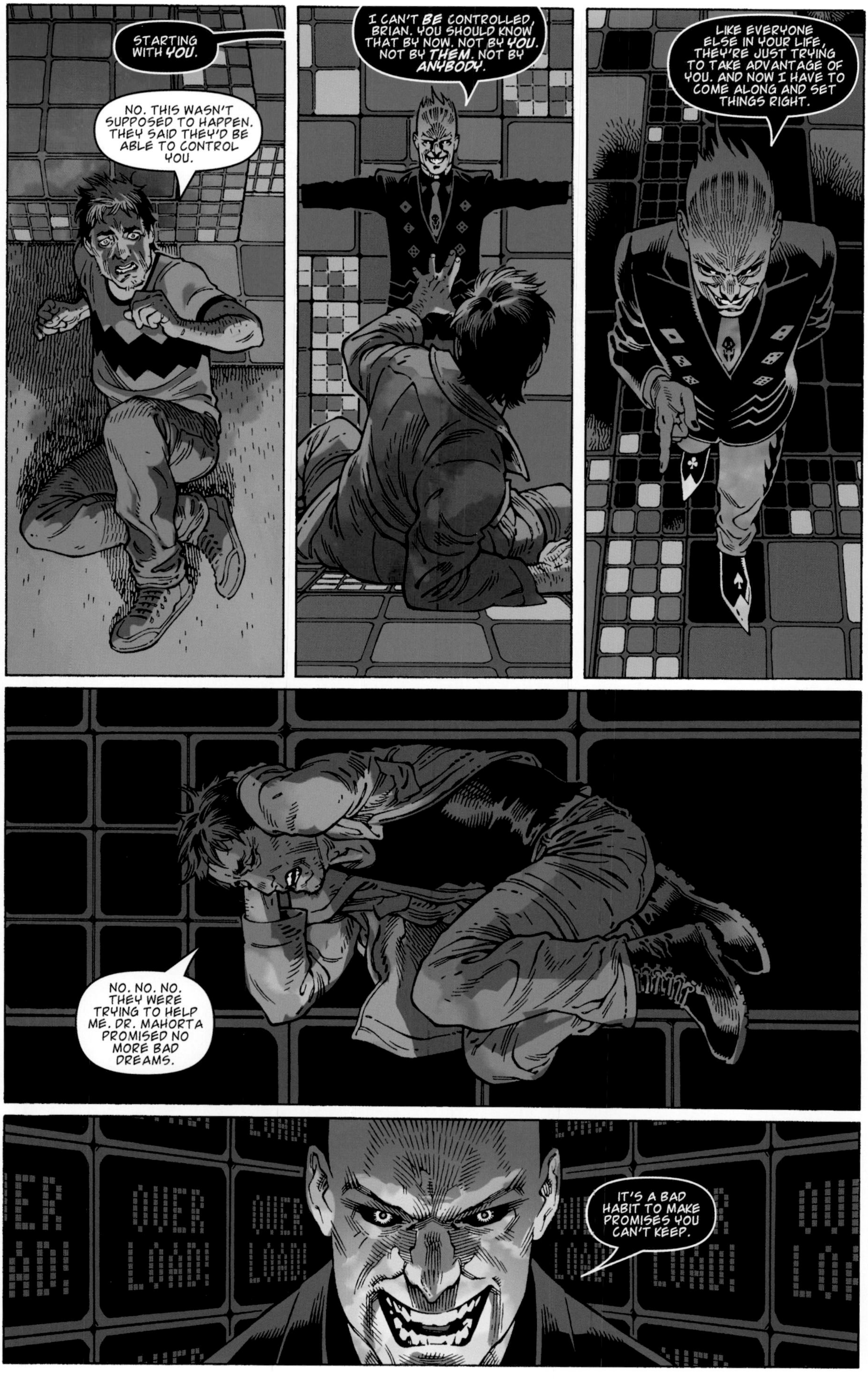
STARTING WITH YOU.
NO. THIS WASN'T SUPPOSED TO HAPPEN. THEY SAID THEY'D BE ABLE TO CONTROL YOU.
I CAN'T BE CONTROLLED, BRIAN. YOU SHOULD KNOW THAT BY NOW. NOT BY YOU. NOT BY THEM. NOT BY ANYBODY.
LIKE EVERYONE ELSE IN YOUR LIFE, THEY'RE JUST TRYING TO TAKE ADVANTAGE OF YOU. AND NOW I HAVE TO COME ALONG AND SET THINGS RIGHT.
NO. NO. NO. THEY WERE TRYING TO HELP ME. DR. MAHORTA PROMISED NO MORE BAD DREAMS.
OVER LOAD!
IT'S A BAD HABIT TO MAKE PROMISES YOU CAN'T KEEP.

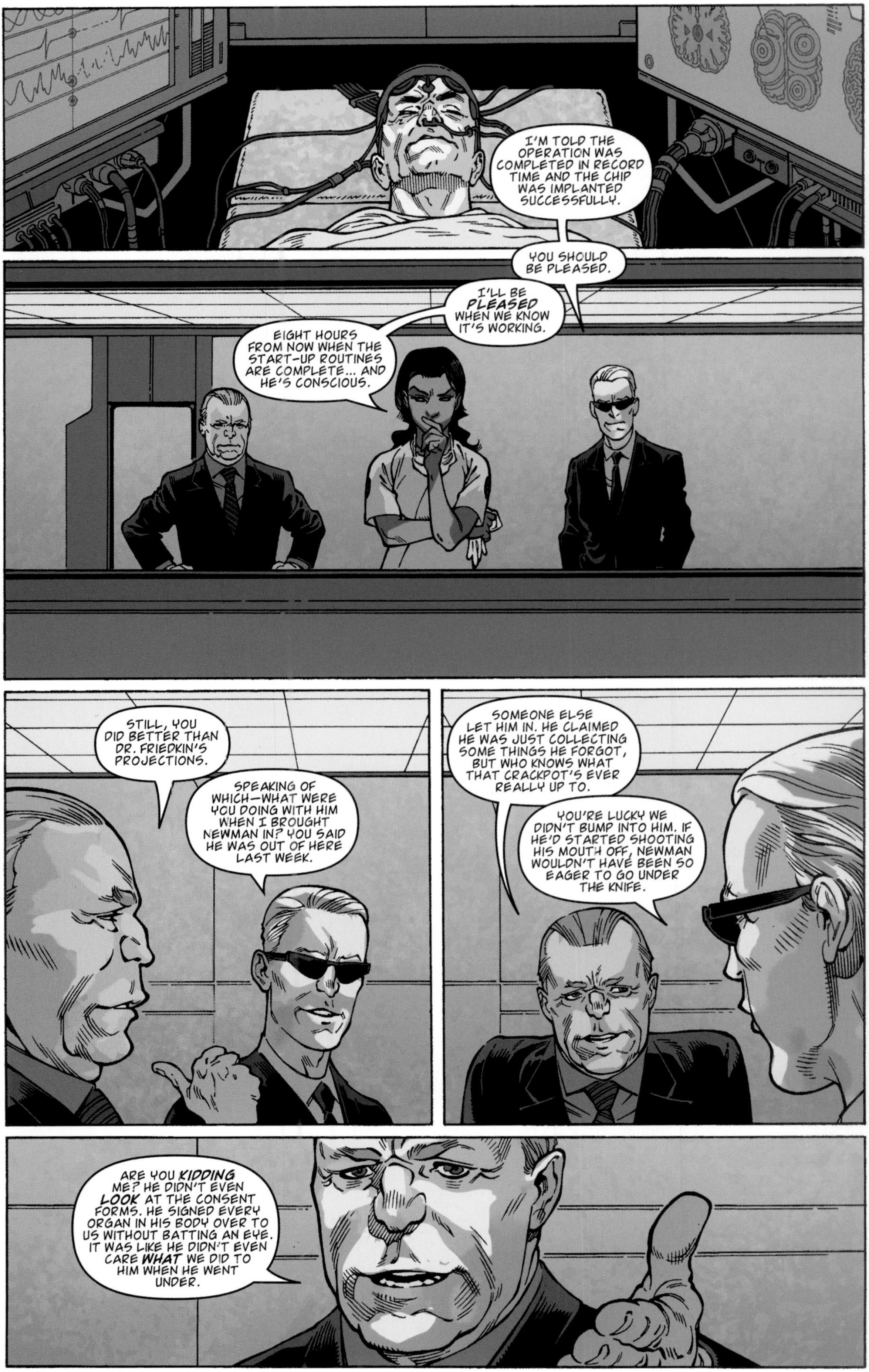
I'M TOLD THE OPERATION WAS COMPLETED IN RECORD TIME AND THE CHIP WAS IMPLANTED SUCCESSFULLY.
YOU SHOULD BE PLEASED.
I'LL BE PLEASED WHEN WE KNOW IT'S WORKING.
EIGHT HOURS FROM NOW WHEN THE START-UP ROUTINES ARE COMPLETE... AND HE'S CONSCIOUS.
STILL, YOU DID BETTER THAN DR. FRIEDKIN'S PROJECTIONS.
SPEAKING OF WHICH—WHAT WERE YOU DOING WITH HIM WHEN I BROUGHT NEWMAN IN? YOU SAID HE WAS OUT OF HERE LAST WEEK.
SOMEONE ELSE LET HIM IN. HE CLAIMED HE WAS JUST COLLECTING SOME THINGS HE FORGOT, BUT WHO KNOWS WHAT THAT CRACKPOT'S EVER REALLY UP TO.
YOU'RE LUCKY WE DIDN'T BUMP INTO HIM. IF HE'D STARTED SHOOTING HIS MOUTH OFF, NEWMAN WOULDN'T HAVE BEEN SO EAGER TO GO UNDER THE KNIFE.
ARE YOU KIDDING ME? HE DIDN'T EVEN LOOK AT THE CONSENT FORMS. HE SIGNED EVERY ORGAN IN HIS BODY OVER TO US WITHOUT BATTING AN EYE. IT WAS LIKE HE DIDN'T EVEN CARE WHAT WE DID TO HIM WHEN HE WENT UNDER.

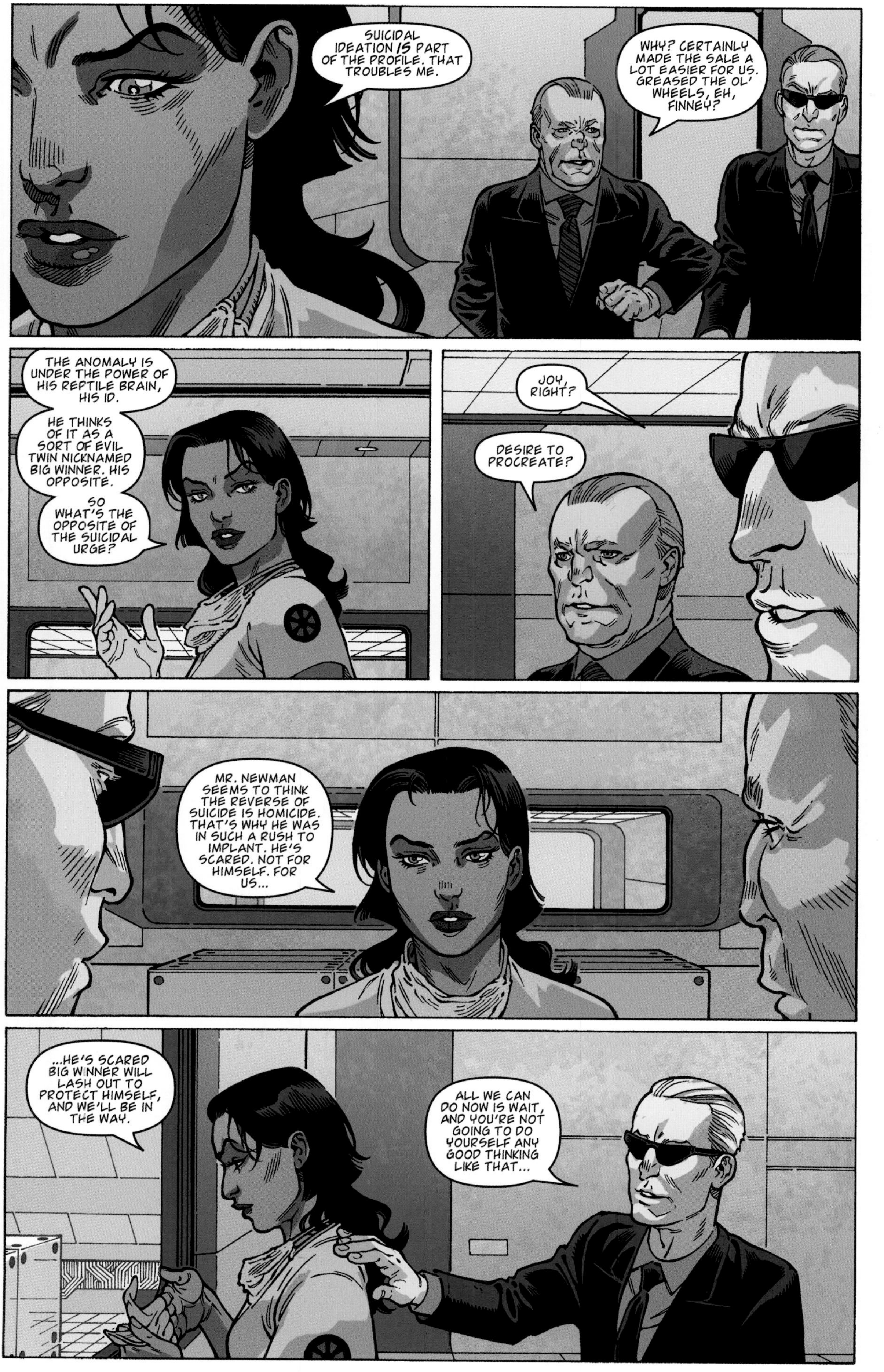
SUICIDAL IDEATION IS PART OF THE PROFILE. THAT TROUBLES ME.
WHY? CERTAINLY MADE THE SALE A LOT EASIER FOR US. GREASED THE OL' WHEELS, EH, FINNEY?
THE ANOMALY IS UNDER THE POWER OF HIS REPTILE BRAIN, HIS ID.
HE THINKS OF IT AS A SORT OF EVIL TWIN NICKNAMED BIG WINNER. HIS OPPOSITE.
SO WHAT'S THE OPPOSITE OF THE SUICIDAL URGE?
JOY, RIGHT?
DESIRE TO PROCREATE?
MR. NEWMAN SEEMS TO THINK THE REVERSE OF SUICIDE IS HOMICIDE. THAT'S WHY HE WAS IN SUCH A RUSH TO IMPLANT. HE'S SCARED. NOT FOR HIMSELF. FOR US...
...HE'S SCARED BIG WINNER WILL LASH OUT TO PROTECT HIMSELF, AND WE'LL BE IN THE WAY.
ALL WE CAN DO NOW IS WAIT, AND YOU'RE NOT GOING TO DO YOURSELF ANY GOOD THINKING LIKE THAT...

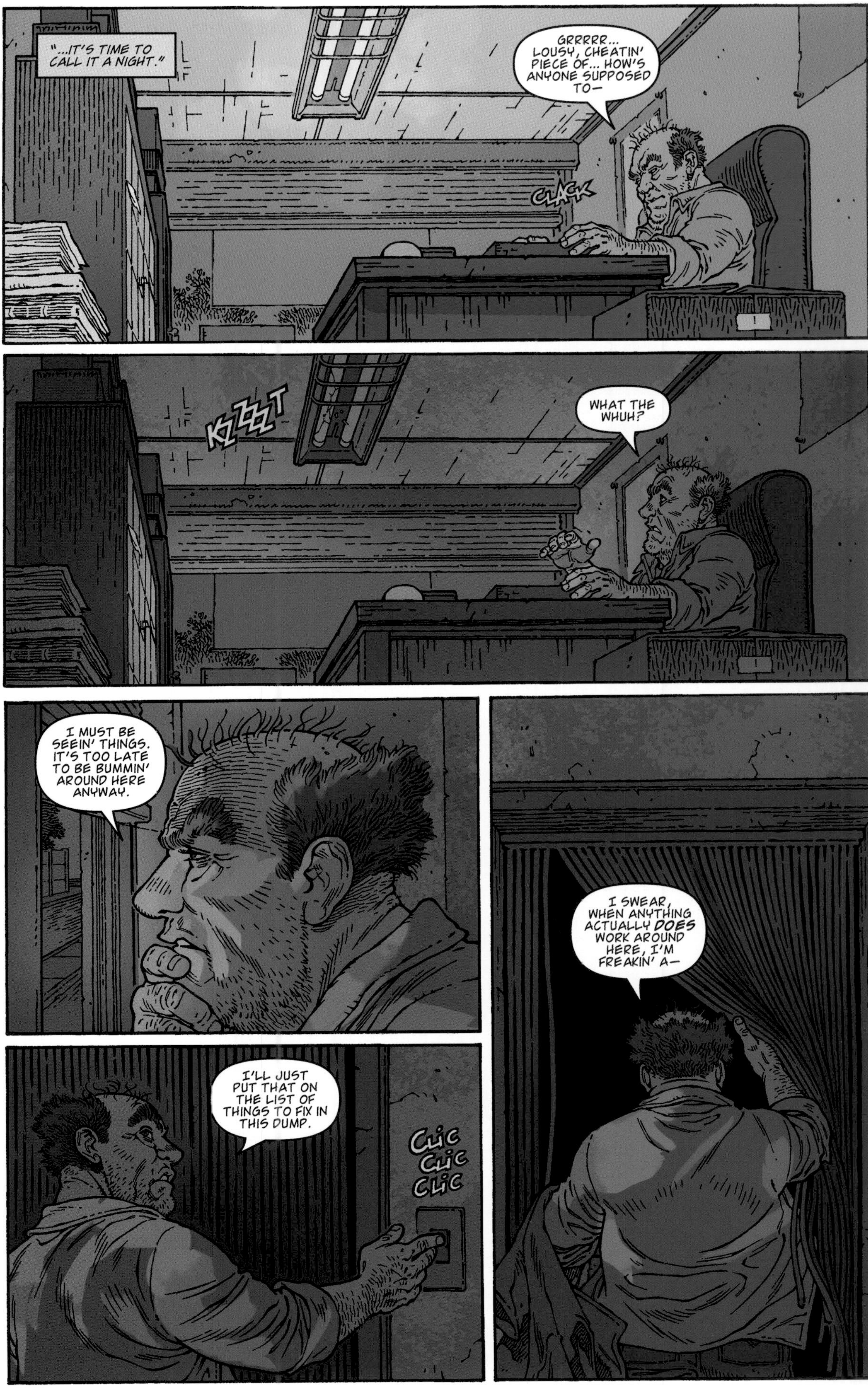
"...IT'S TIME TO CALL IT A NIGHT."
GRRRRR... LOUSY, CHEATIN' PIECE OF... HOW'S ANYONE SUPPOSED TO—
CLACK
KZZZZT
WHAT THE WHUH?
I MUST BE SEEIN' THINGS. IT'S TOO LATE TO BE BUMMIN' AROUND HERE ANYWAY.
I SWEAR, WHEN ANYTHING ACTUALLY DOES WORK AROUND HERE, I'M FREAKIN' A—
I'LL JUST PUT THAT ON THE LIST OF THINGS TO FIX IN THIS DUMP.
CLIC CLIC CLIC

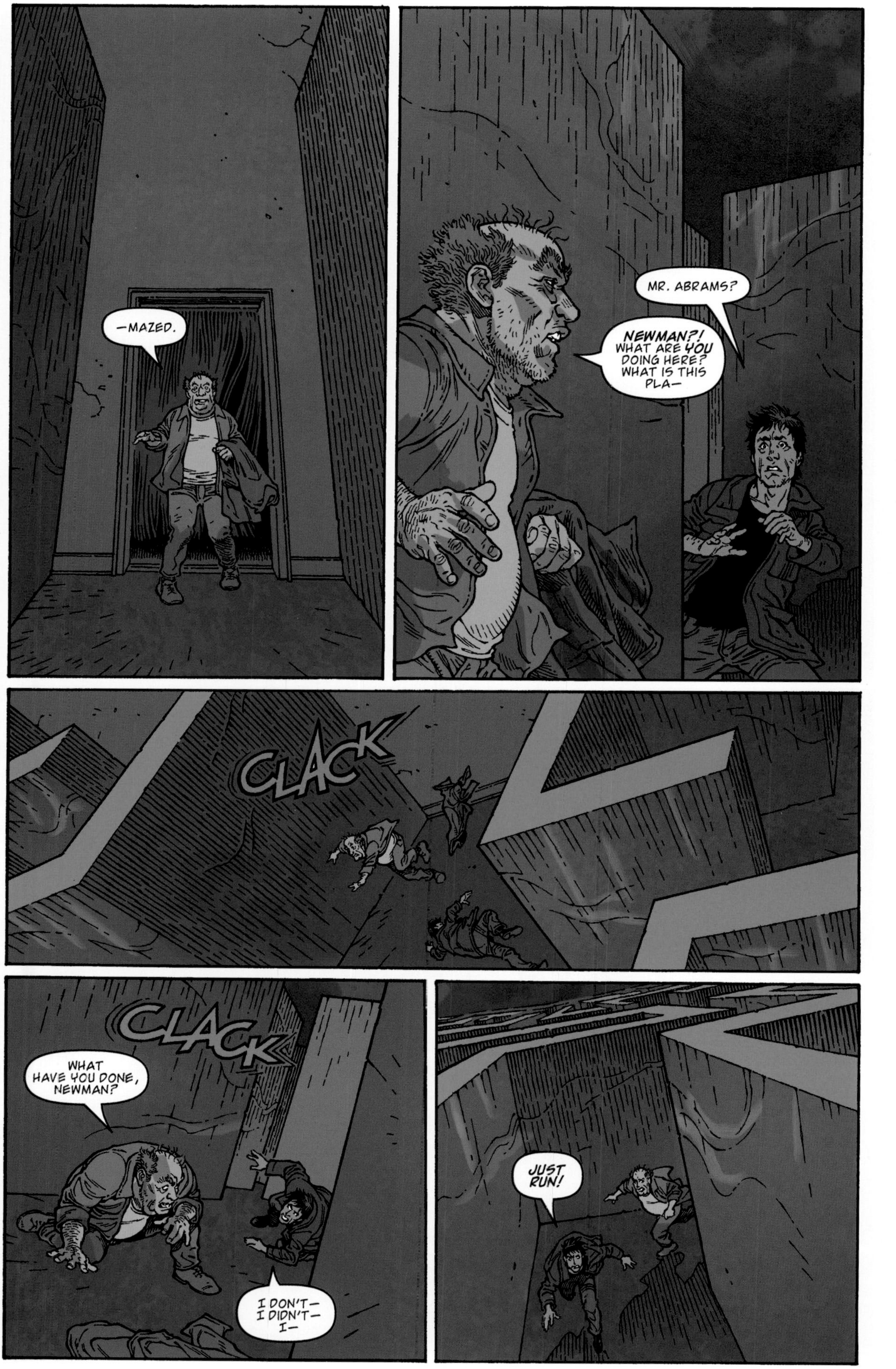

—MAZED.
MR. ABRAMS?
NEWMAN?! WHAT ARE YOU DOING HERE? WHAT IS THIS PLA—
CLACK
CLACK
WHAT HAVE YOU DONE, NEWMAN?
I DON'T— I DIDN'T— I—
JUST RUN!

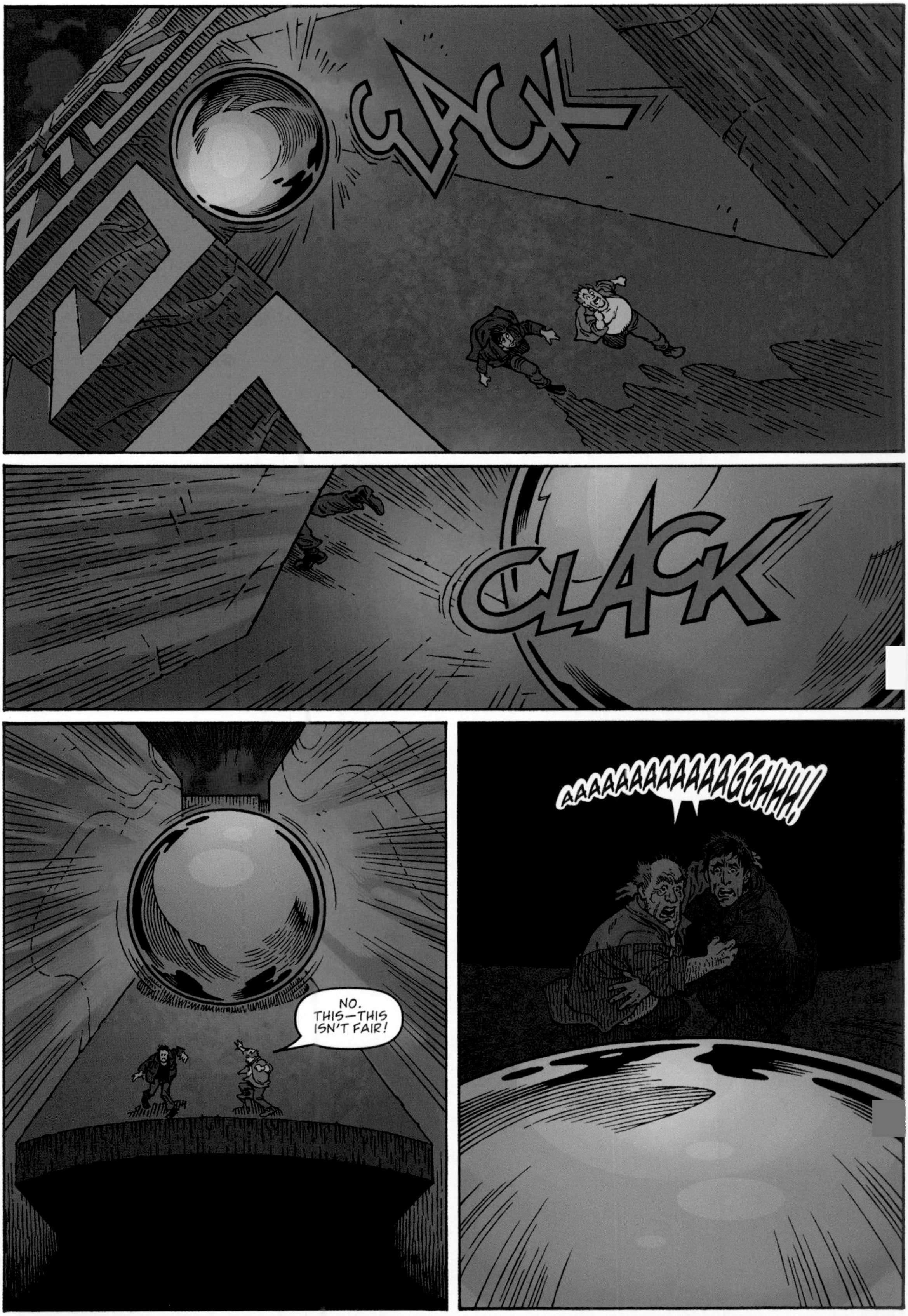
CLACK
CLACK
NO. THIS—THIS ISN'T FAIR!
AAAAAAAAAAAAGGHHH!

[redacted]

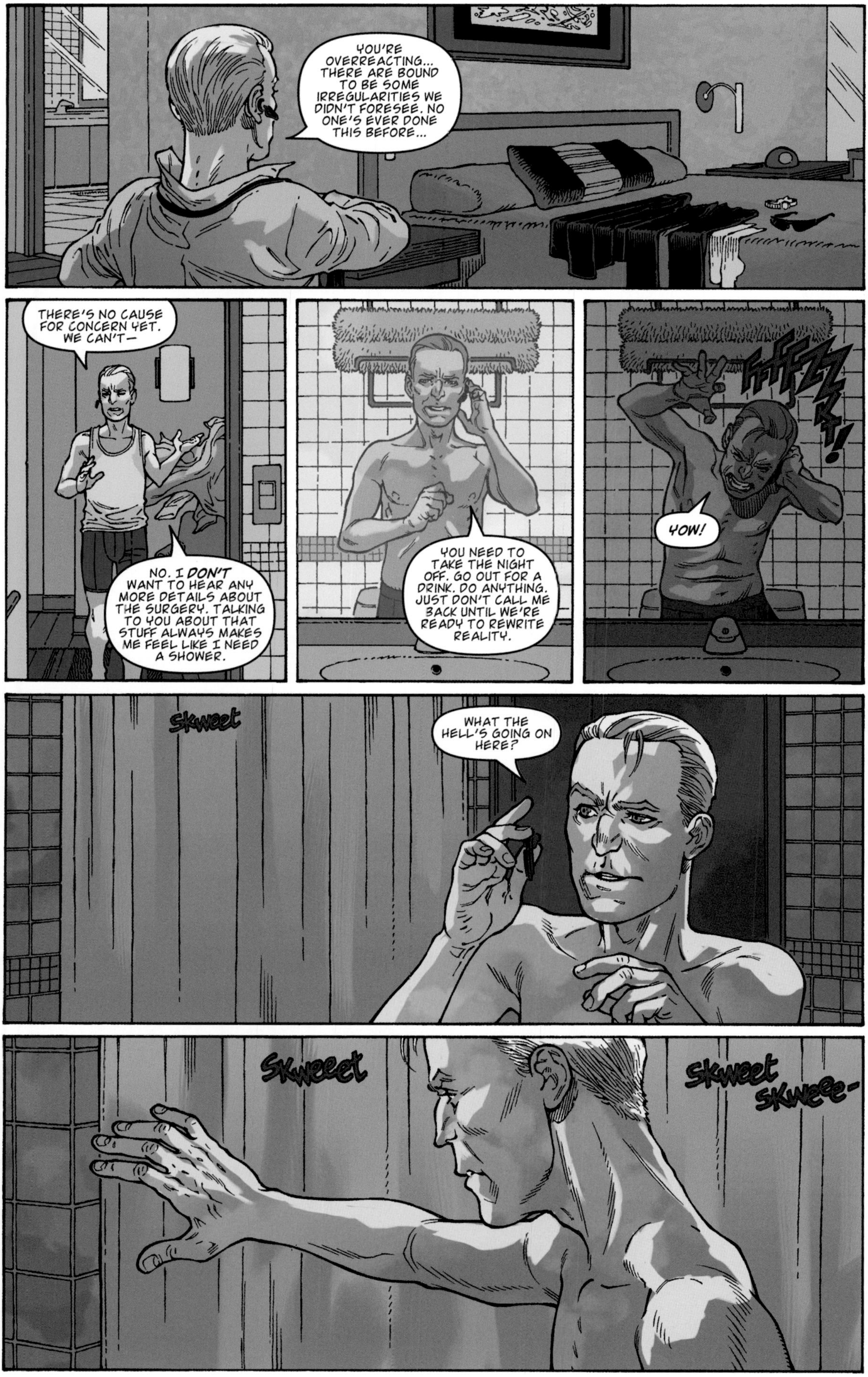
YOU'RE OVERREACTING... THERE ARE BOUND TO BE SOME IRREGULARITIES WE DIDN'T FORESEE. NO ONE'S EVER DONE THIS BEFORE...
THERE'S NO CAUSE FOR CONCERN YET. WE CAN'T—
NO. I DON'T WANT TO HEAR ANY MORE DETAILS ABOUT THE SURGERY. TALKING TO YOU ABOUT THAT STUFF ALWAYS MAKES ME FEEL LIKE I NEED A SHOWER.
YOU NEED TO TAKE THE NIGHT OFF. GO OUT FOR A DRINK. DO ANYTHING. JUST DON'T CALL ME BACK UNTIL WE'RE READY TO REWRITE REALITY.
FFFZZZKT!
YOW!
SKWEET
WHAT THE HELL'S GOING ON HERE?
SKWEEET
SKWEET
SKWEEE-

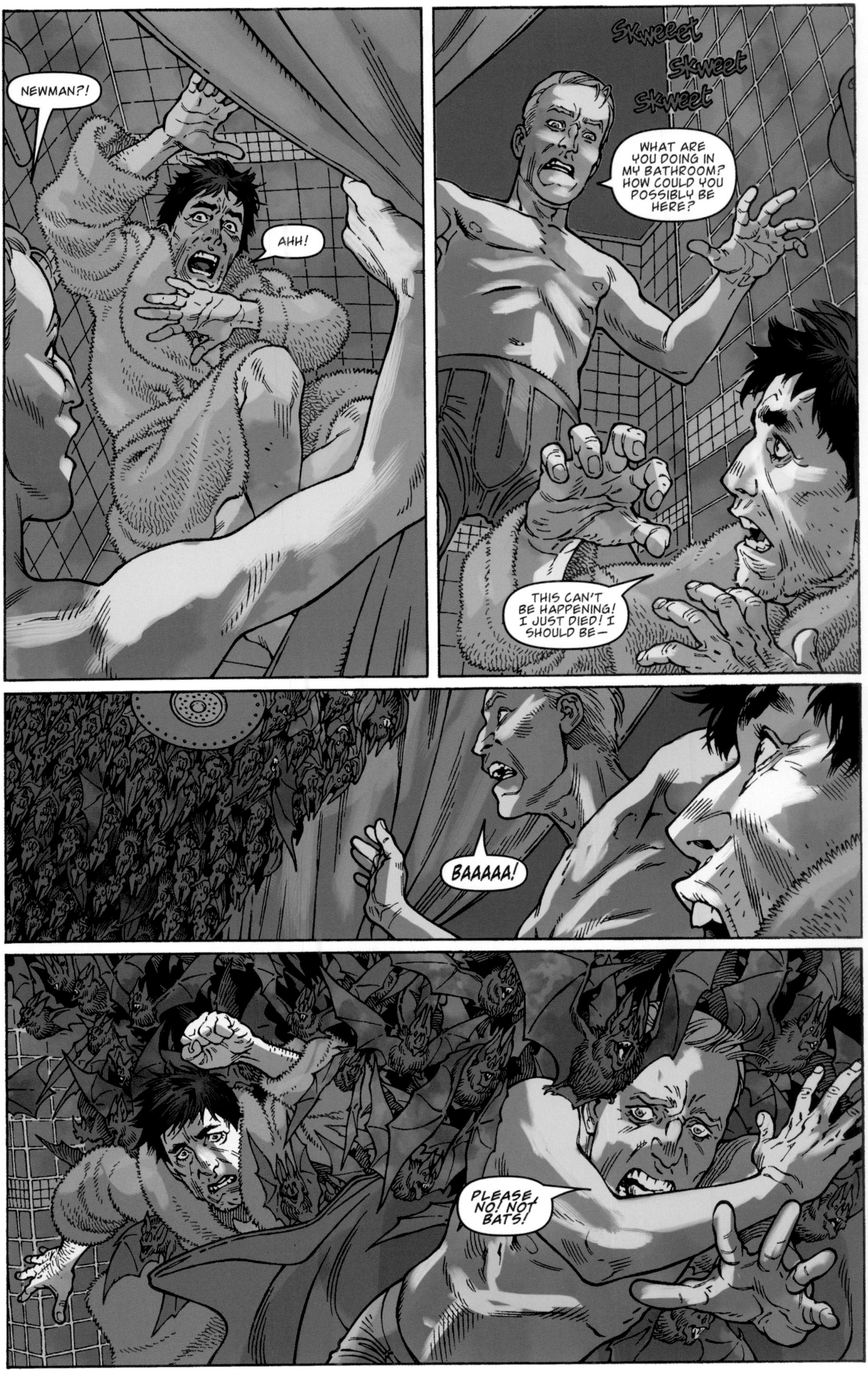
NEWMAN?!
AHH!
SKWEEET
SKWEET
SKWEET
WHAT ARE YOU DOING IN MY BATHROOM? HOW COULD YOU POSSIBLY BE HERE?
THIS CAN'T BE HAPPENING! I JUST DIED! I SHOULD BE—
BAAAAA!
PLEASE, NO! NOT BATS!

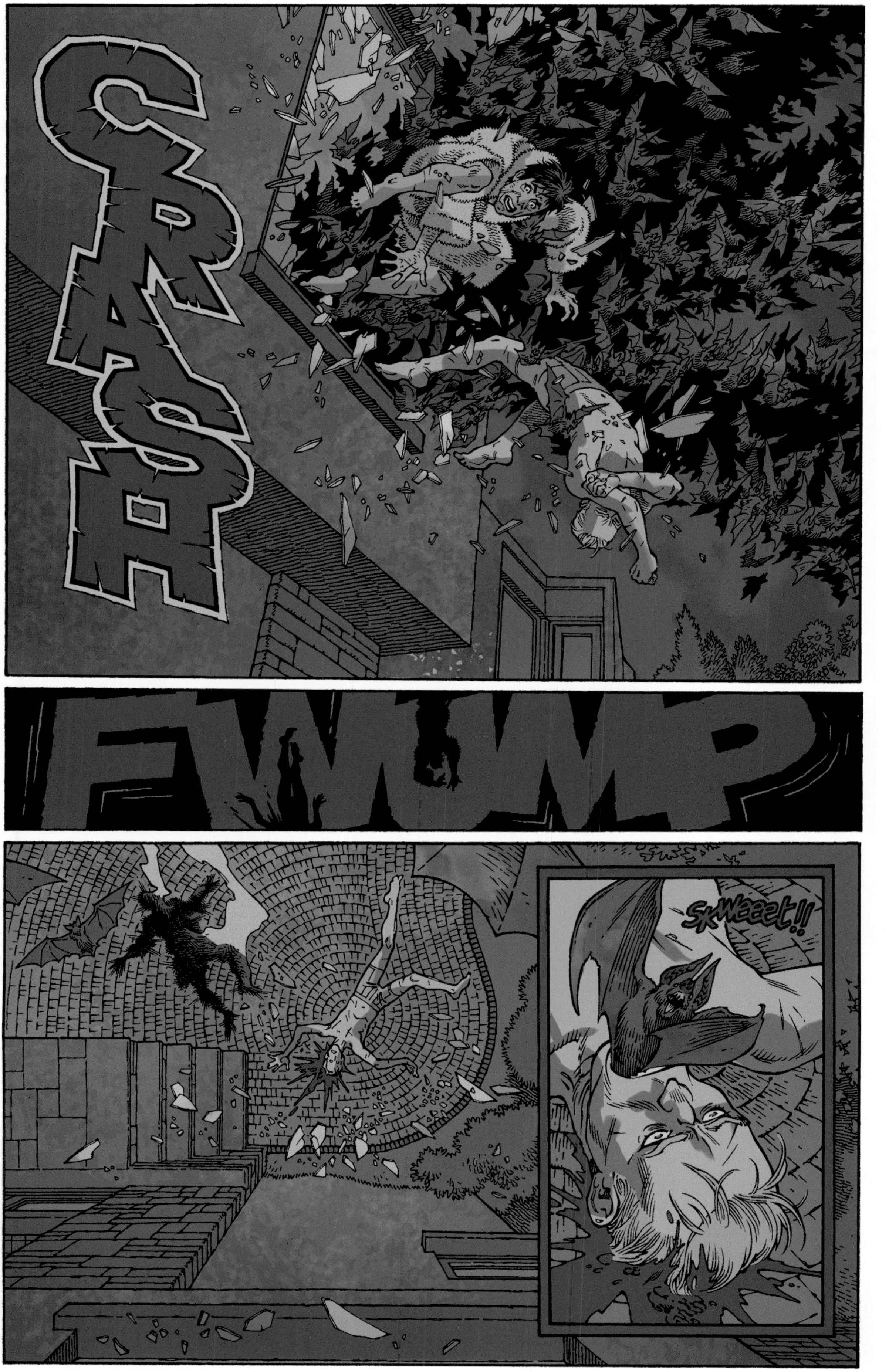
CRASH
FWUMP
SKWEEET!!

THIS BETTER BE WORTH DRAGGING MY ASS DOWN HERE IN THE MIDDLE OF THE NIGHT.

WE THOUGHT YOU'D WANT TO SEE THIS FIRSTHAND, SIR.

WH—WHERE THE HELL IS HE?

WE BELIEVE HE'S... *INSIDE,* SIR.

WELL, GET HIM OUT OF THERE ALREADY.

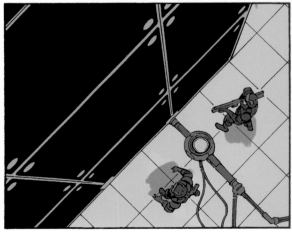

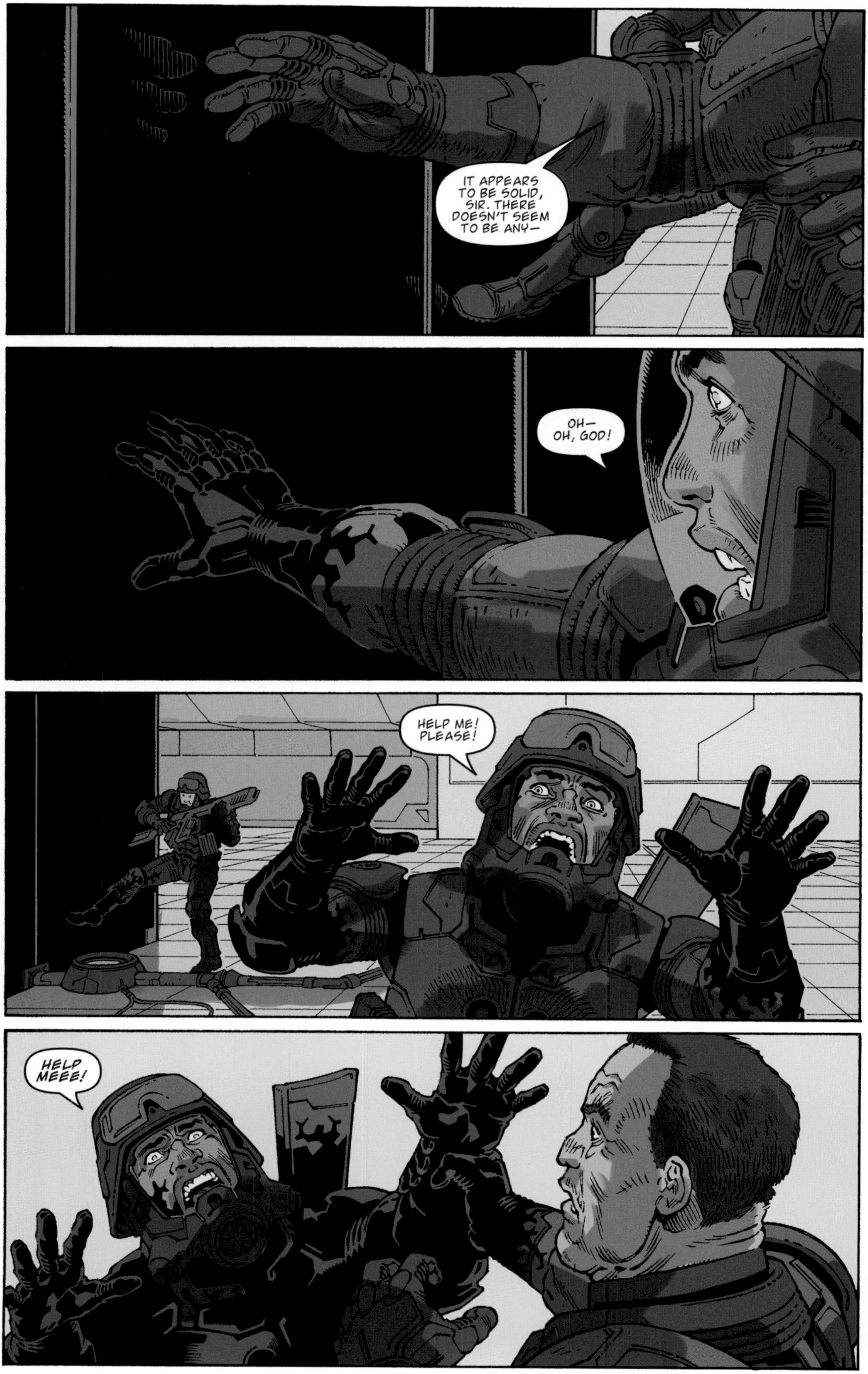
IT APPEARS TO BE SOLID, SIR. THERE DOESN'T SEEM TO BE ANY—
OH— OH, GOD!
HELP ME! PLEASE!
HELP MEEE!

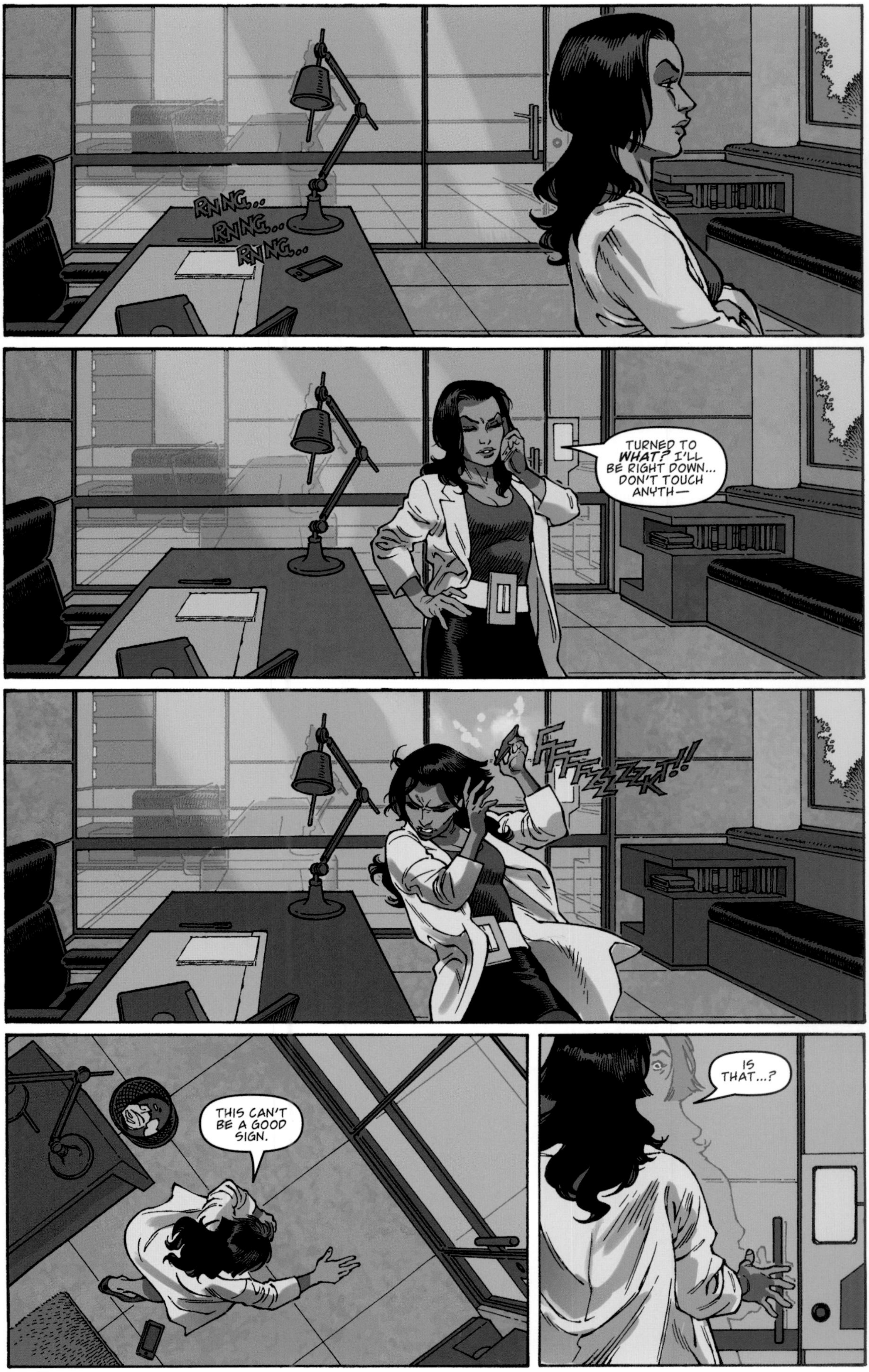
RNNG..
RNNG..
RNNG..
TURNED TO WHAT? I'LL BE RIGHT DOWN... DON'T TOUCH ANYTH—
FFFFZZZZKT!!
THIS CAN'T BE A GOOD SIGN.
IS THAT...?

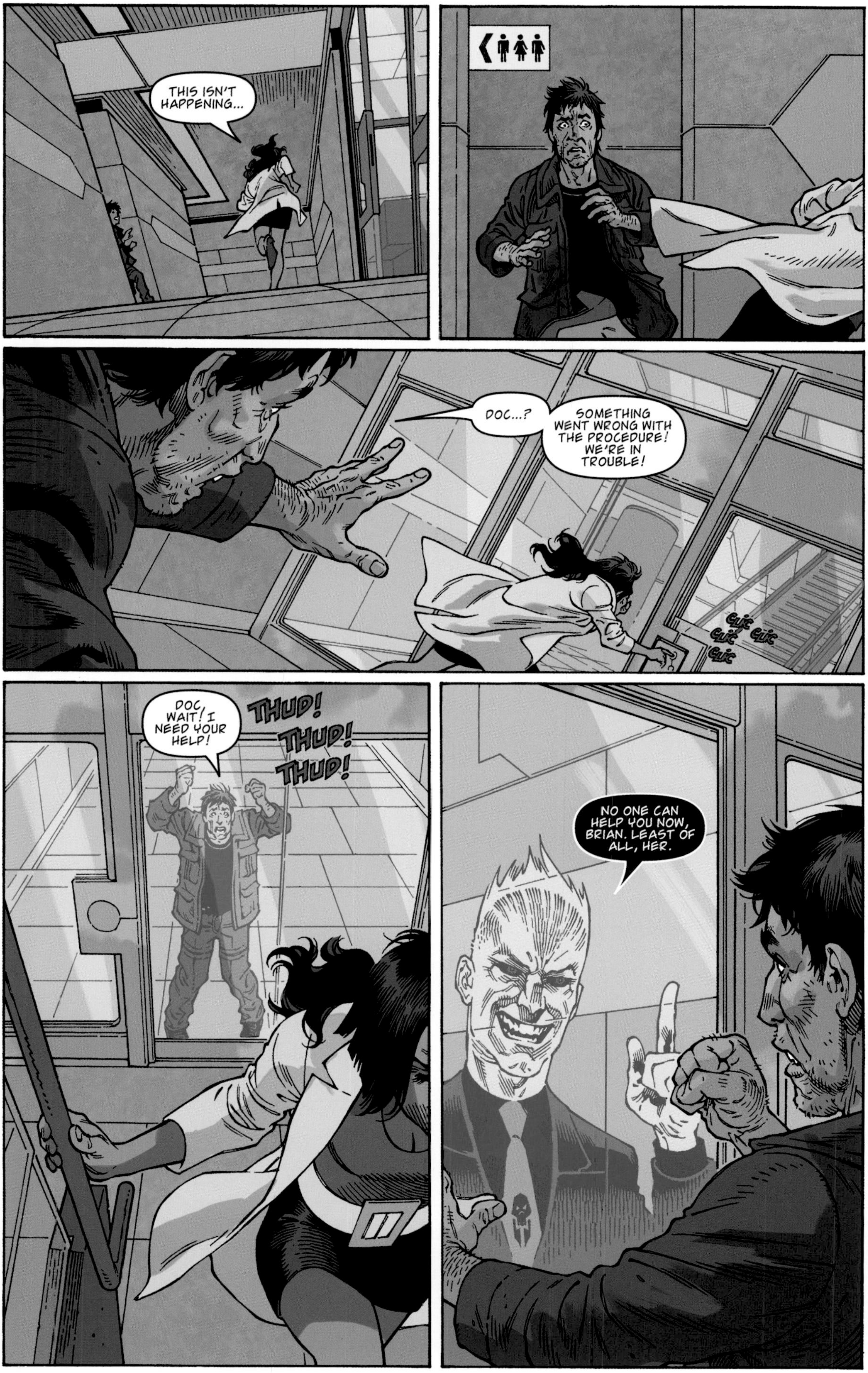
THIS ISN'T HAPPENING...
DOC...?
SOMETHING WENT WRONG WITH THE PROCEDURE! WE'RE IN TROUBLE!
CLIC
CLIC
CLIC
CLIC
DOC, WAIT! I NEED YOUR HELP!
THUD! THUD! THUD!
NO ONE CAN HELP YOU NOW, BRIAN. LEAST OF ALL, HER.

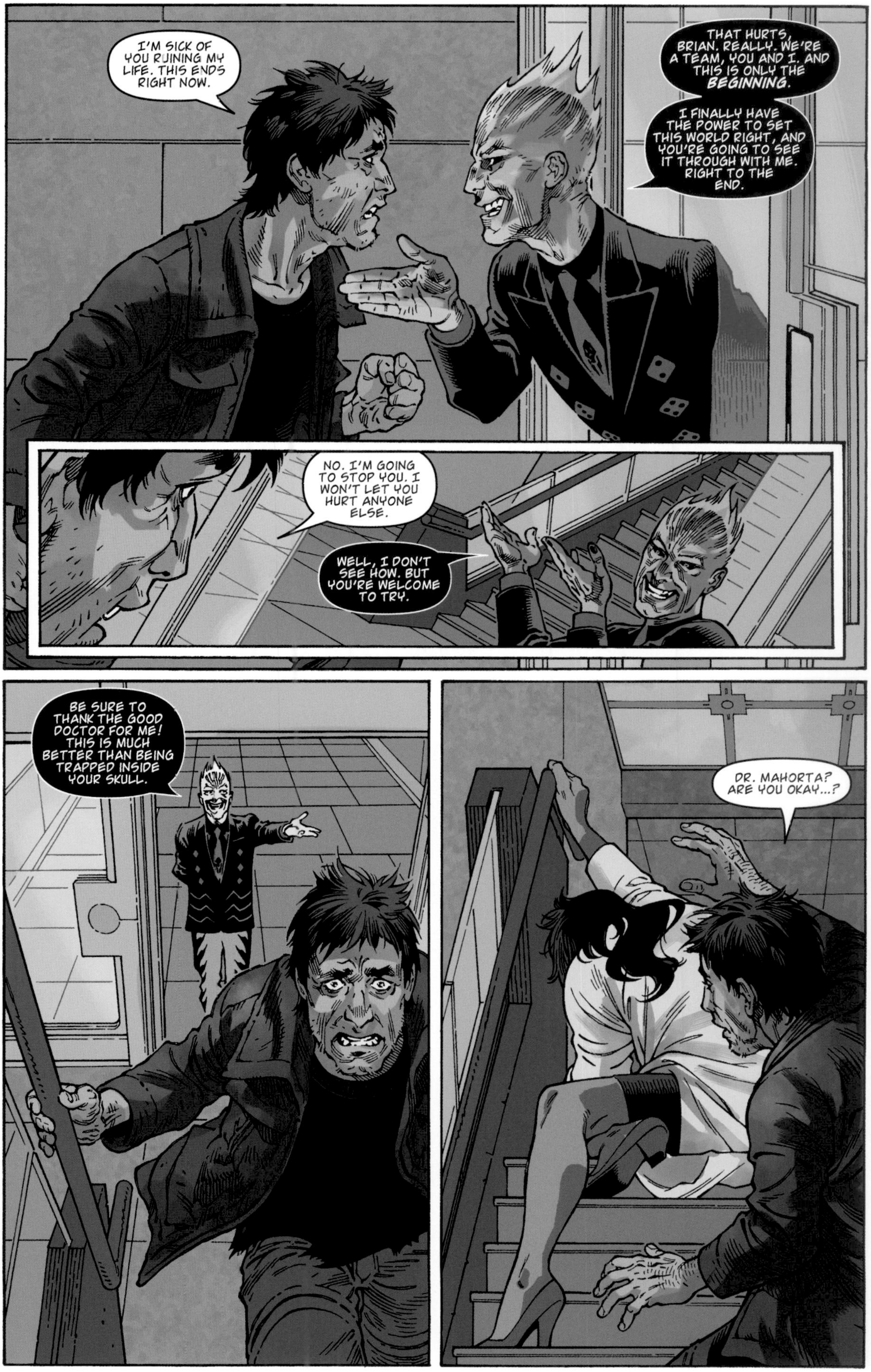
I'M SICK OF YOU RUINING MY LIFE. THIS ENDS RIGHT NOW.
THAT HURTS, BRIAN. REALLY. WE'RE A TEAM, YOU AND I. AND THIS IS ONLY THE *BEGINNING*.
I FINALLY HAVE THE POWER TO SET THIS WORLD RIGHT, AND YOU'RE GOING TO SEE IT THROUGH WITH ME. RIGHT TO THE END.
NO. I'M GOING TO STOP YOU. I WON'T LET YOU HURT ANYONE ELSE.
WELL, I DON'T SEE HOW. BUT YOU'RE WELCOME TO TRY.
BE SURE TO THANK THE GOOD DOCTOR FOR ME! THIS IS MUCH BETTER THAN BEING TRAPPED INSIDE YOUR SKULL.
DR. MAHORTA? ARE YOU OKAY...?

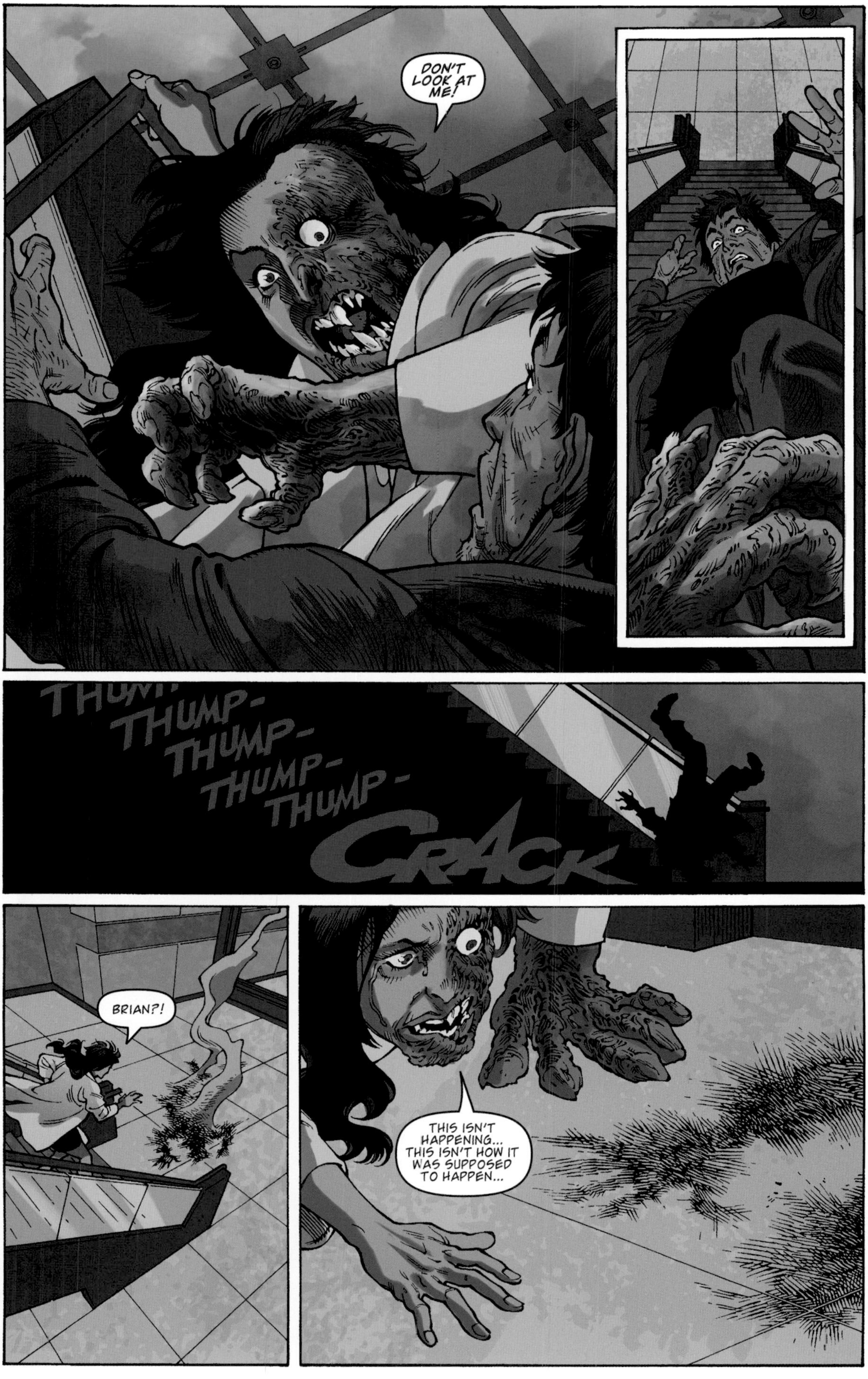
DON'T LOOK AT ME!
THUMP-
THUMP-
THUMP-
THUMP-
THUMP-
CRACK
BRIAN?!
THIS ISN'T HAPPENING... THIS ISN'T HOW IT WAS SUPPOSED TO HAPPEN...

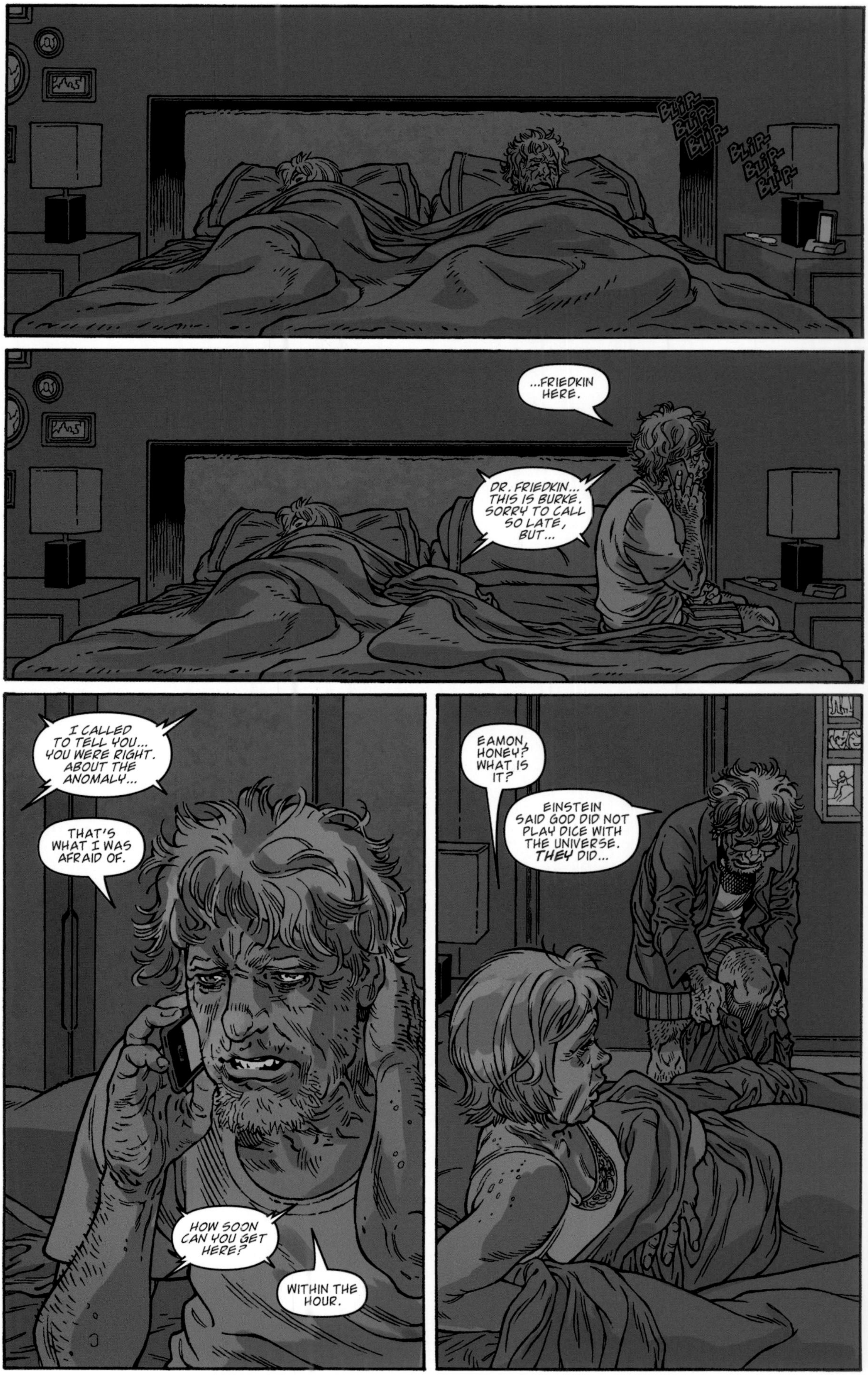
BLIP-BLIP-BLIP-
BLIP-BLIP-BLIP-
...FRIEDKIN HERE.
DR. FRIEDKIN... THIS IS BURKE. SORRY TO CALL SO LATE, BUT...
I CALLED TO TELL YOU... YOU WERE RIGHT. ABOUT THE ANOMALY...
THAT'S WHAT I WAS AFRAID OF.
HOW SOON CAN YOU GET HERE?
WITHIN THE HOUR.
EAMON, HONEY? WHAT IS IT?
EINSTEIN SAID GOD DID NOT PLAY DICE WITH THE UNIVERSE. THEY DID...

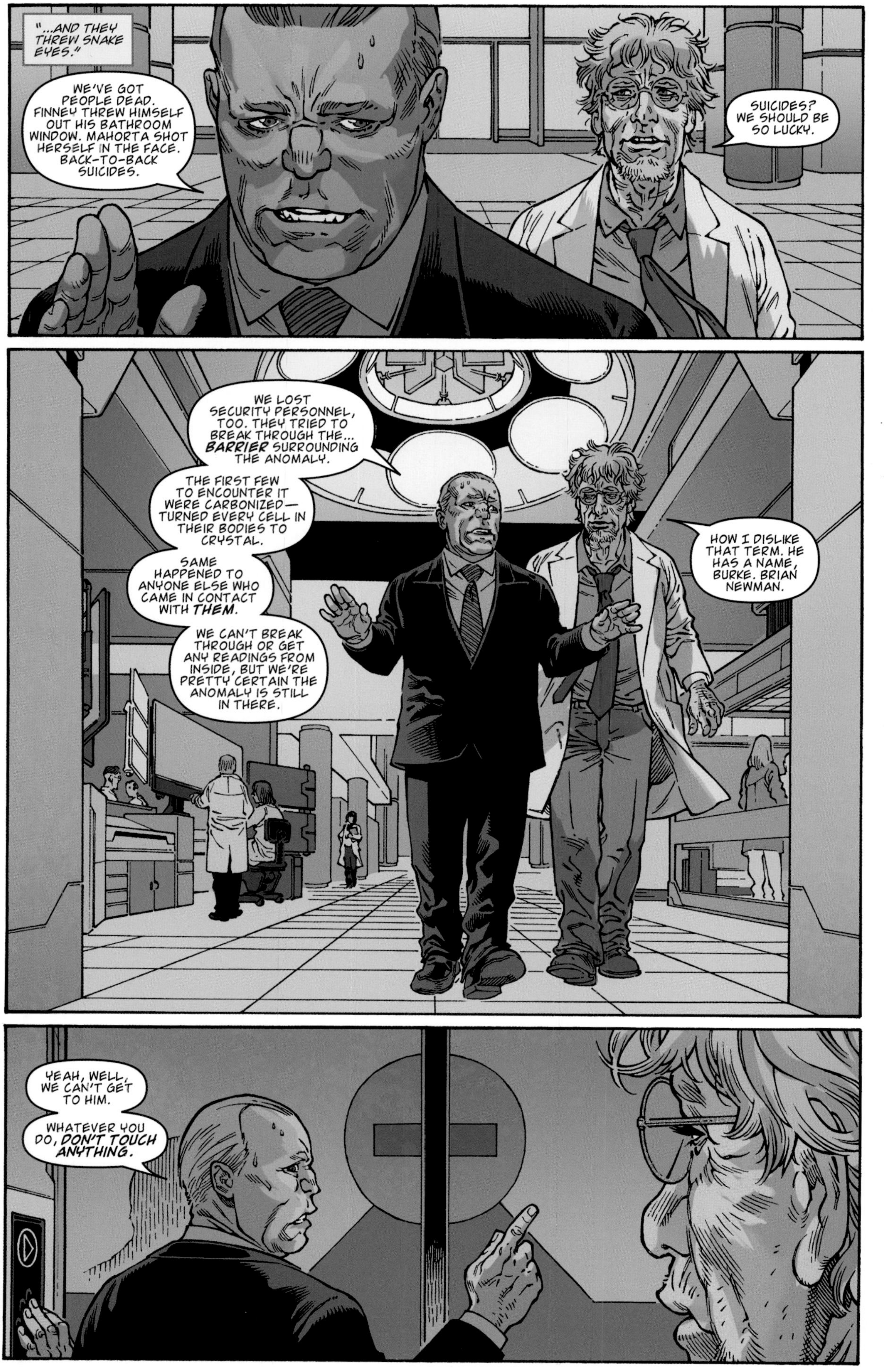
"...AND THEY THREW SNAKE EYES."
WE'VE GOT PEOPLE DEAD. FINNEY THREW HIMSELF OUT HIS BATHROOM WINDOW. MAHORTA SHOT HERSELF IN THE FACE. BACK-TO-BACK SUICIDES.
SUICIDES? WE SHOULD BE SO LUCKY.
WE LOST SECURITY PERSONNEL, TOO. THEY TRIED TO BREAK THROUGH THE... BARRIER SURROUNDING THE ANOMALY.
THE FIRST FEW TO ENCOUNTER IT WERE CARBONIZED— TURNED EVERY CELL IN THEIR BODIES TO CRYSTAL.
SAME HAPPENED TO ANYONE ELSE WHO CAME IN CONTACT WITH THEM.
WE CAN'T BREAK THROUGH OR GET ANY READINGS FROM INSIDE, BUT WE'RE PRETTY CERTAIN THE ANOMALY IS STILL IN THERE.
HOW I DISLIKE THAT TERM. HE HAS A NAME, BURKE. BRIAN NEWMAN.
YEAH, WELL, WE CAN'T GET TO HIM.
WHATEVER YOU DO, DON'T TOUCH ANYTHING.

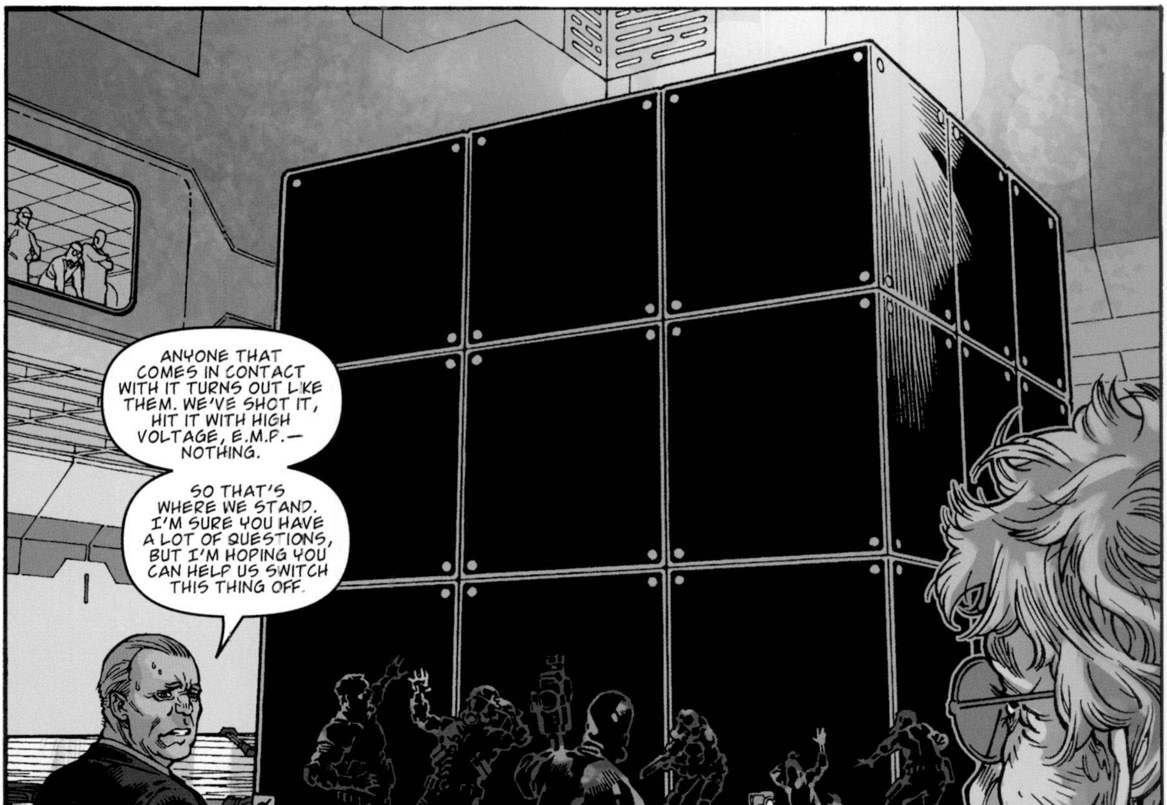
ANYONE THAT COMES IN CONTACT WITH IT TURNS OUT LIKE THEM. WE'VE SHOT IT, HIT IT WITH HIGH VOLTAGE, E.M.P.— NOTHING.
SO THAT'S WHERE WE STAND. I'M SURE YOU HAVE A LOT OF QUESTIONS, BUT I'M HOPING YOU CAN HELP US SWITCH THIS THING OFF.

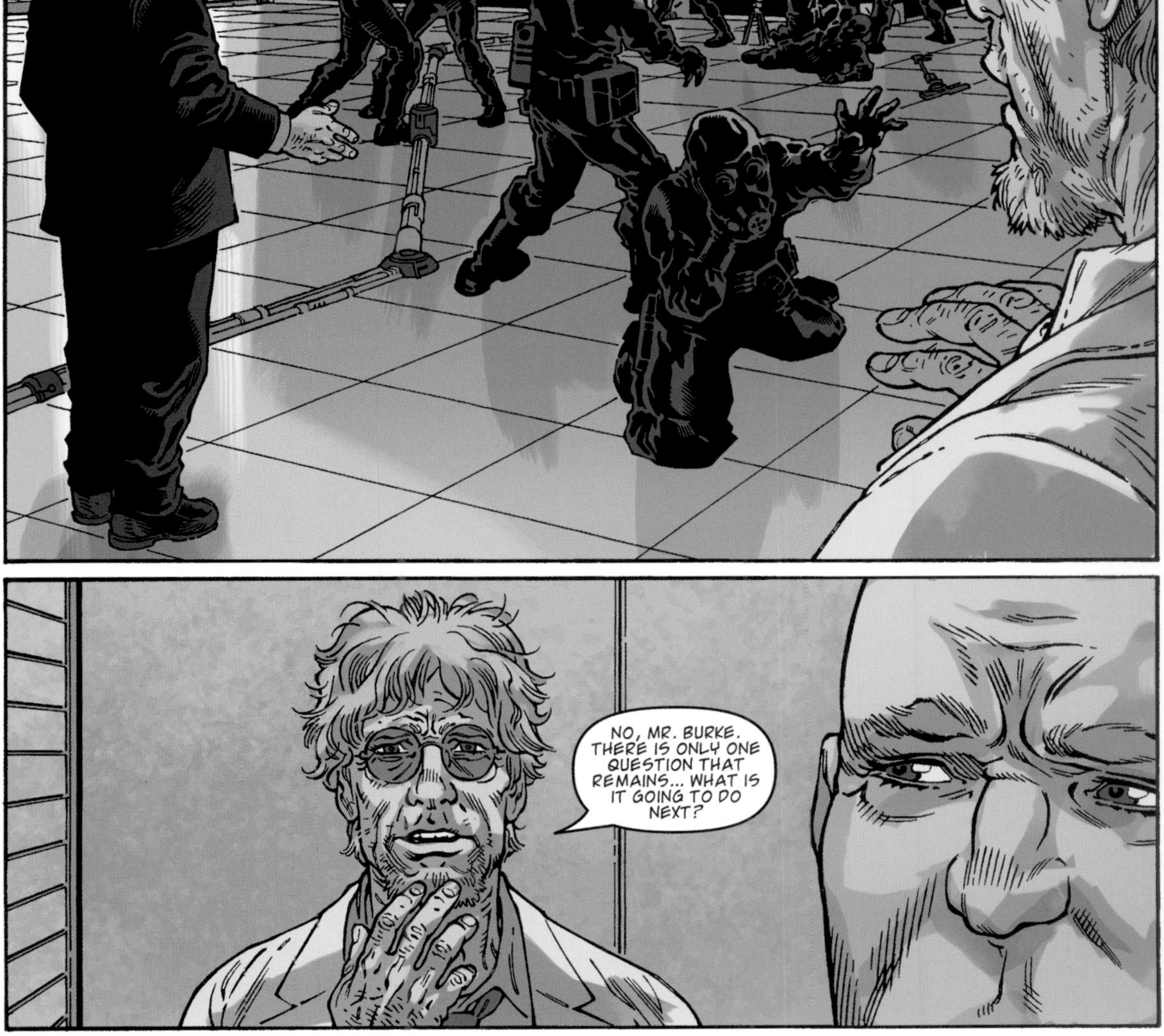
NO, MR. BURKE. THERE IS ONLY ONE QUESTION THAT REMAINS... WHAT IS IT GOING TO DO NEXT?

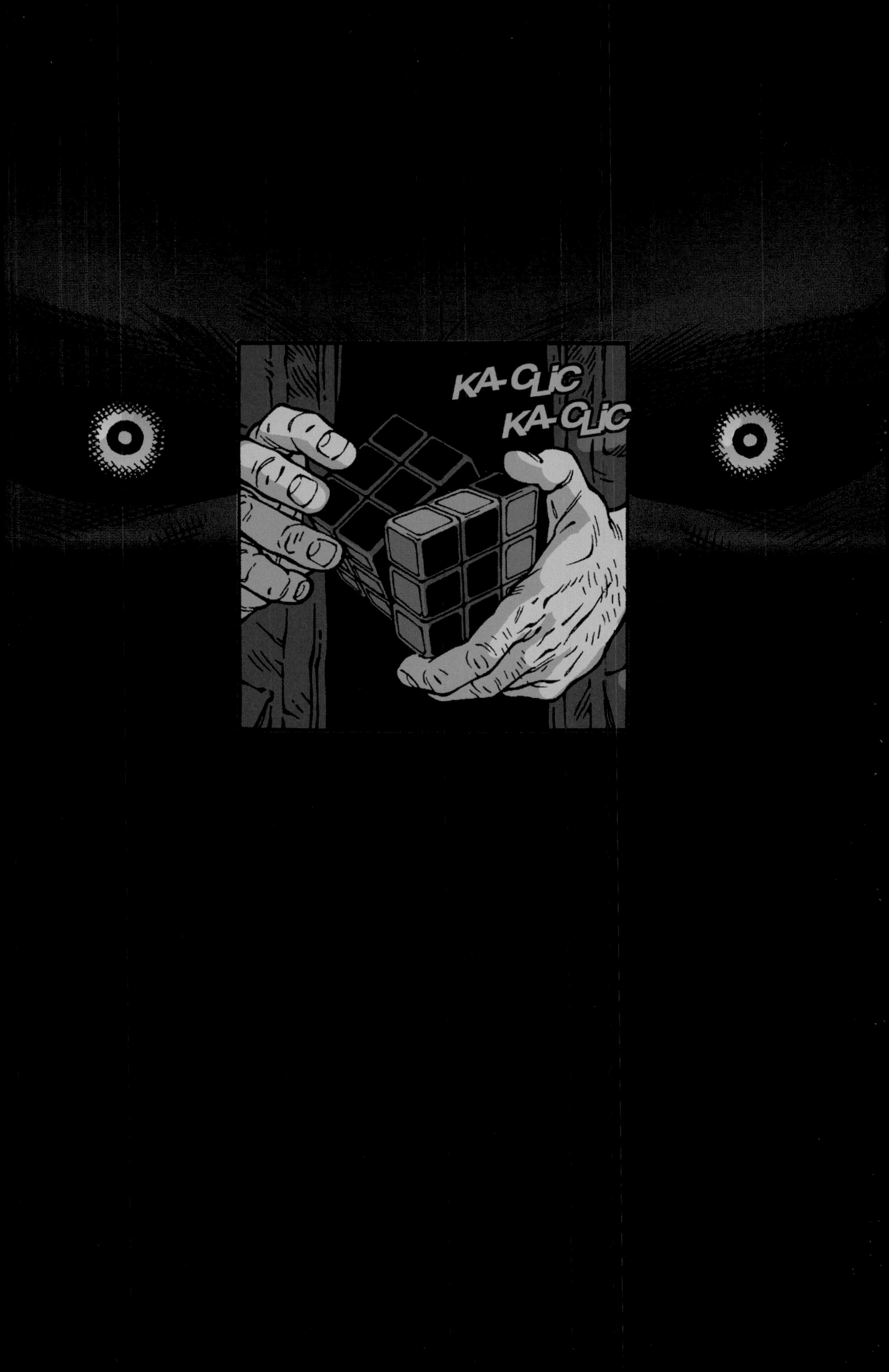
KA-CLIC
KA-CLIC

A WINDOW OPENS

ART BY GABRIEL RODRIGUEZ
COLORS BY RYAN HILL

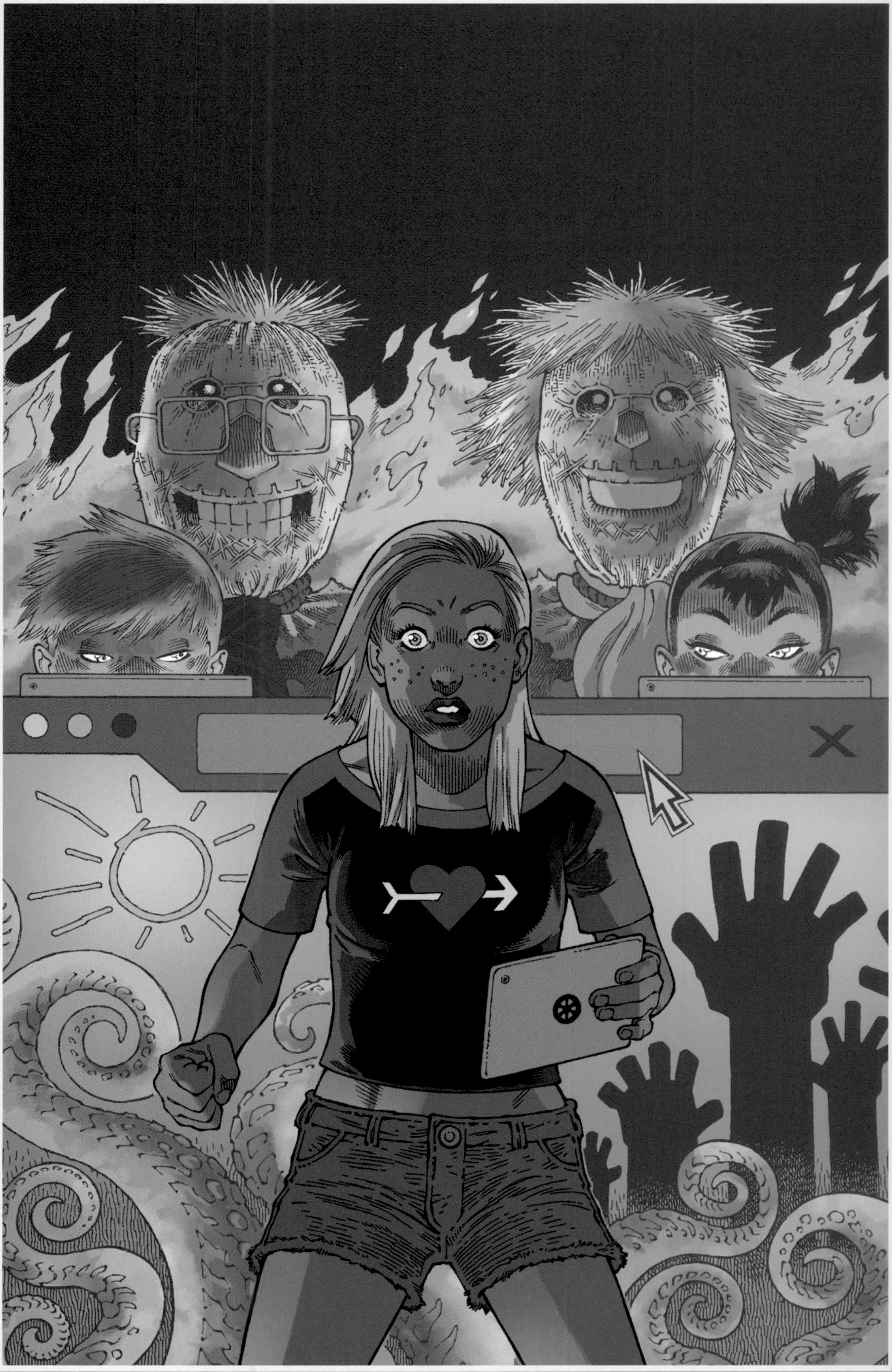

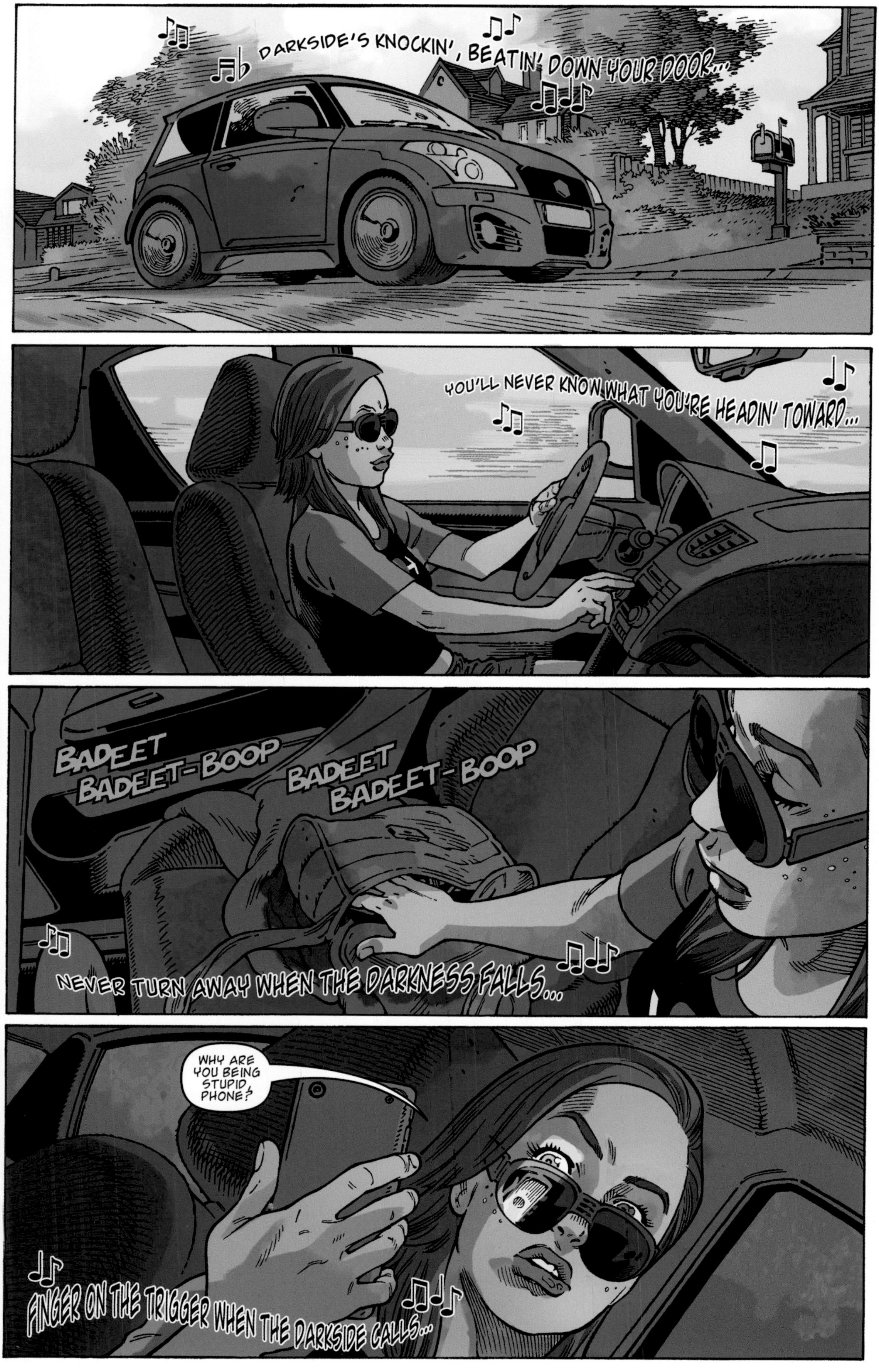
DARKSIDE'S KNOCKIN', BEATIN' DOWN YOUR DOOR...
YOU'LL NEVER KNOW WHAT YOU'RE HEADIN' TOWARD...
BADEET BADEET-BOOP
BADEET BADEET-BOOP
NEVER TURN AWAY WHEN THE DARKNESS FALLS...
WHY ARE YOU BEING STUPID, PHONE?
FINGER ON THE TRIGGER WHEN THE DARKSIDE CALLS...

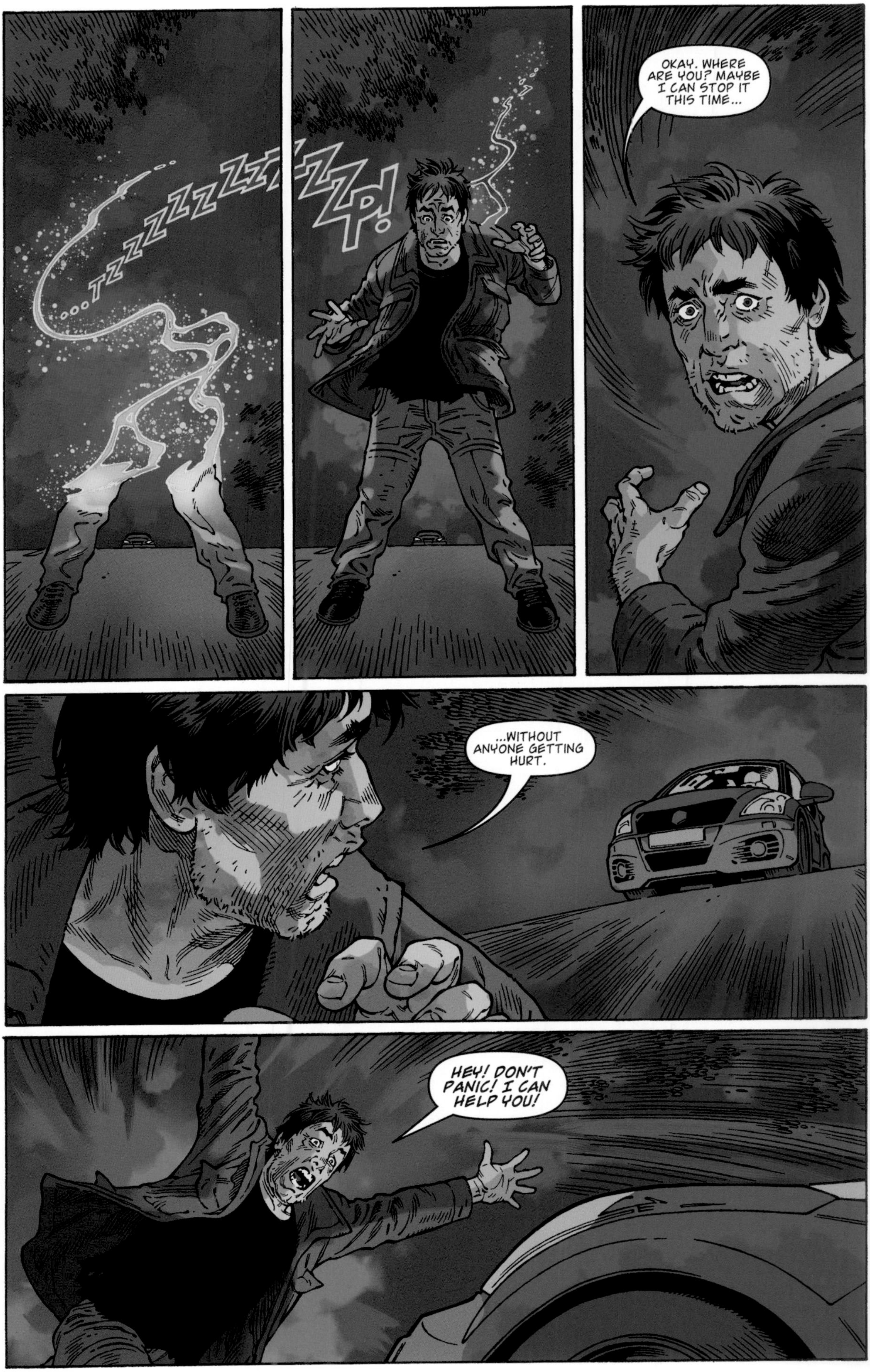
TZZZZZZZZZZZP!
OKAY. WHERE ARE YOU? MAYBE I CAN STOP IT THIS TIME...
...WITHOUT ANYONE GETTING HURT.
HEY! DON'T PANIC! I CAN HELP YOU!

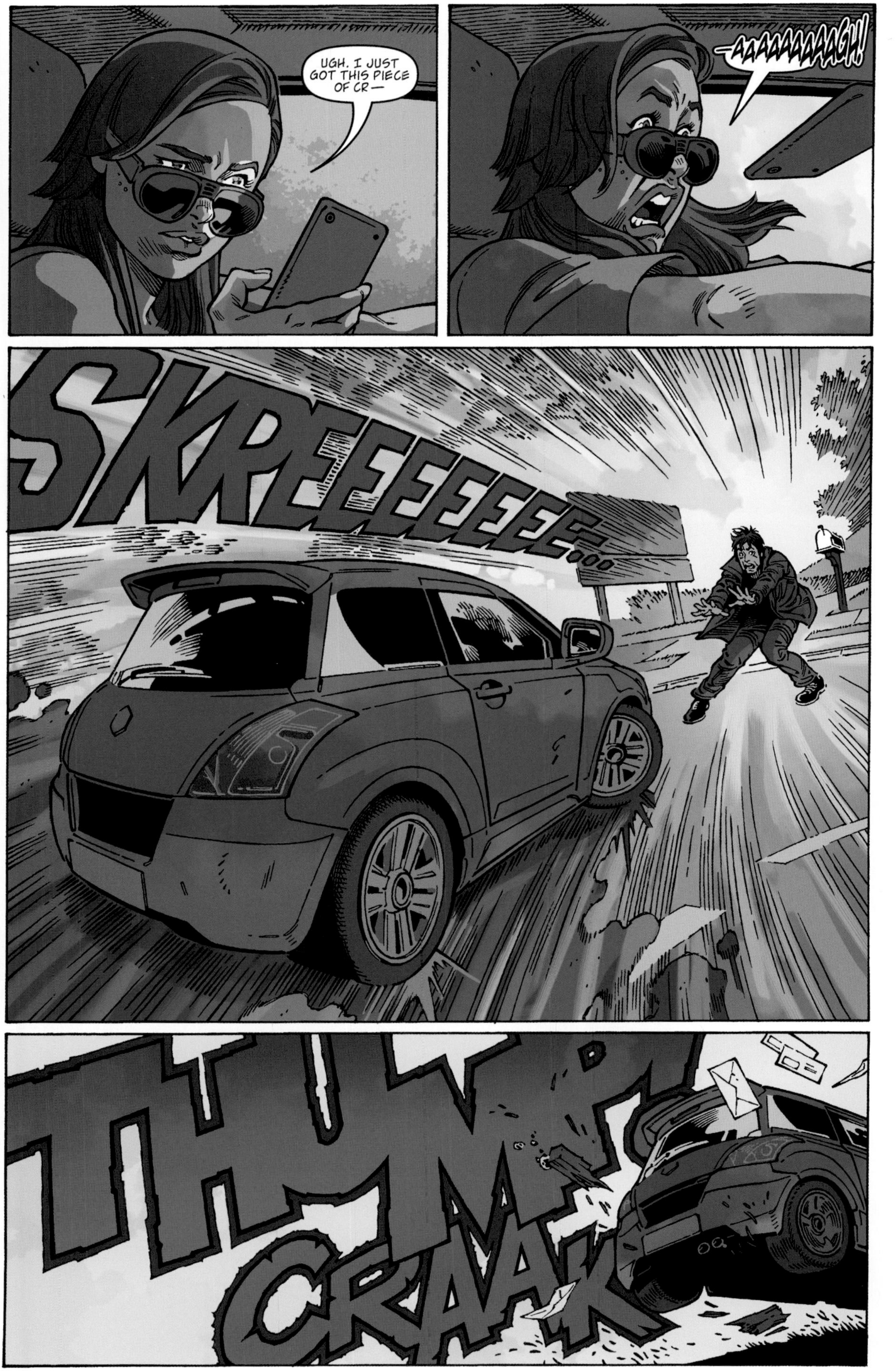
UGH. I JUST GOT THIS PIECE OF CR—
—AAAAAAAAAGH!
SKREEEEEEEEE...
THUMP
CRAAK

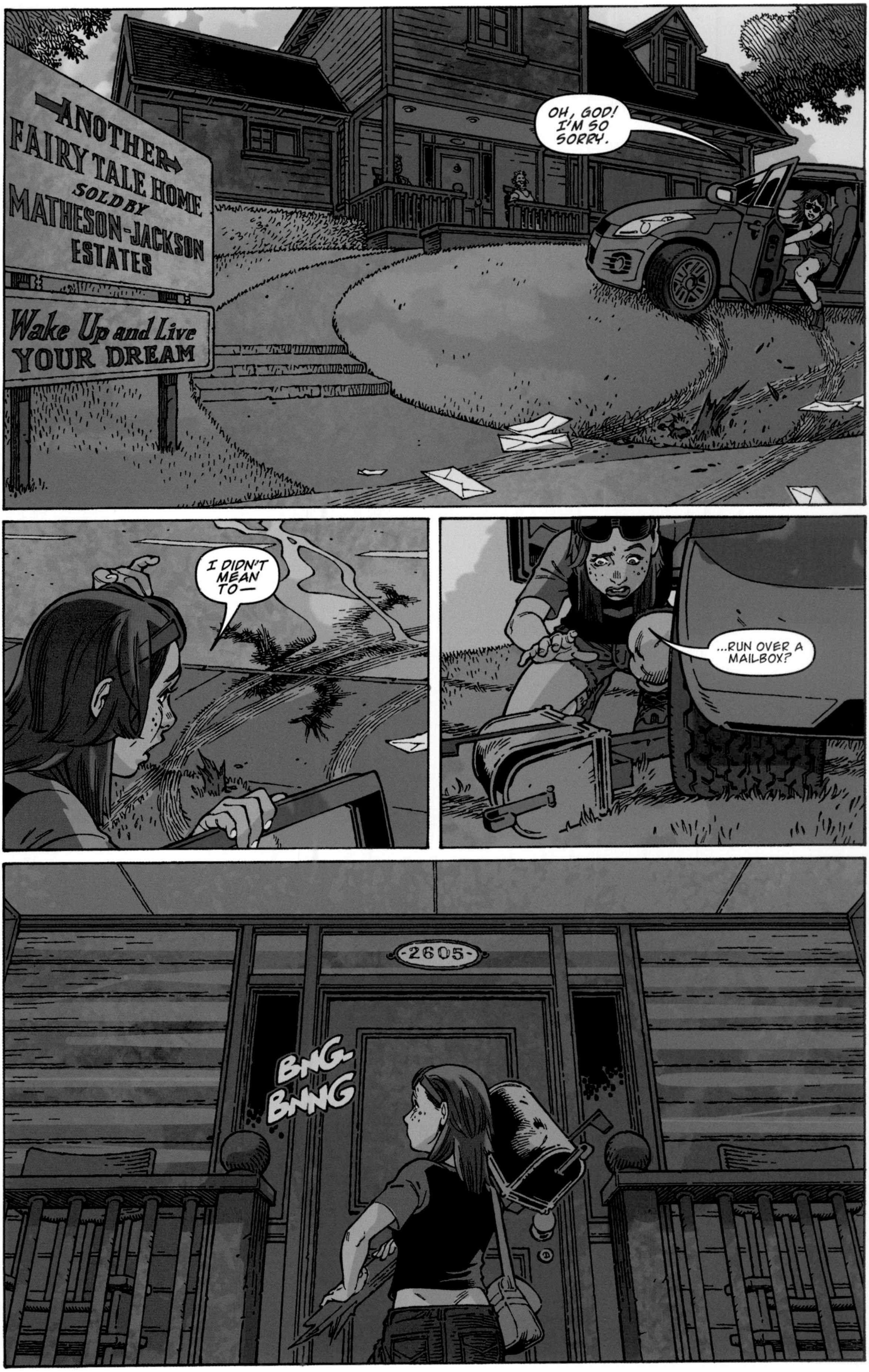
ANOTHER
FAIRY TALE HOME
SOLD BY
MATHESON-JACKSON
ESTATES
Wake Up and Live
YOUR DREAM
OH, GOD! I'M SO SORRY.
I DIDN'T MEAN TO—
...RUN OVER A MAILBOX?
2605
BNG BNNG

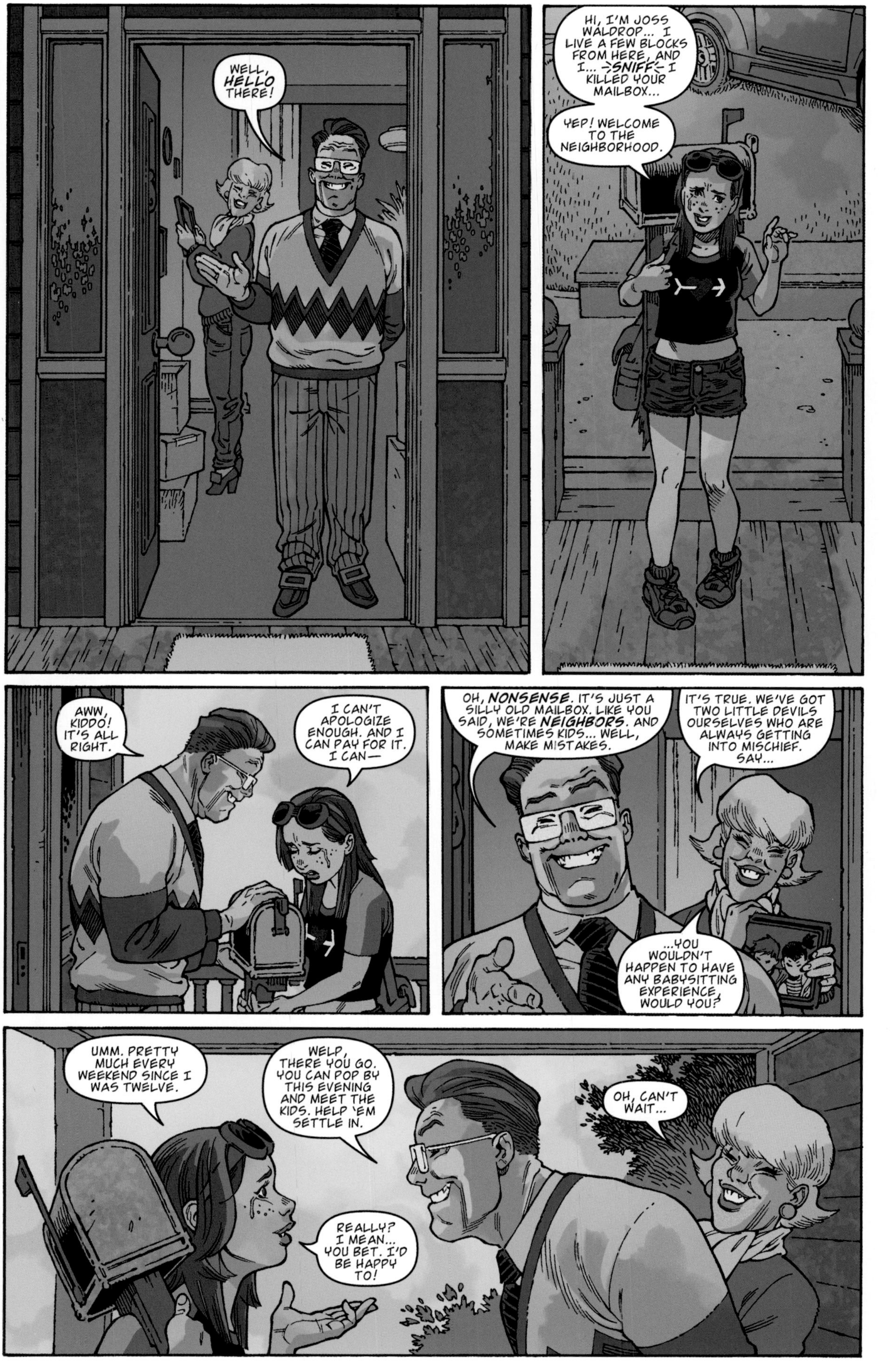
WELL, HELLO THERE!
HI, I'M JOSS WALDROP... I LIVE A FEW BLOCKS FROM HERE, AND I... SNIFF I KILLED YOUR MAILBOX...
YEP! WELCOME TO THE NEIGHBORHOOD.
AWW, KIDDO! IT'S ALL RIGHT.
I CAN'T APOLOGIZE ENOUGH. AND I CAN PAY FOR IT. I CAN—
OH, NONSENSE. IT'S JUST A SILLY OLD MAILBOX. LIKE YOU SAID, WE'RE NEIGHBORS. AND SOMETIMES KIDS... WELL, MAKE MISTAKES.
IT'S TRUE. WE'VE GOT TWO LITTLE DEVILS OURSELVES WHO ARE ALWAYS GETTING INTO MISCHIEF. SAY...
...YOU WOULDN'T HAPPEN TO HAVE ANY BABYSITTING EXPERIENCE, WOULD YOU?
UMM. PRETTY MUCH EVERY WEEKEND SINCE I WAS TWELVE.
WELP, THERE YOU GO. YOU CAN POP BY THIS EVENING AND MEET THE KIDS. HELP 'EM SETTLE IN.
OH, CAN'T WAIT...
REALLY? I MEAN... YOU BET. I'D BE HAPPY TO!

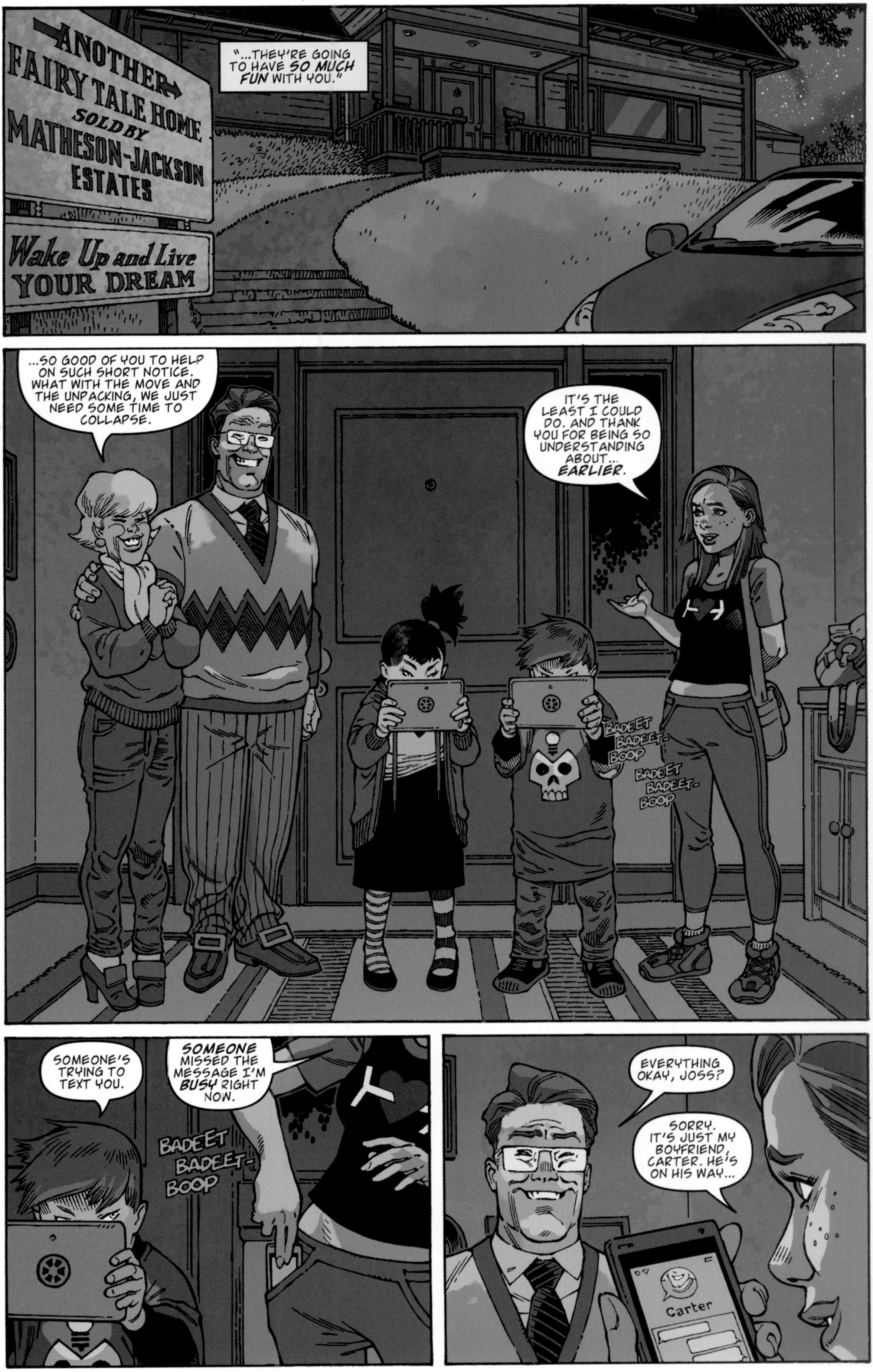
ANOTHER
FAIRY TALE HOME
SOLD BY
MATHESON-JACKSON
ESTATES
Wake Up and Live
YOUR DREAM
"...THEY'RE GOING TO HAVE SO MUCH FUN WITH YOU."
...SO GOOD OF YOU TO HELP ON SUCH SHORT NOTICE. WHAT WITH THE MOVE AND THE UNPACKING, WE JUST NEED SOME TIME TO COLLAPSE.
IT'S THE LEAST I COULD DO. AND THANK YOU FOR BEING SO UNDERSTANDING ABOUT... EARLIER.
BADEET BADEET-BOOP
BADEET BADEET-BOOP
SOMEONE'S TRYING TO TEXT YOU.
SOMEONE MISSED THE MESSAGE I'M BUSY RIGHT NOW.
BADEET BADEET-BOOP
EVERYTHING OKAY, JOSS?
SORRY. IT'S JUST MY BOYFRIEND, CARTER. HE'S ON HIS WAY...
Carter

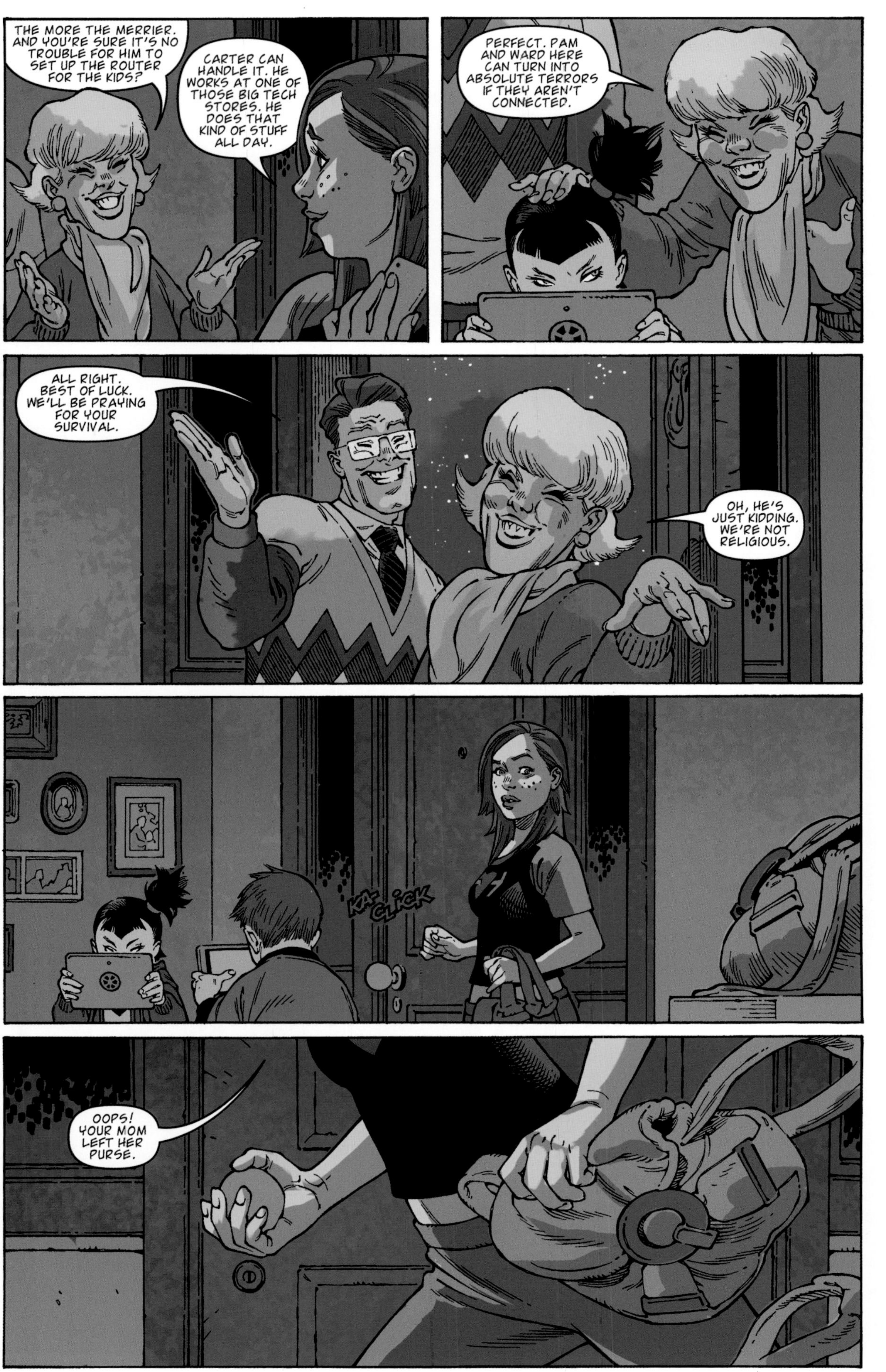
THE MORE THE MERRIER. AND YOU'RE SURE IT'S NO TROUBLE FOR HIM TO SET UP THE ROUTER FOR THE KIDS?
CARTER CAN HANDLE IT. HE WORKS AT ONE OF THOSE BIG TECH STORES. HE DOES THAT KIND OF STUFF ALL DAY.
PERFECT. PAM AND WARD HERE CAN TURN INTO ABSOLUTE TERRORS IF THEY AREN'T CONNECTED.
ALL RIGHT. BEST OF LUCK. WE'LL BE PRAYING FOR YOUR SURVIVAL.
OH, HE'S JUST KIDDING. WE'RE NOT RELIGIOUS.
KA-CLICK
OOPS! YOUR MOM LEFT HER PURSE.

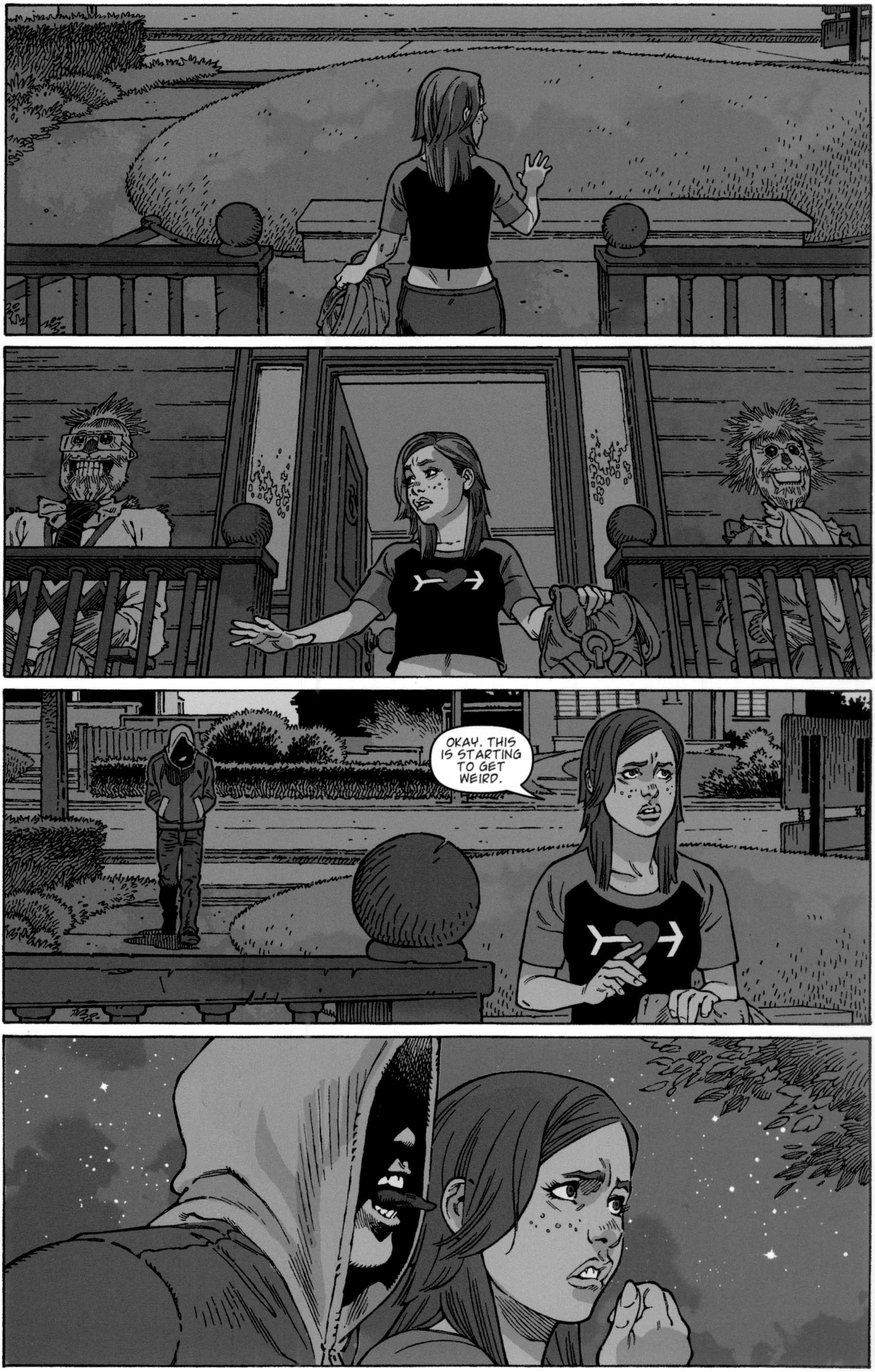
OKAY. THIS IS STARTING TO GET WEIRD.

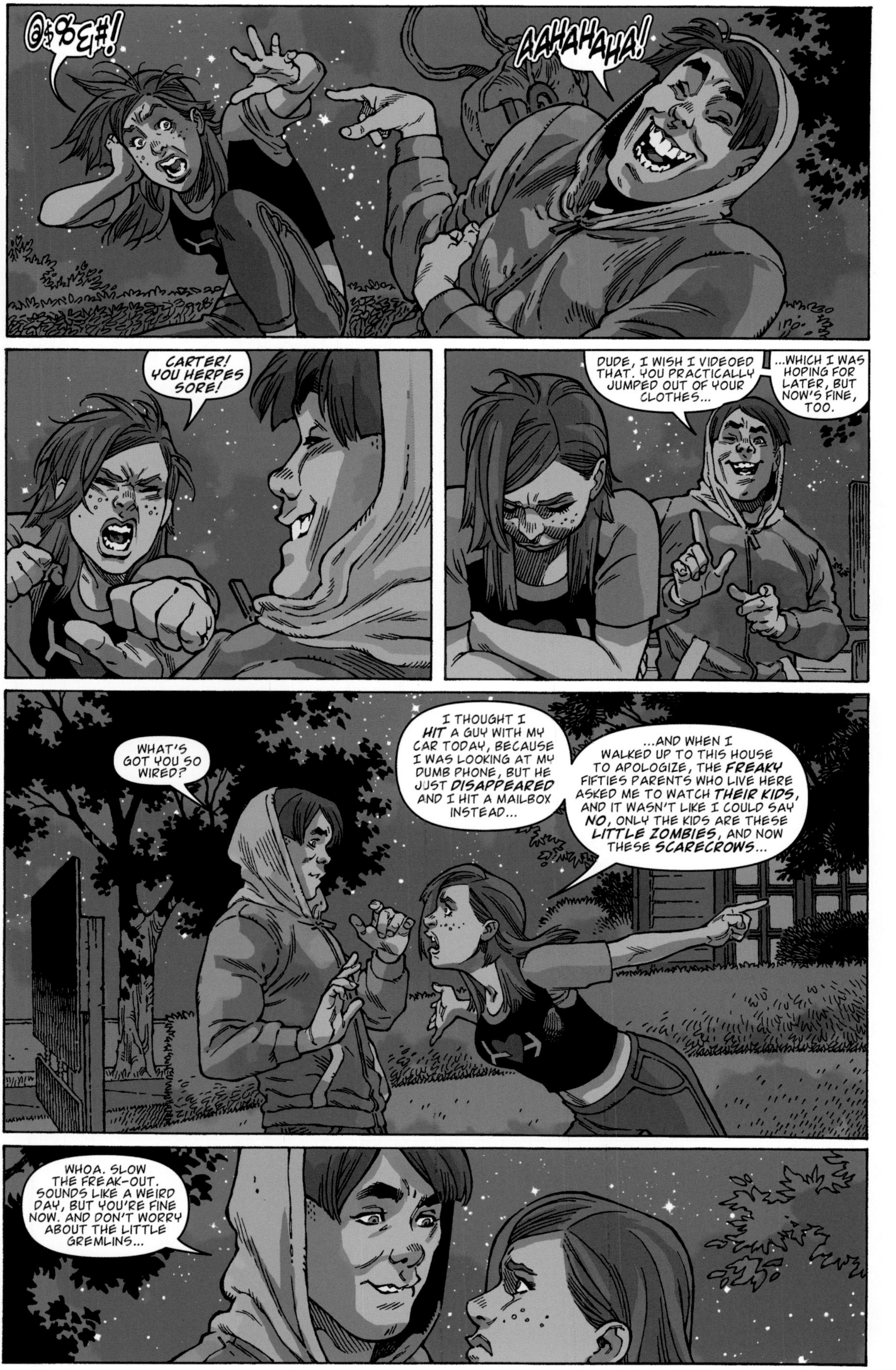
@$%#!
AAHAHAHA!
CARTER! YOU HERPES SORE!
DUDE, I WISH I VIDEOED THAT. YOU PRACTICALLY JUMPED OUT OF YOUR CLOTHES...
...WHICH I WAS HOPING FOR LATER, BUT NOW'S FINE, TOO.
WHAT'S GOT YOU SO WIRED?
I THOUGHT I HIT A GUY WITH MY CAR TODAY, BECAUSE I WAS LOOKING AT MY DUMB PHONE, BUT HE JUST DISAPPEARED AND I HIT A MAILBOX INSTEAD...
...AND WHEN I WALKED UP TO THIS HOUSE TO APOLOGIZE, THE FREAKY FIFTIES PARENTS WHO LIVE HERE ASKED ME TO WATCH THEIR KIDS, AND IT WASN'T LIKE I COULD SAY NO, ONLY THE KIDS ARE THESE LITTLE ZOMBIES, AND NOW THESE SCARECROWS...
WHOA. SLOW THE FREAK-OUT. SOUNDS LIKE A WEIRD DAY, BUT YOU'RE FINE NOW. AND DON'T WORRY ABOUT THE LITTLE GREMLINS...

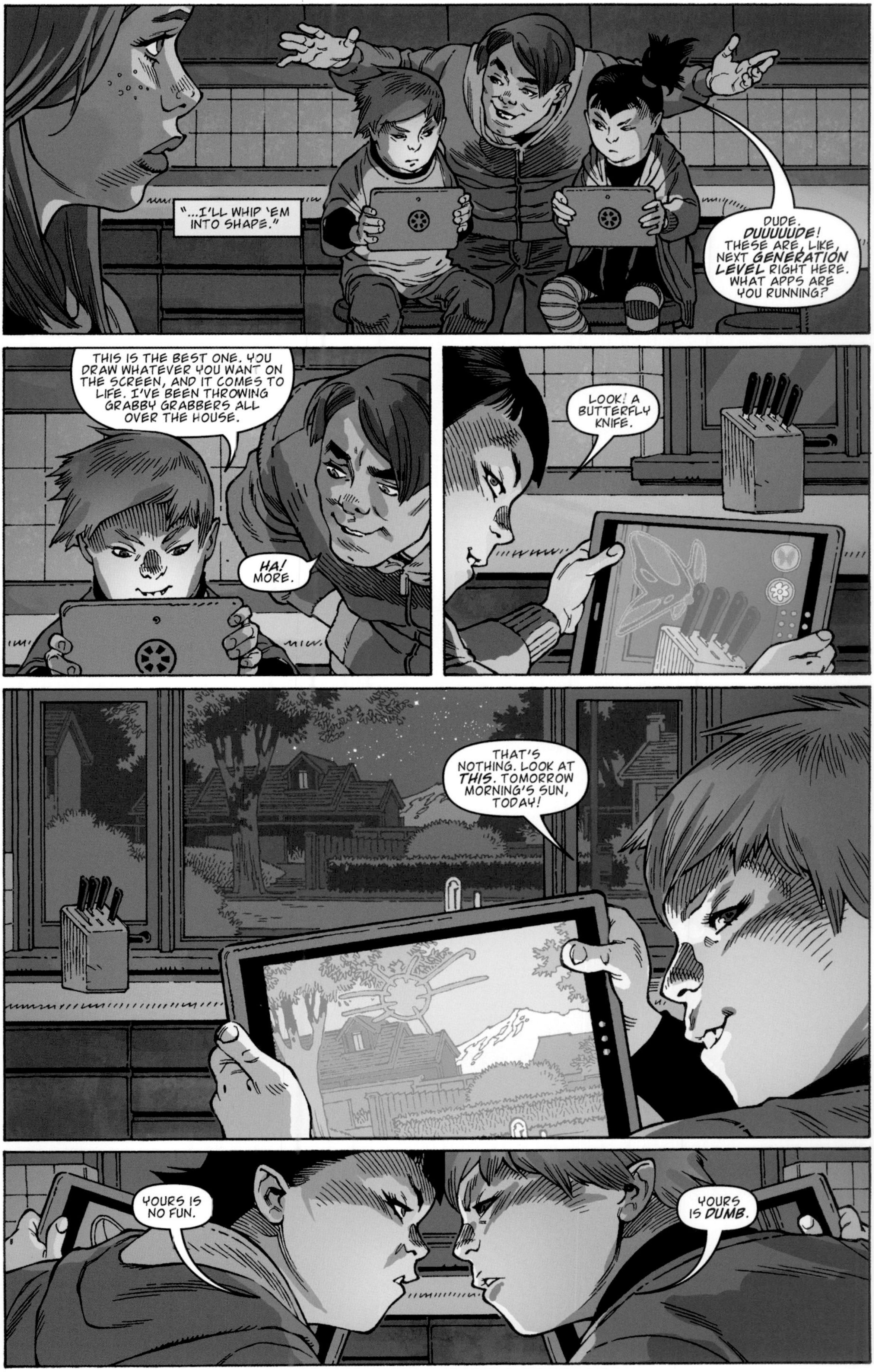
"...I'LL WHIP 'EM INTO SHAPE."
DUDE. DUUUUUDE! THESE ARE, LIKE, NEXT GENERATION LEVEL RIGHT HERE. WHAT APPS ARE YOU RUNNING?
THIS IS THE BEST ONE. YOU DRAW WHATEVER YOU WANT ON THE SCREEN, AND IT COMES TO LIFE. I'VE BEEN THROWING GRABBY GRABBERS ALL OVER THE HOUSE.
HA! MORE.
LOOK! A BUTTERFLY KNIFE.
THAT'S NOTHING. LOOK AT THIS. TOMORROW MORNING'S SUN, TODAY!
YOURS IS NO FUN.
YOURS IS DUMB.

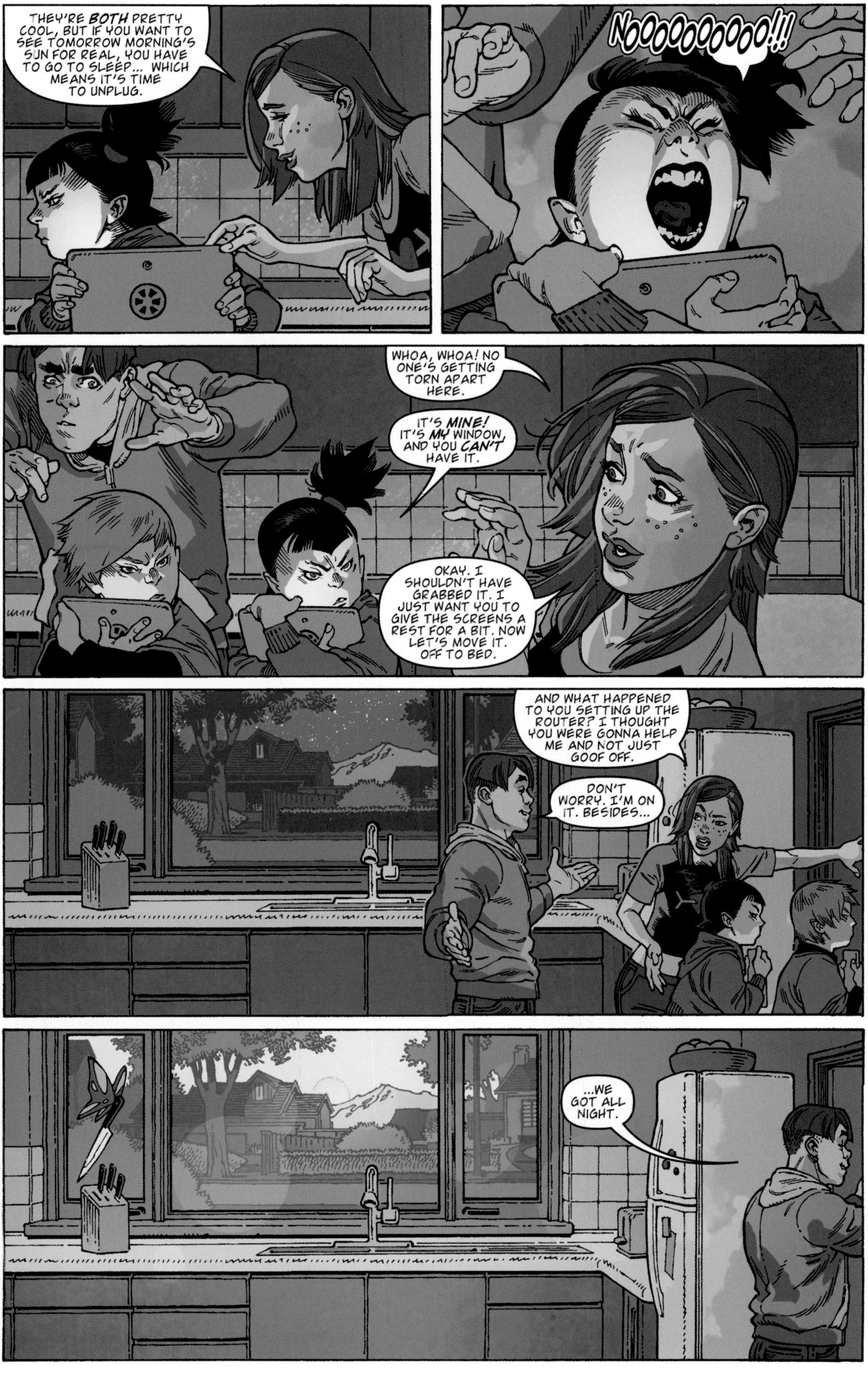
THEY'RE BOTH PRETTY COOL, BUT IF YOU WANT TO SEE TOMORROW MORNING'S SUN FOR REAL, YOU HAVE TO GO TO SLEEP... WHICH MEANS IT'S TIME TO UNPLUG.
NOOOOOOOOOO!!!
WHOA, WHOA! NO ONE'S GETTING TORN APART HERE.
IT'S MINE! IT'S MY WINDOW, AND YOU CAN'T HAVE IT.
OKAY. I SHOULDN'T HAVE GRABBED IT. I JUST WANT YOU TO GIVE THE SCREENS A REST FOR A BIT. NOW LET'S MOVE IT. OFF TO BED.
AND WHAT HAPPENED TO YOU SETTING UP THE ROUTER? I THOUGHT YOU WERE GONNA HELP ME AND NOT JUST GOOF OFF.
DON'T WORRY. I'M ON IT. BESIDES...
...WE GOT ALL NIGHT.

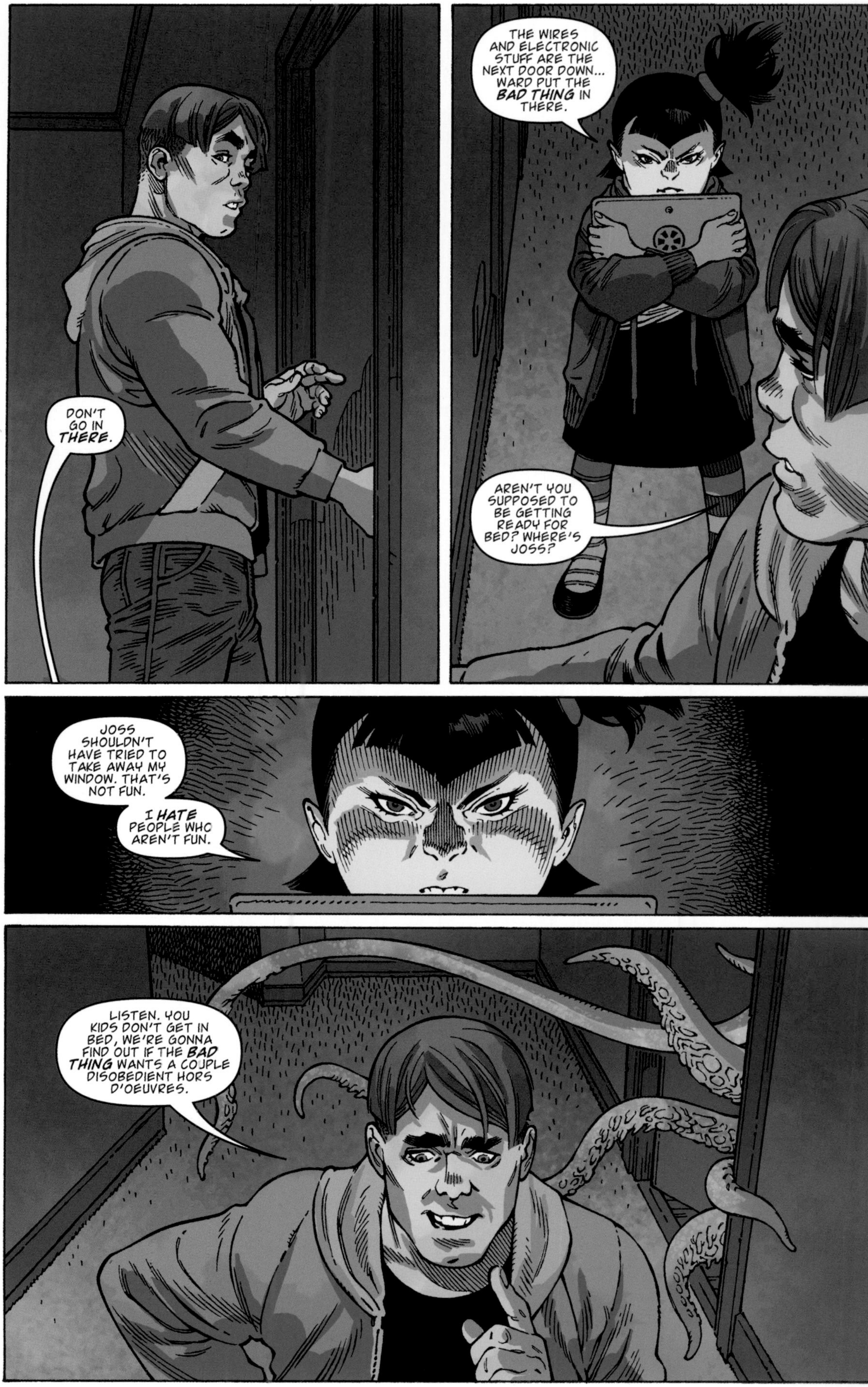
DON'T GO IN *THERE*.
THE WIRES AND ELECTRONIC STUFF ARE THE NEXT DOOR DOWN... WARD PUT THE *BAD THING* IN THERE.
AREN'T YOU SUPPOSED TO BE GETTING READY FOR BED? WHERE'S JOSS?
JOSS SHOULDN'T HAVE TRIED TO TAKE AWAY MY WINDOW. THAT'S NOT FUN.
I *HATE* PEOPLE WHO AREN'T FUN.
LISTEN. YOU KIDS DON'T GET IN BED, WE'RE GONNA FIND OUT IF THE *BAD THING* WANTS A COUPLE DISOBEDIENT HORS D'OEUVRES.

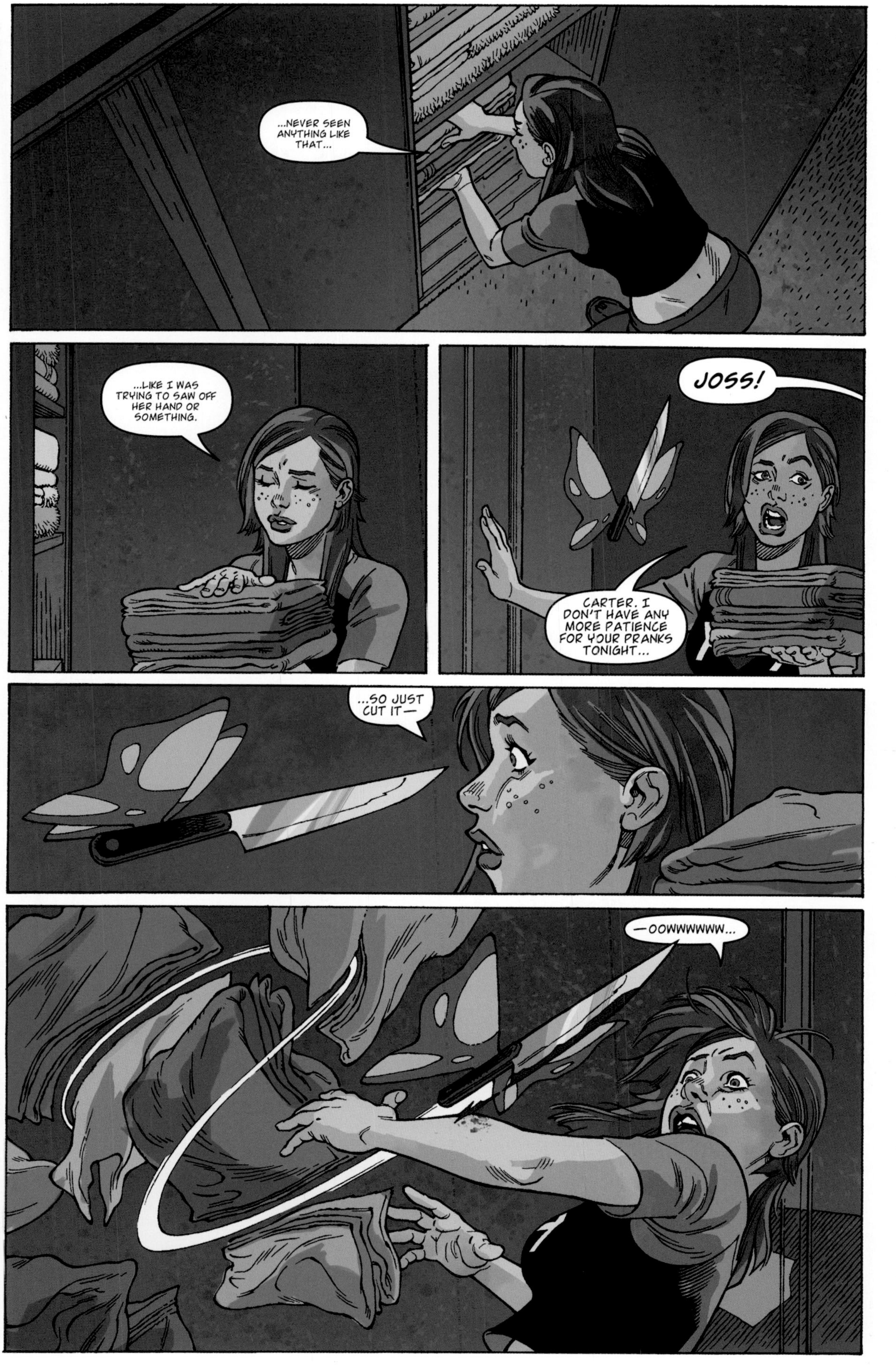
...NEVER SEEN ANYTHING LIKE THAT...
...LIKE I WAS TRYING TO SAW OFF HER HAND OR SOMETHING.
JOSS!
CARTER. I DON'T HAVE ANY MORE PATIENCE FOR YOUR PRANKS TONIGHT...
...SO JUST CUT IT—
—OOWWWWWW...

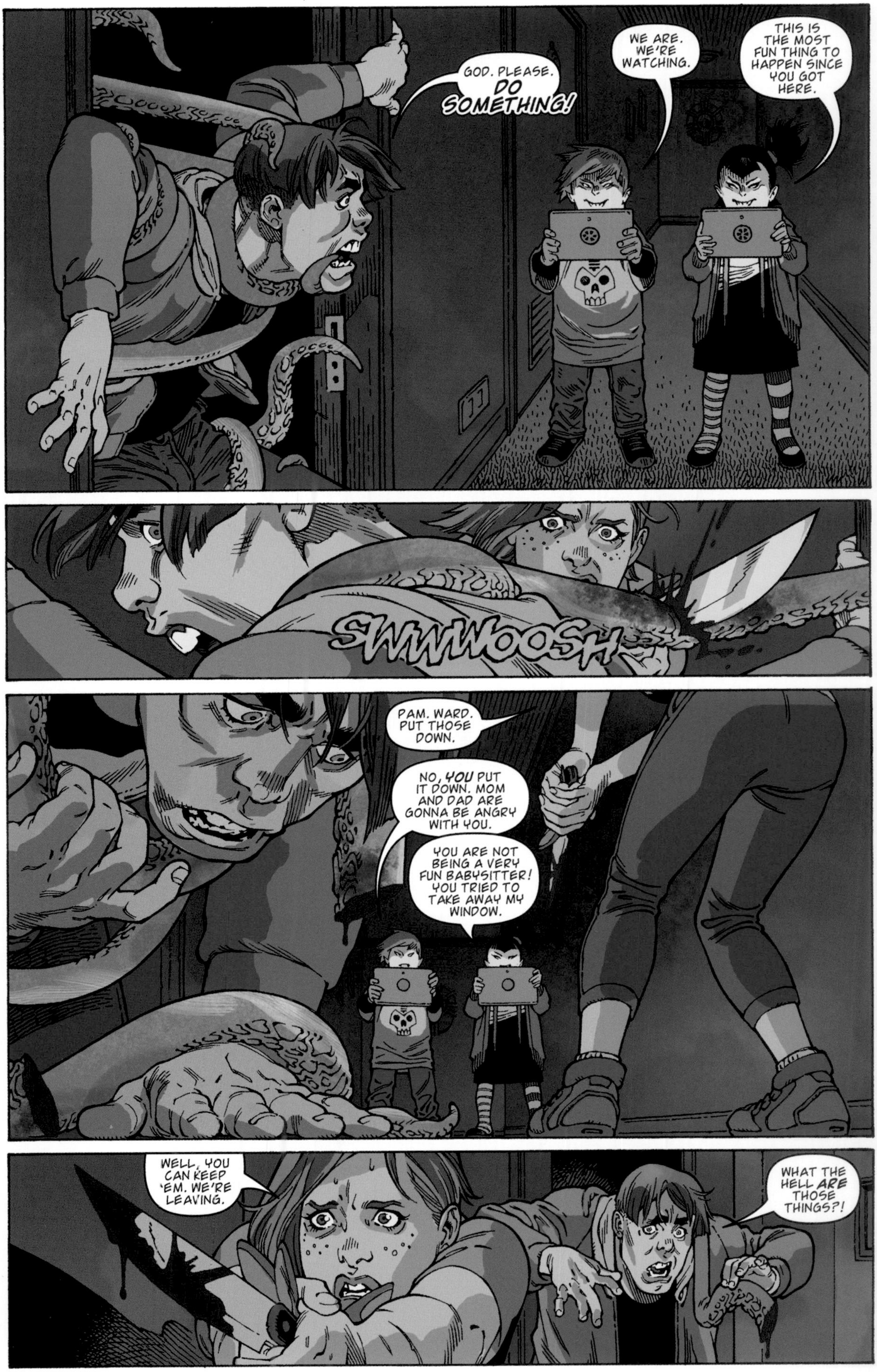
GOD. PLEASE. ***DO SOMETHING!***
WE ARE. WE'RE WATCHING.
THIS IS THE MOST FUN THING TO HAPPEN SINCE YOU GOT HERE.
SWWOOSH
PAM. WARD. PUT THOSE DOWN.
NO, ***YOU*** PUT IT DOWN. MOM AND DAD ARE GONNA BE ANGRY WITH YOU.
YOU ARE NOT BEING A VERY FUN BABYSITTER! YOU TRIED TO TAKE AWAY MY WINDOW.
WELL, YOU CAN KEEP 'EM. WE'RE LEAVING.
WHAT THE HELL ***ARE*** THOSE THINGS?!

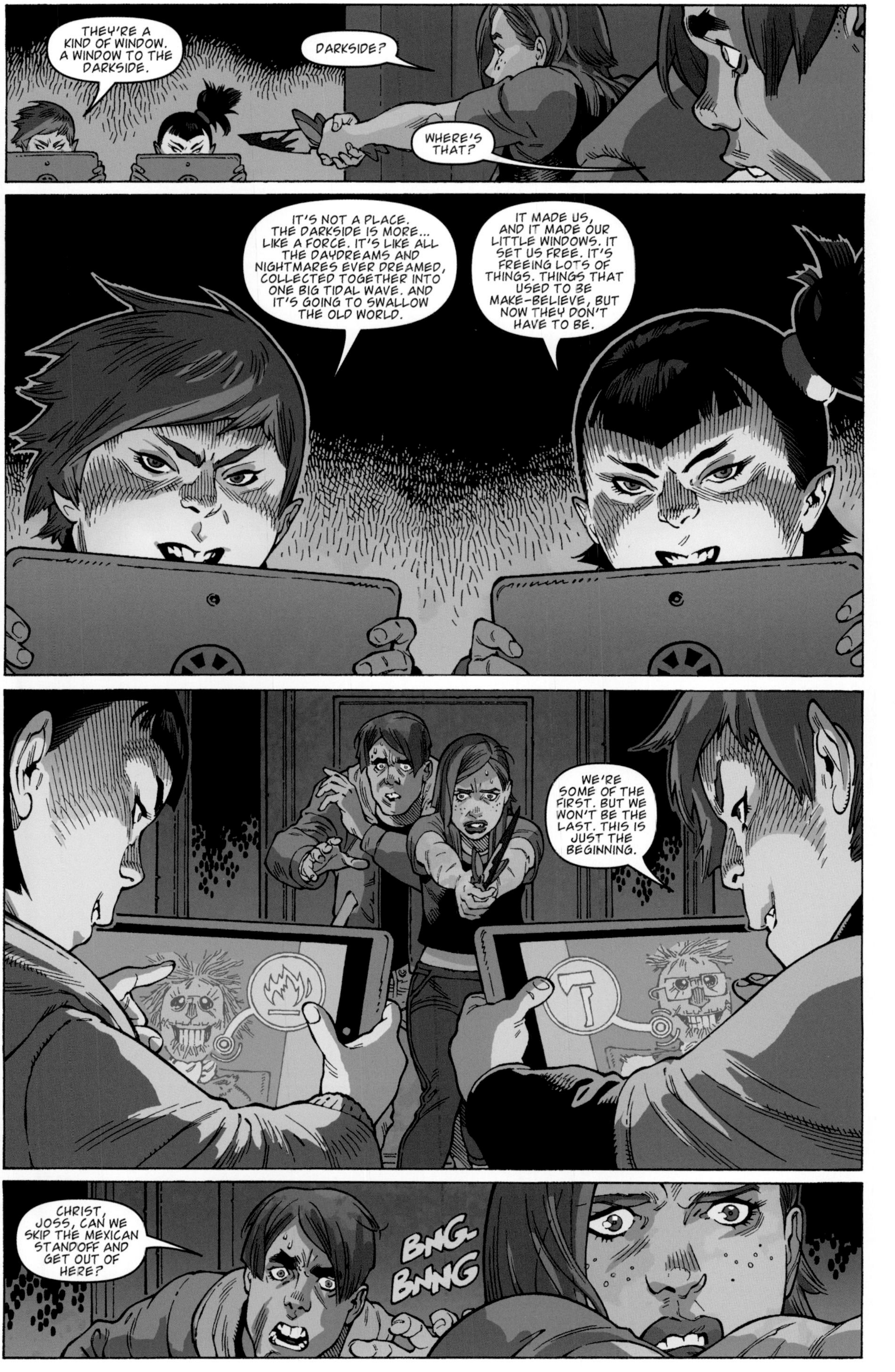
THEY'RE A KIND OF WINDOW. A WINDOW TO THE DARKSIDE.
DARKSIDE?
WHERE'S THAT?
IT'S NOT A PLACE. THE DARKSIDE IS MORE... LIKE A FORCE. IT'S LIKE ALL THE DAYDREAMS AND NIGHTMARES EVER DREAMED, COLLECTED TOGETHER INTO ONE BIG TIDAL WAVE. AND IT'S GOING TO SWALLOW THE OLD WORLD.
IT MADE US, AND IT MADE OUR LITTLE WINDOWS. IT SET US FREE. IT'S FREEING LOTS OF THINGS. THINGS THAT USED TO BE MAKE-BELIEVE, BUT NOW THEY DON'T HAVE TO BE.
WE'RE SOME OF THE FIRST. BUT WE WON'T BE THE LAST. THIS IS JUST THE BEGINNING.
CHRIST, JOSS, CAN WE SKIP THE MEXICAN STANDOFF AND GET OUT OF HERE?
BNG BNNG

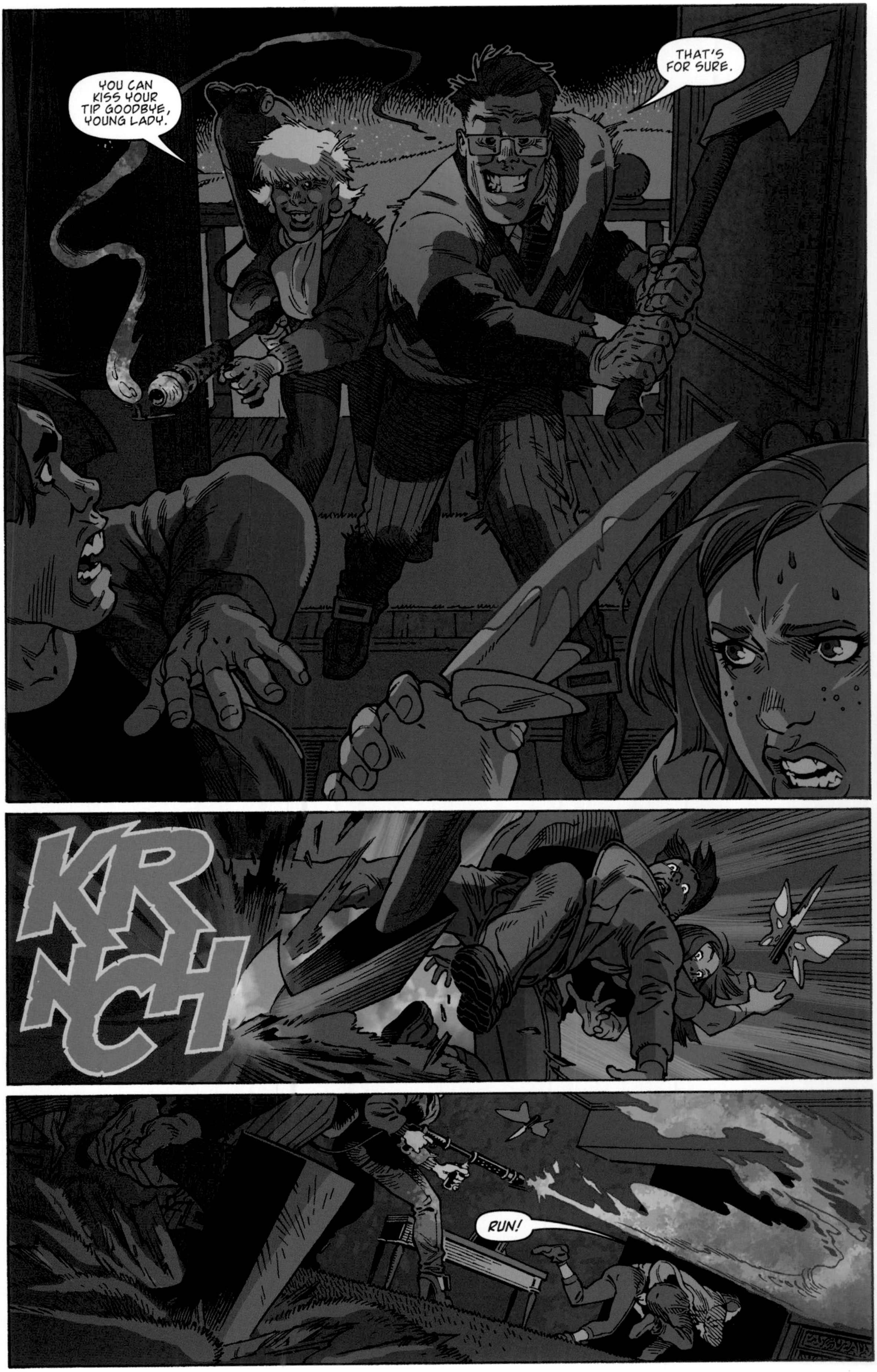
YOU CAN KISS YOUR TIP GOODBYE, YOUNG LADY.
THAT'S FOR SURE.
KRNCH
RUN!

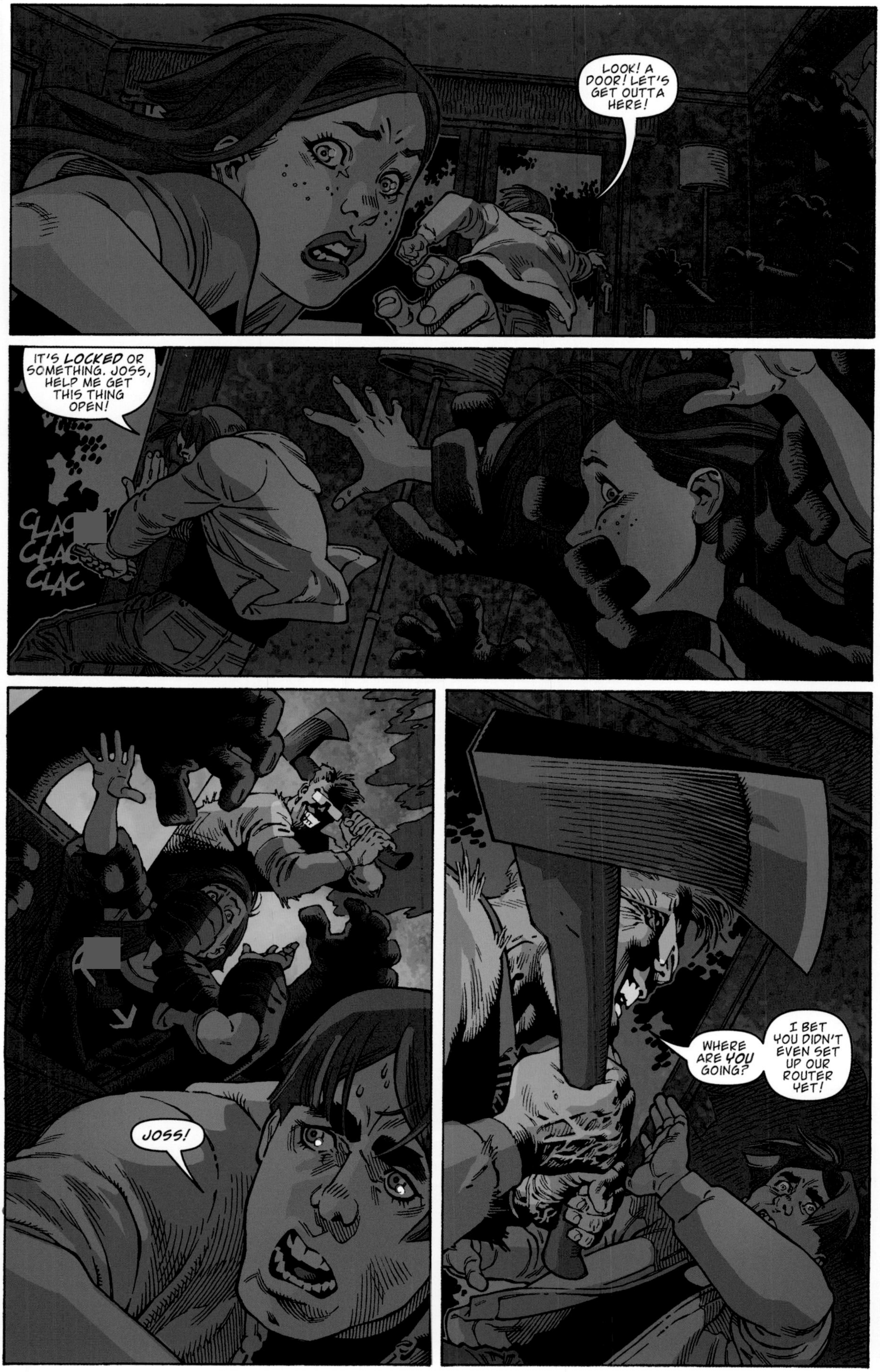
LOOK! A DOOR! LET'S GET OUTTA HERE!
IT'S LOCKED OR SOMETHING. JOSS, HELP ME GET THIS THING OPEN!
CLAC
JOSS!
WHERE ARE YOU GOING?
I BET YOU DIDN'T EVEN SET UP OUR ROUTER YET!

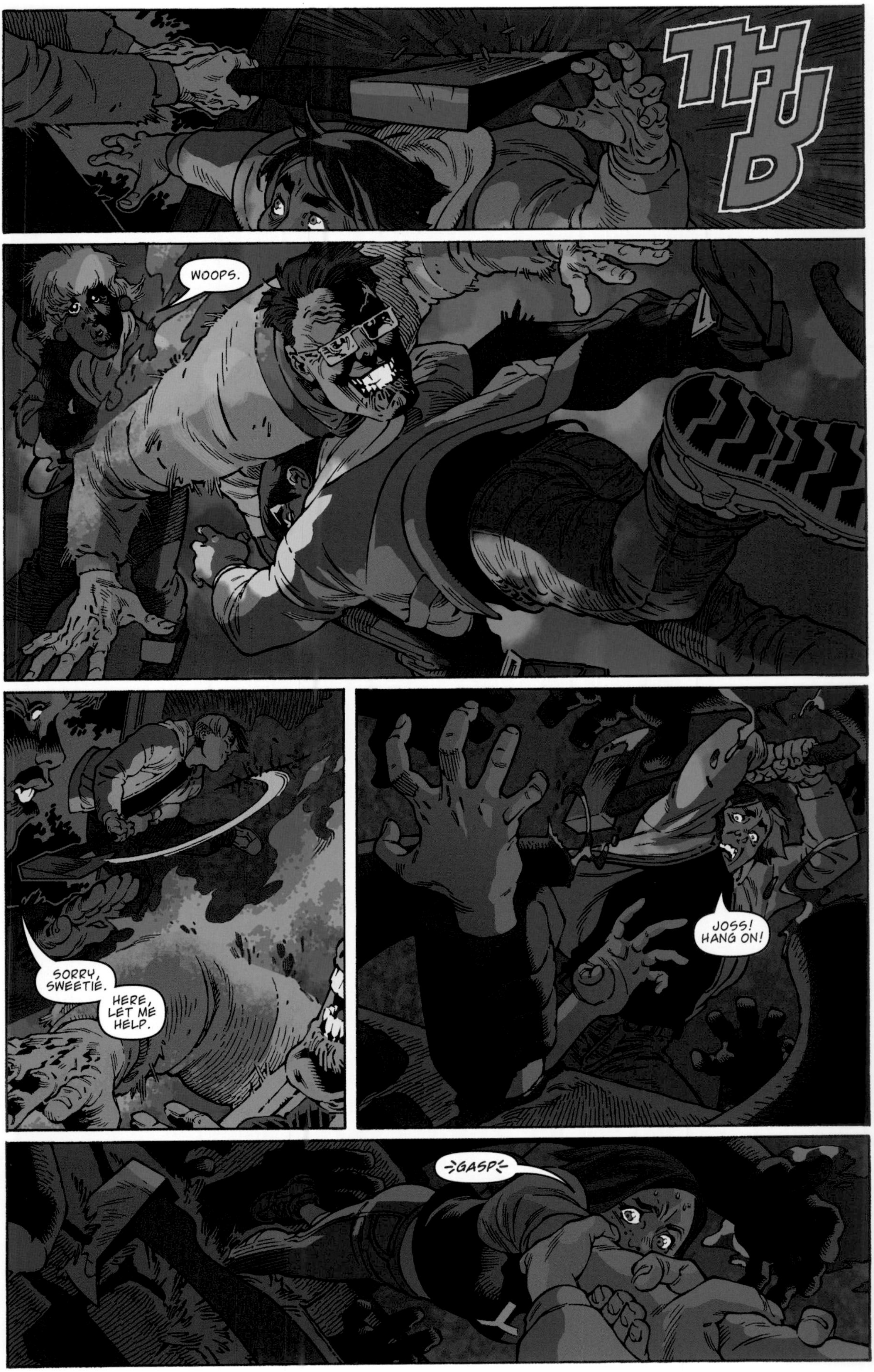
THUD
WOOPS.
SORRY, SWEETIE.
HERE, LET ME HELP.
JOSS! HANG ON!
GASP

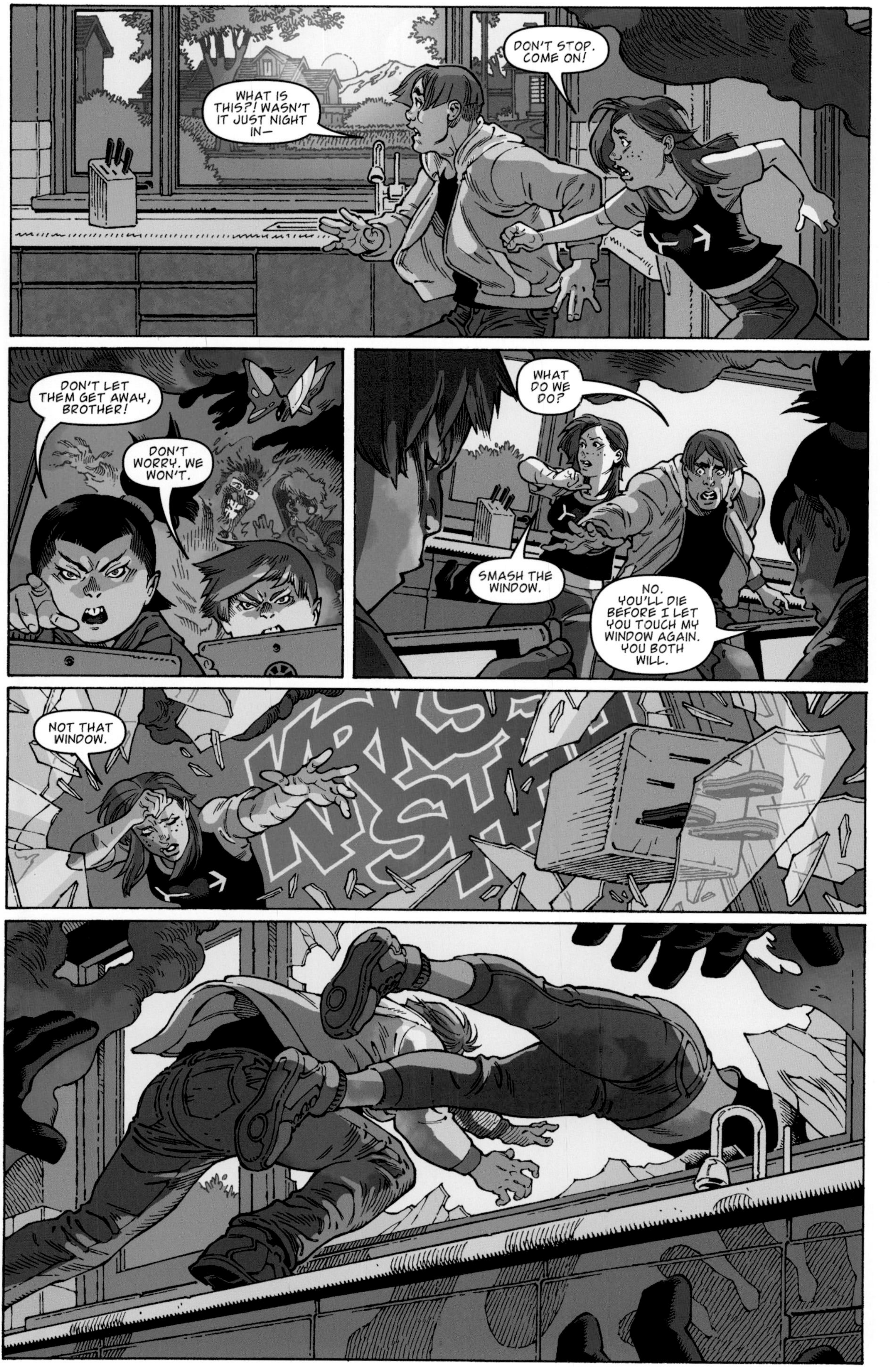
WHAT IS THIS?! WASN'T IT JUST NIGHT IN—
DON'T STOP. COME ON!
DON'T LET THEM GET AWAY, BROTHER!
DON'T WORRY. WE WON'T.
WHAT DO WE DO?
SMASH THE WINDOW.
NO. YOU'LL DIE BEFORE I LET YOU TOUCH MY WINDOW AGAIN. YOU BOTH WILL.
NOT THAT WINDOW.

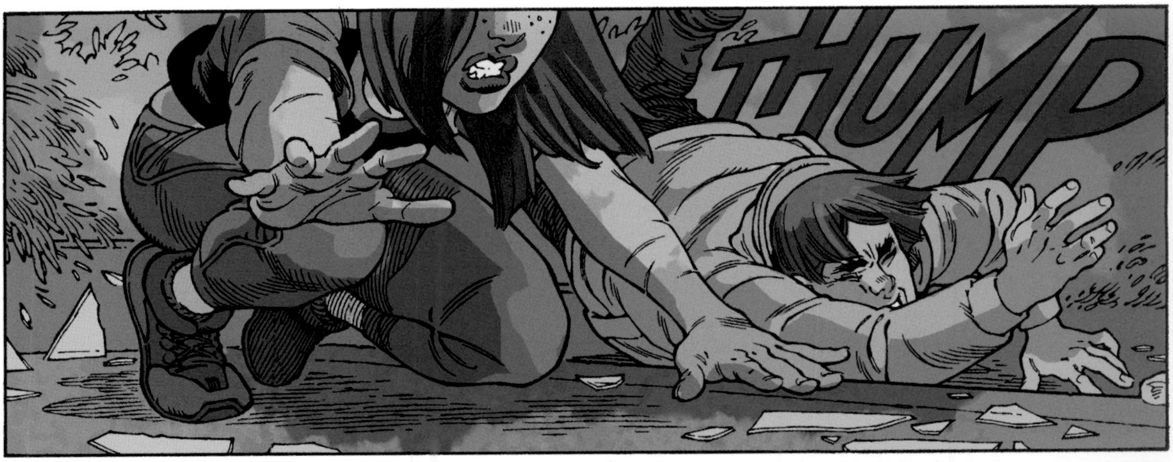
THUMP

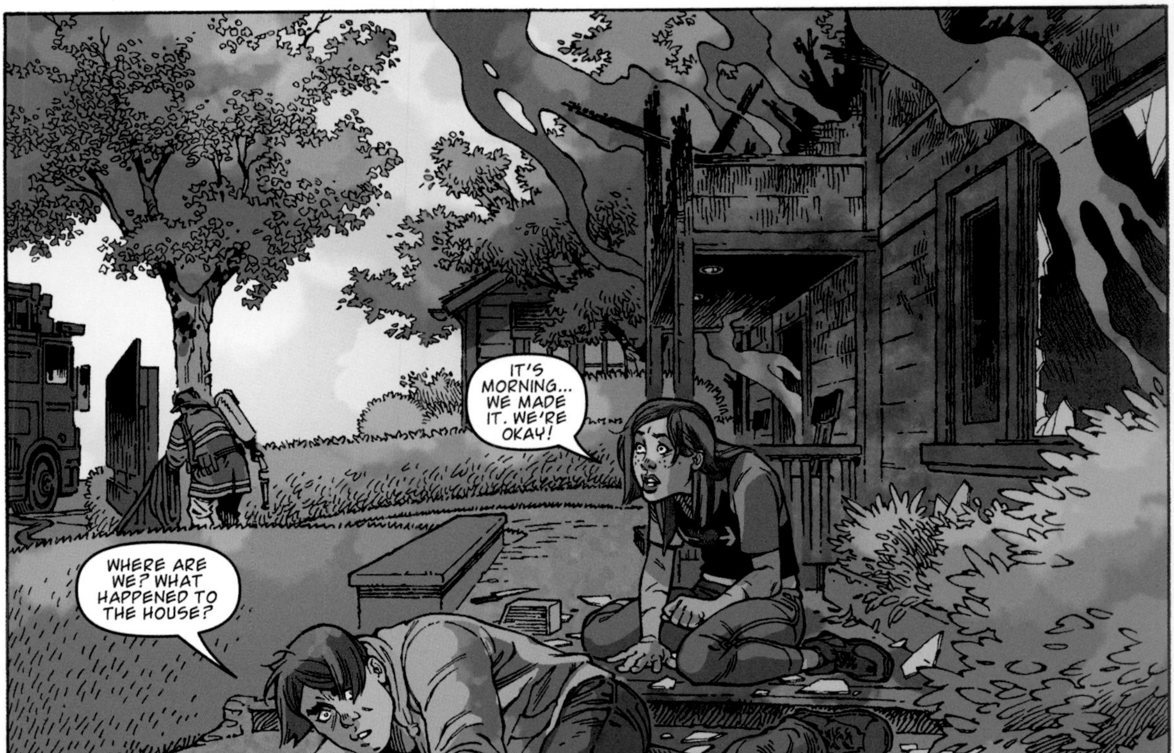
IT'S MORNING... WE MADE IT. WE'RE OKAY!
WHERE ARE WE? WHAT HAPPENED TO THE HOUSE?

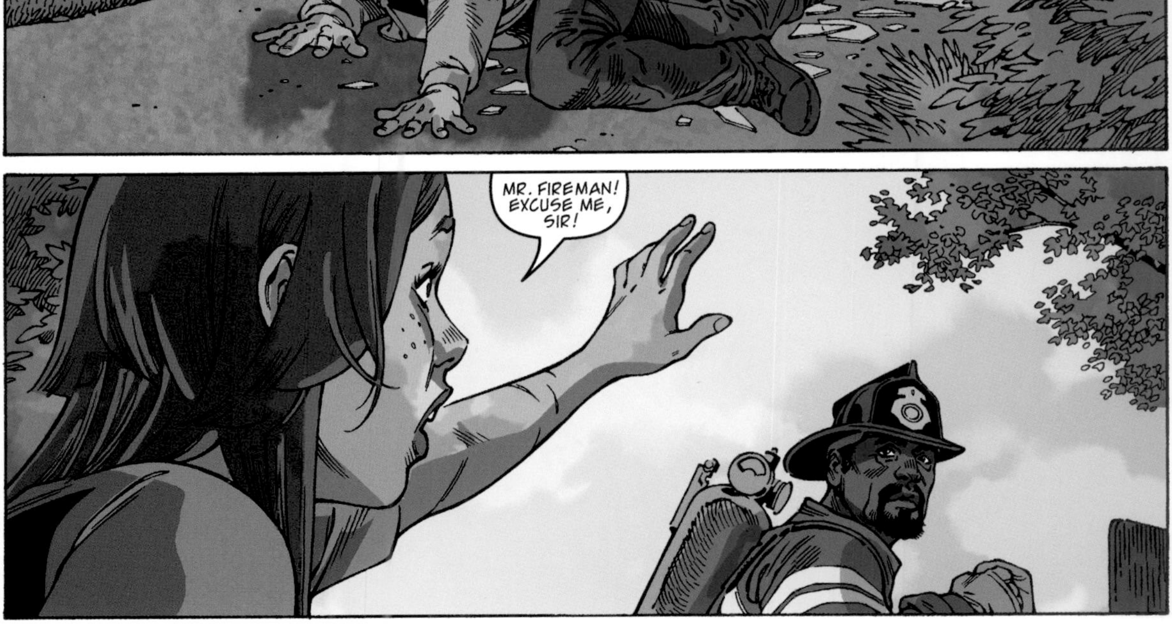
MR. FIREMAN! EXCUSE ME, SIR!

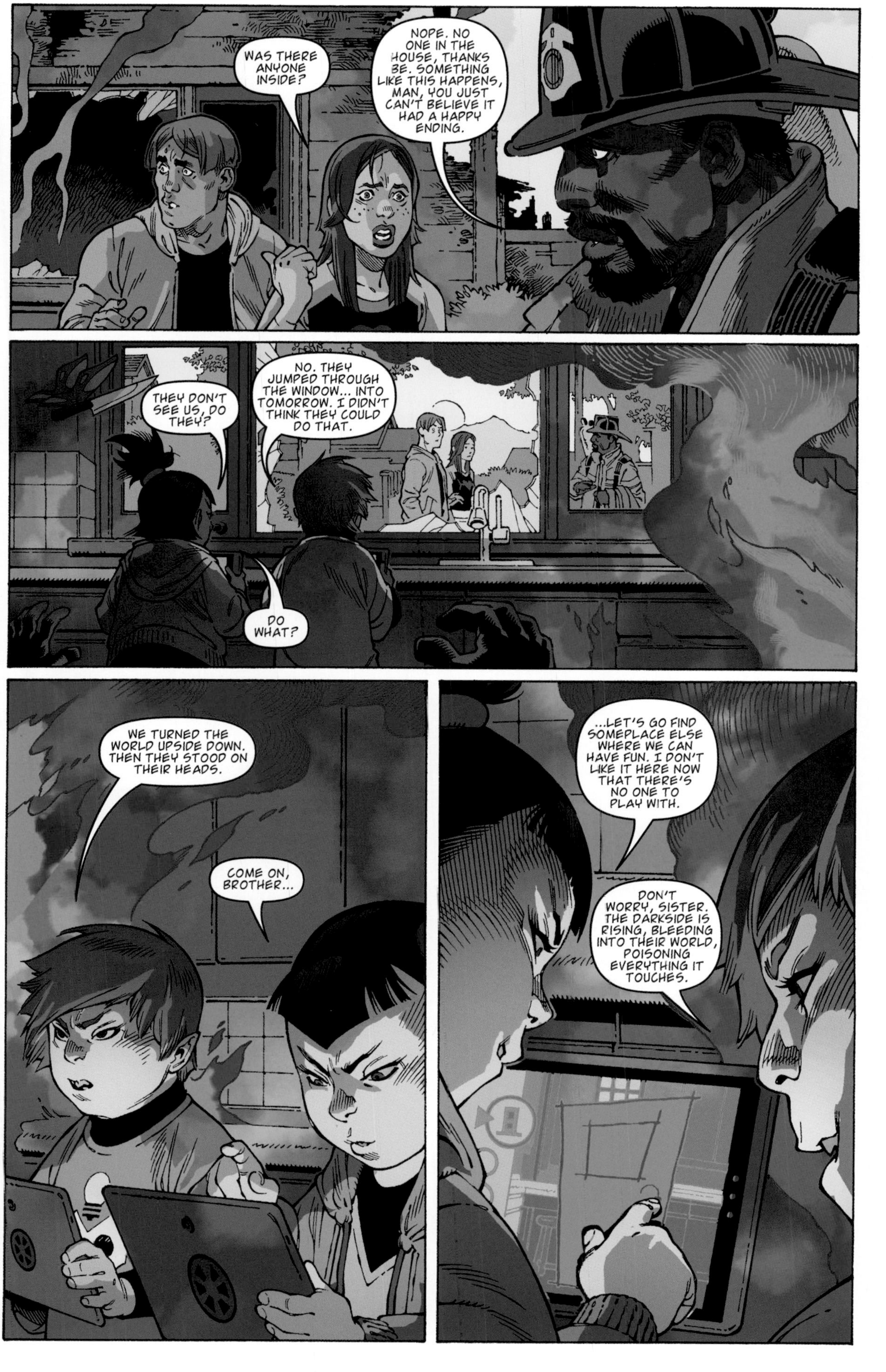
WAS THERE ANYONE INSIDE?
NOPE. NO ONE IN THE HOUSE, THANKS BE. SOMETHING LIKE THIS HAPPENS, MAN, YOU JUST CAN'T BELIEVE IT HAD A HAPPY ENDING.
THEY DON'T SEE US, DO THEY?
NO. THEY JUMPED THROUGH THE WINDOW... INTO TOMORROW. I DIDN'T THINK THEY COULD DO THAT.
DO WHAT?
WE TURNED THE WORLD UPSIDE DOWN. THEN THEY STOOD ON THEIR HEADS.
COME ON, BROTHER...
...LET'S GO FIND SOMEPLACE ELSE WHERE WE CAN HAVE FUN. I DON'T LIKE IT HERE NOW THAT THERE'S NO ONE TO PLAY WITH.
DON'T WORRY, SISTER. THE DARKSIDE IS RISING, BLEEDING INTO THEIR WORLD, POISONING EVERYTHING IT TOUCHES.

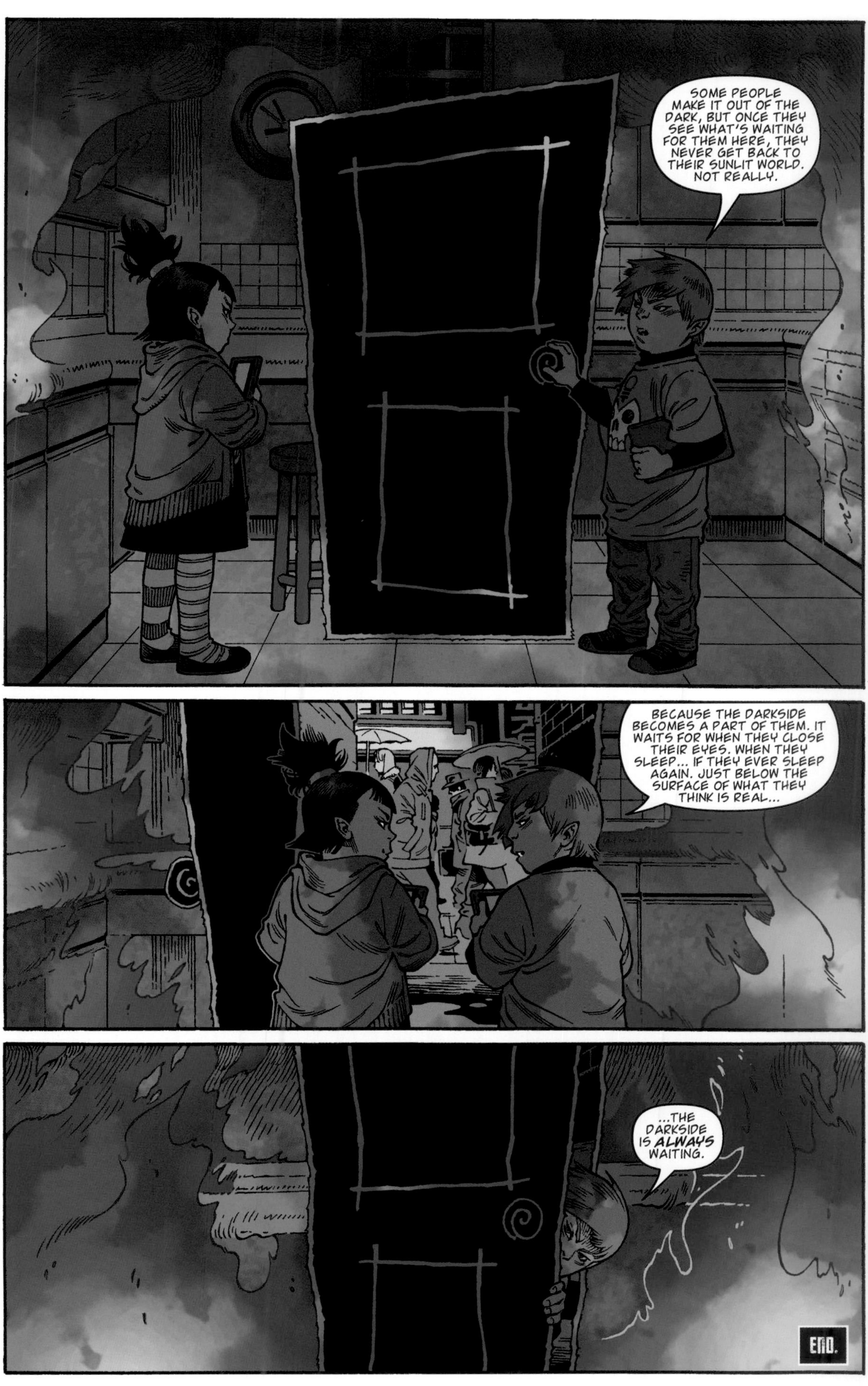
SOME PEOPLE MAKE IT OUT OF THE DARK, BUT ONCE THEY SEE WHAT'S WAITING FOR THEM HERE, THEY NEVER GET BACK TO THEIR SUNLIT WORLD. NOT REALLY.
BECAUSE THE DARKSIDE BECOMES A PART OF THEM. IT WAITS FOR WHEN THEY CLOSE THEIR EYES. WHEN THEY SLEEP... IF THEY EVER SLEEP AGAIN. JUST BELOW THE SURFACE OF WHAT THEY THINK IS REAL...
...THE DARKSIDE IS ALWAYS WAITING.
END.

TALES FROM THE DARKSIDE

COVER GALLERY

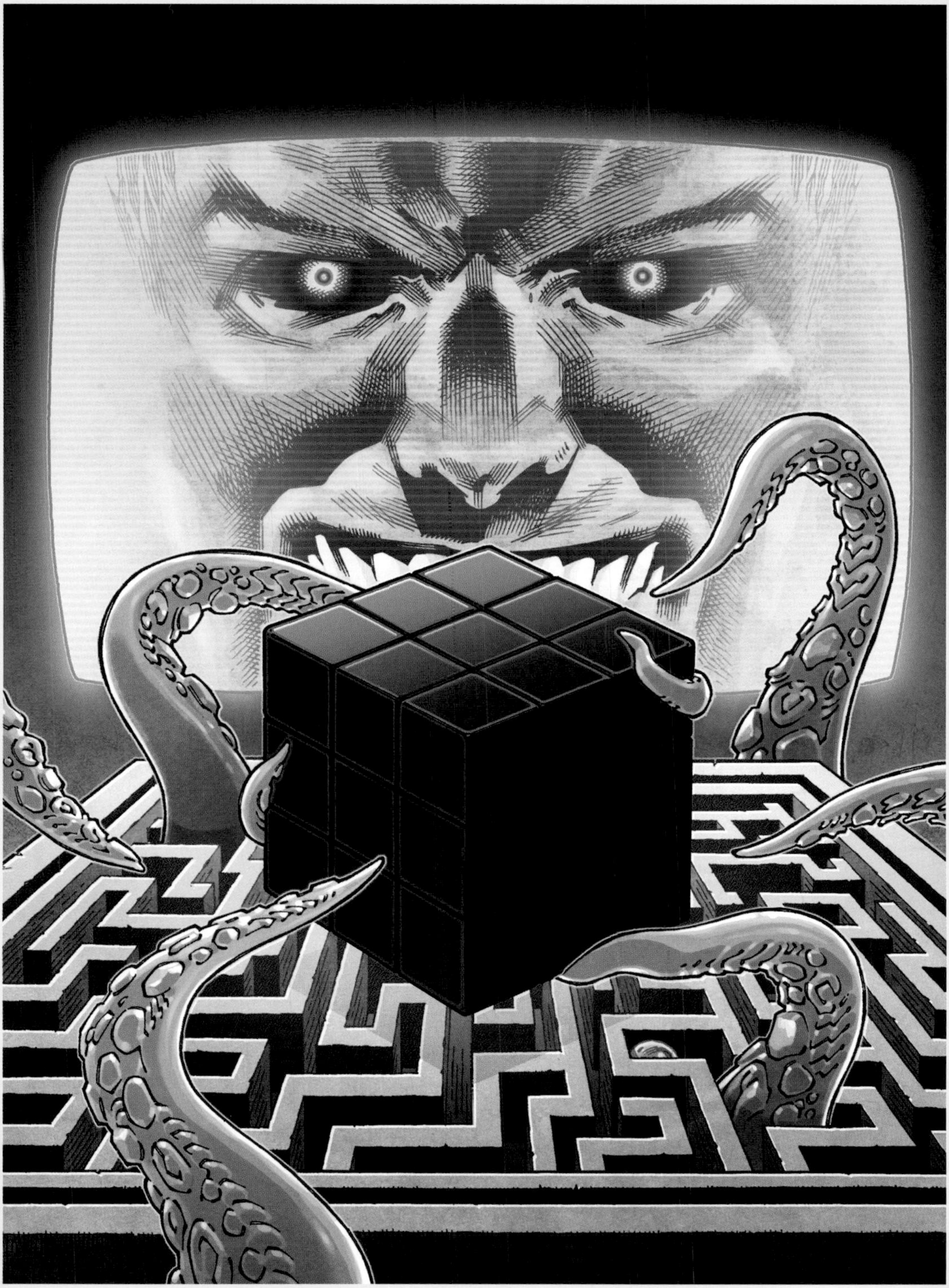

ART BY GABRIEL RODRIGUEZ

NEXT PAGE: ART BY CHARLES PAUL WILSON III

ART BY BEN TEMPLESMITH

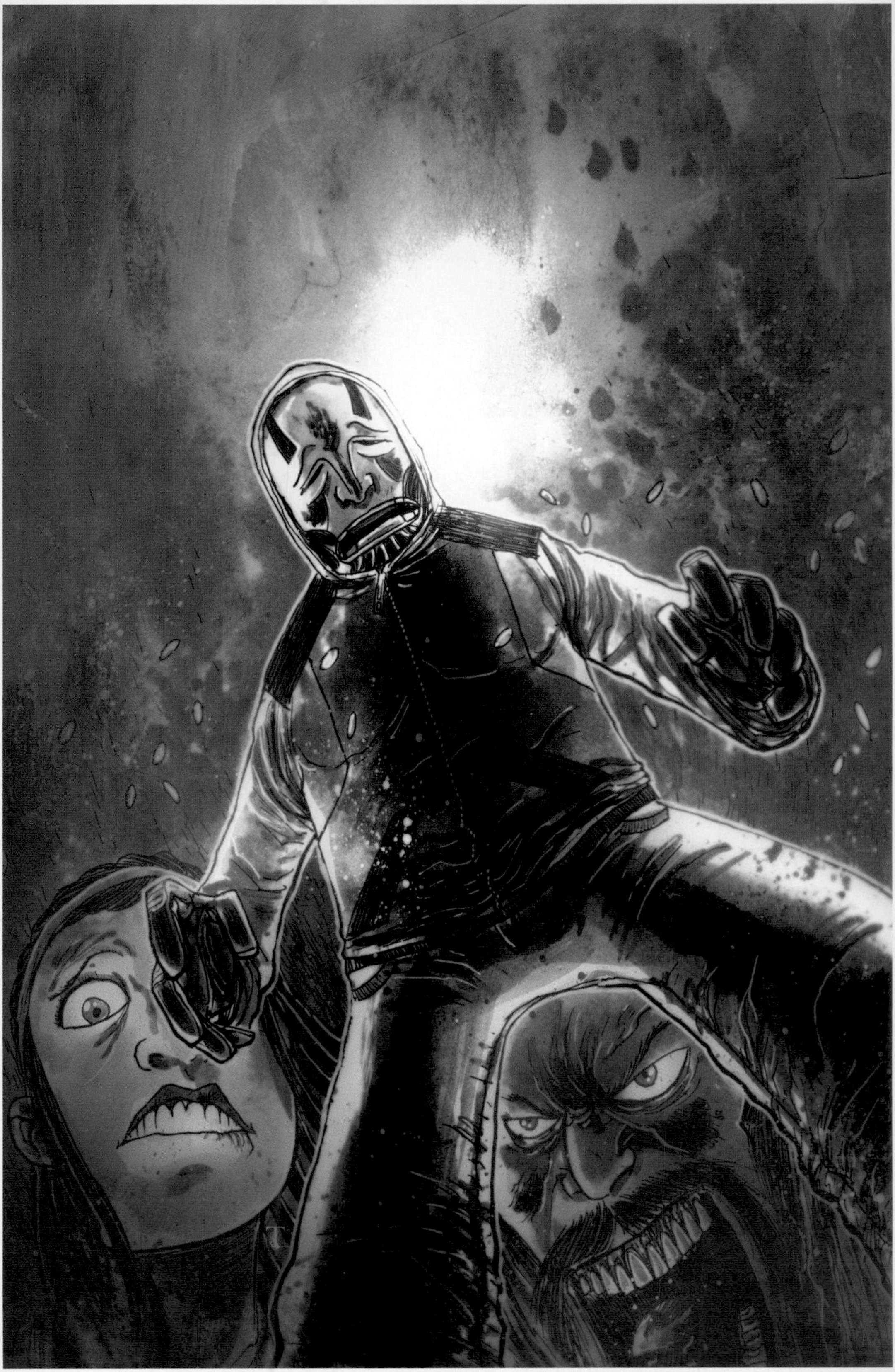

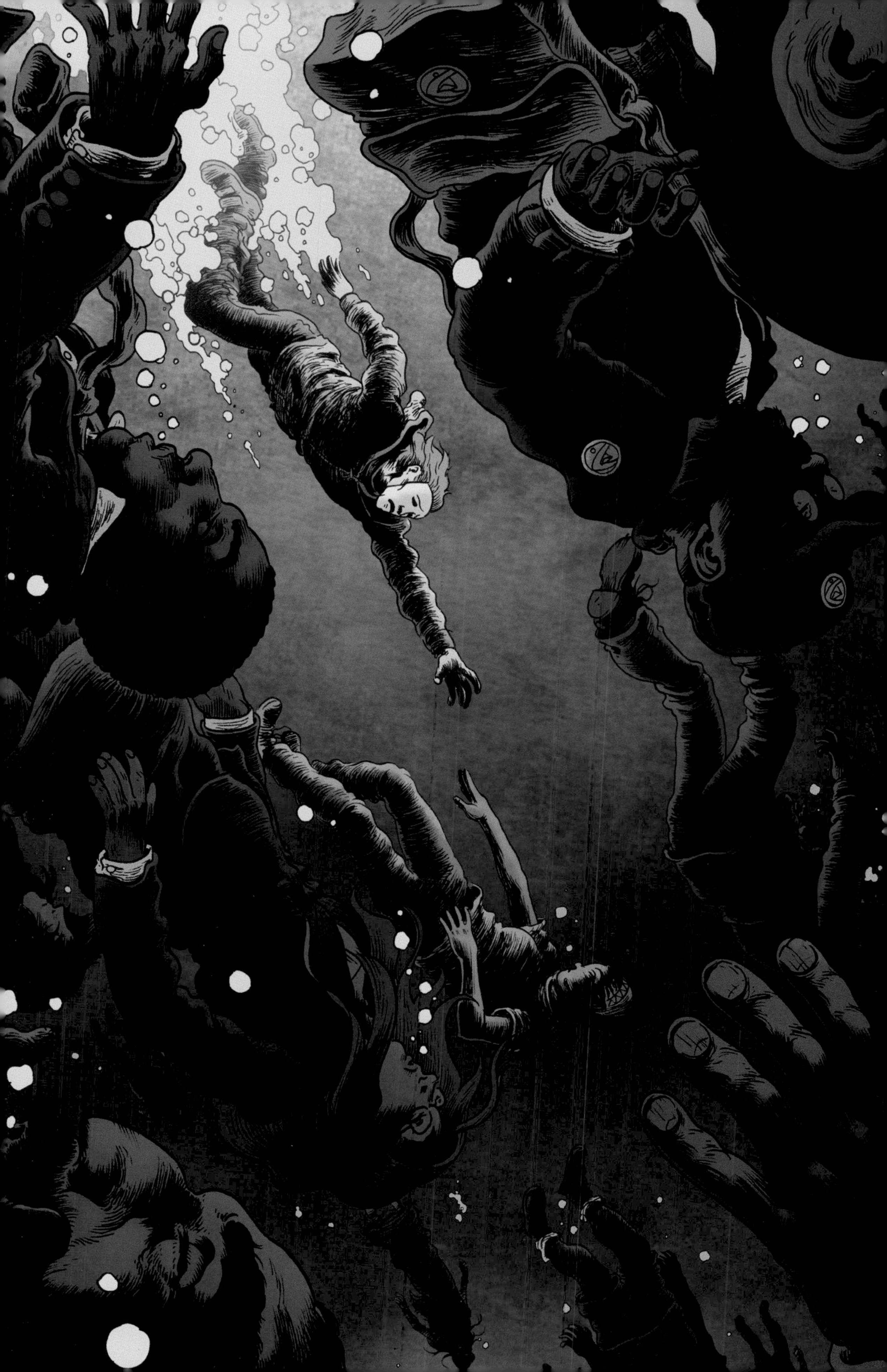

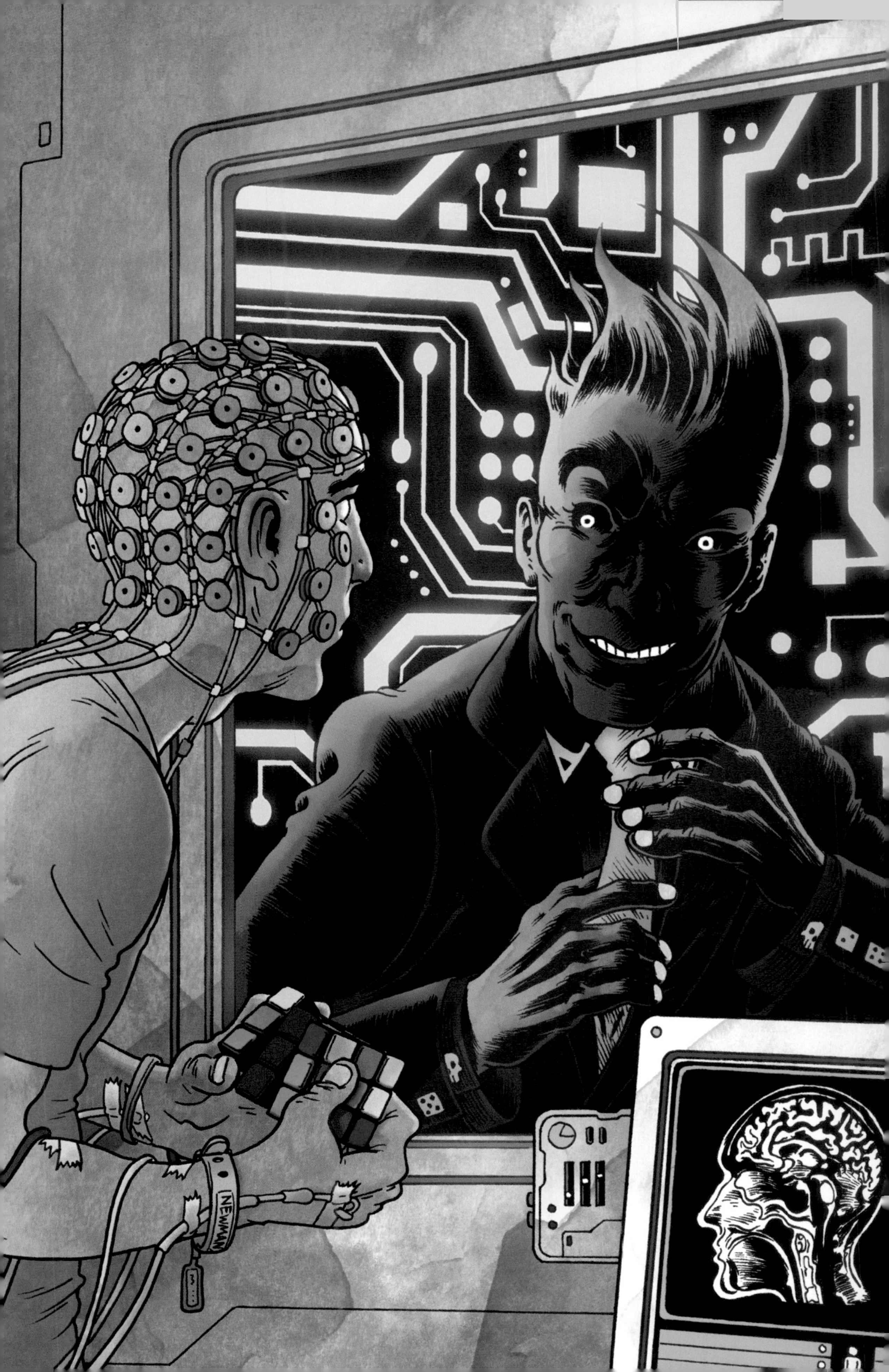
NEWMAN

PREVIOUS PAGE: ART BY CHARLES PAUL WILSON III

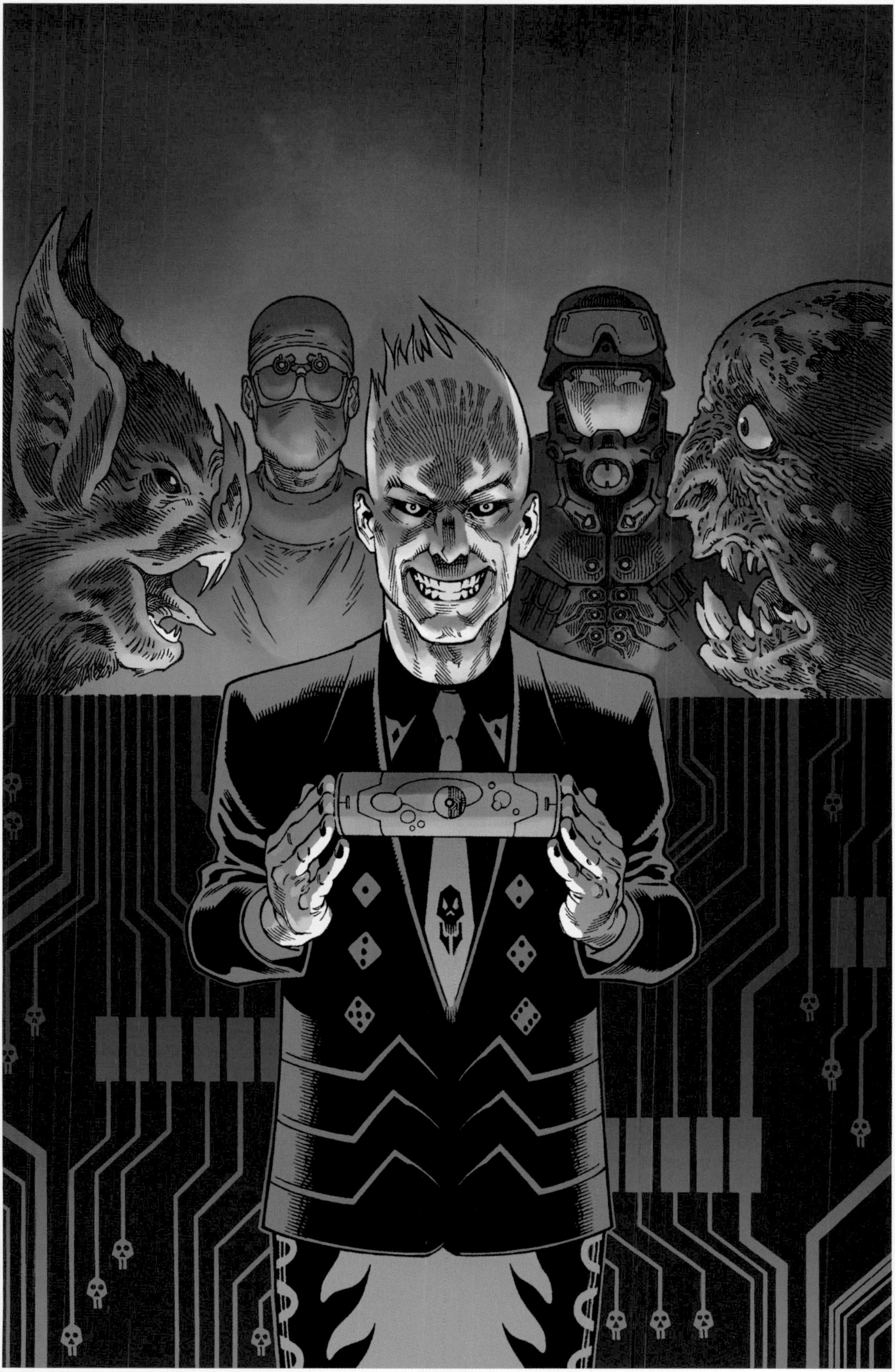

ART BY GABRIEL RODRIGUEZ
COLORS BY RYAN HILL

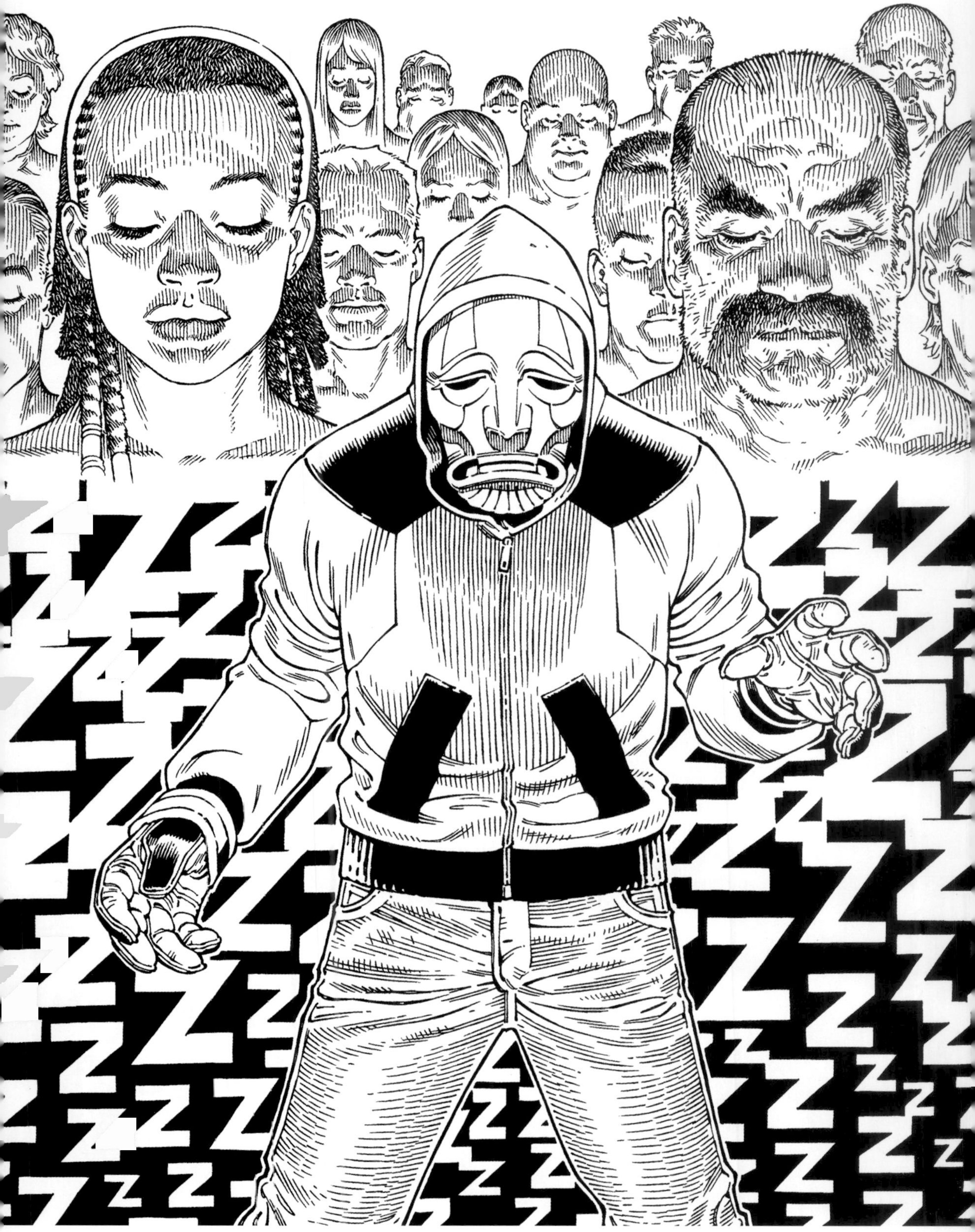

ART BY GABRIEL RODRIGUEZ

ART BY GABRIEL RODRIGUEZ

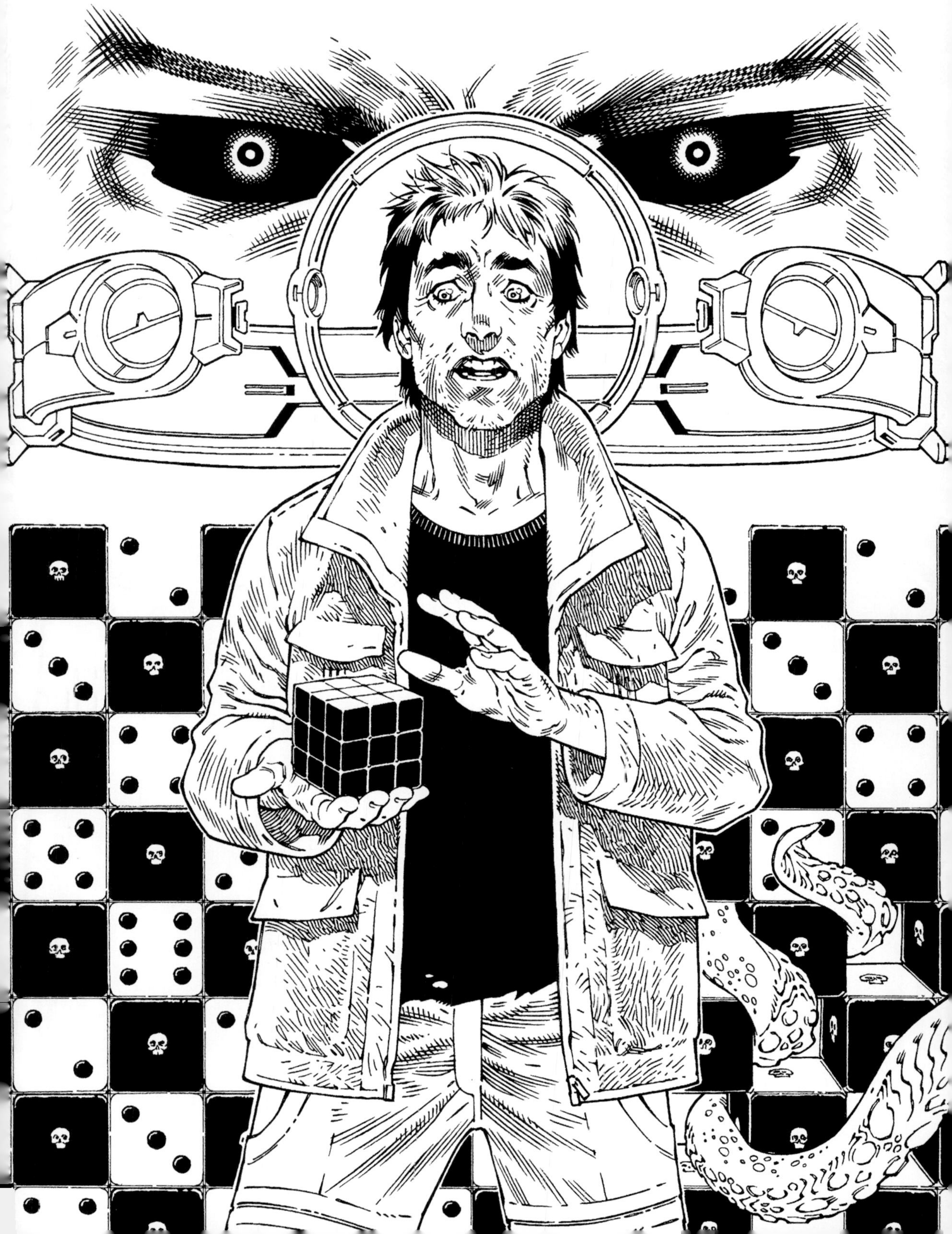

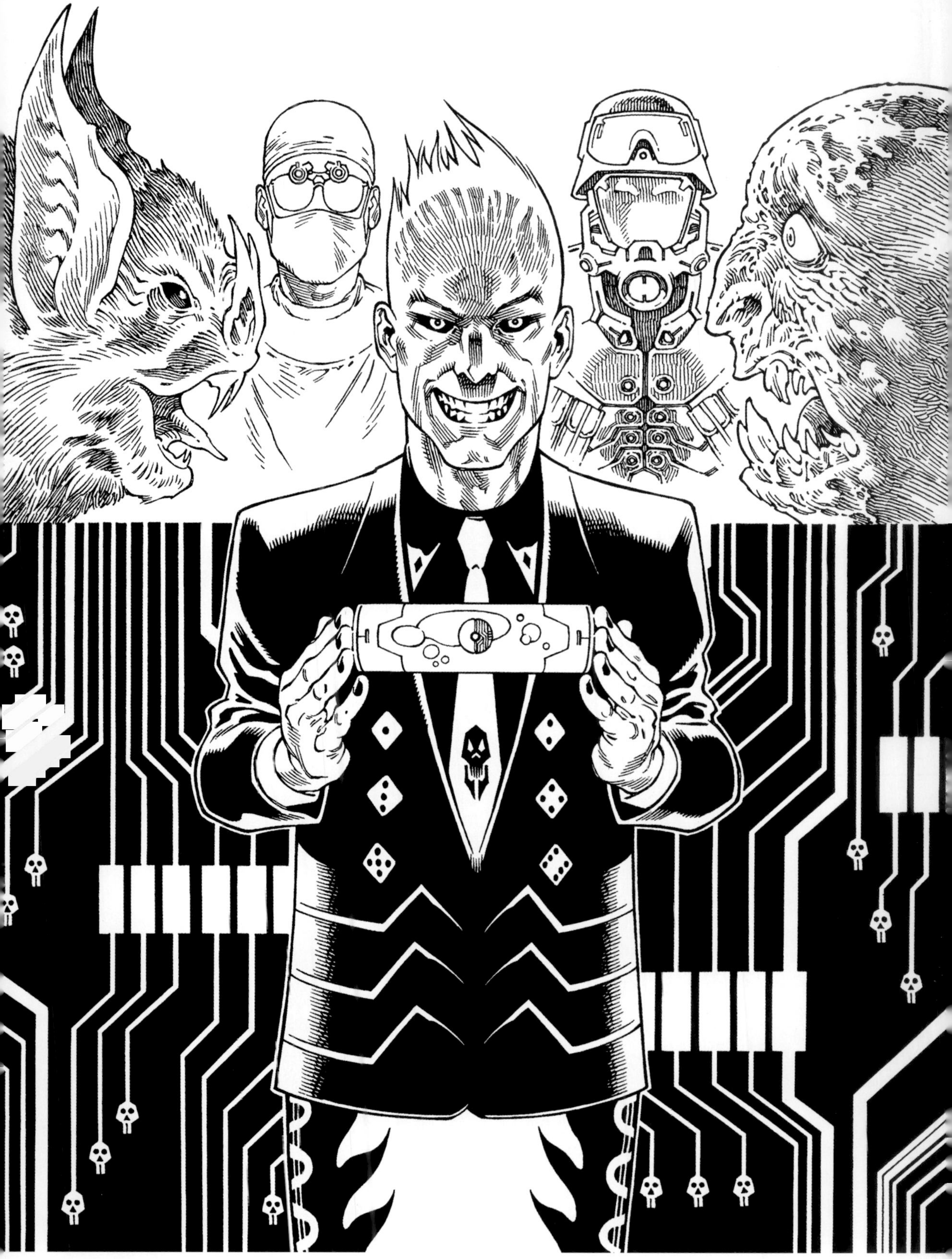

ART BY GABRIEL RODRIGUEZ

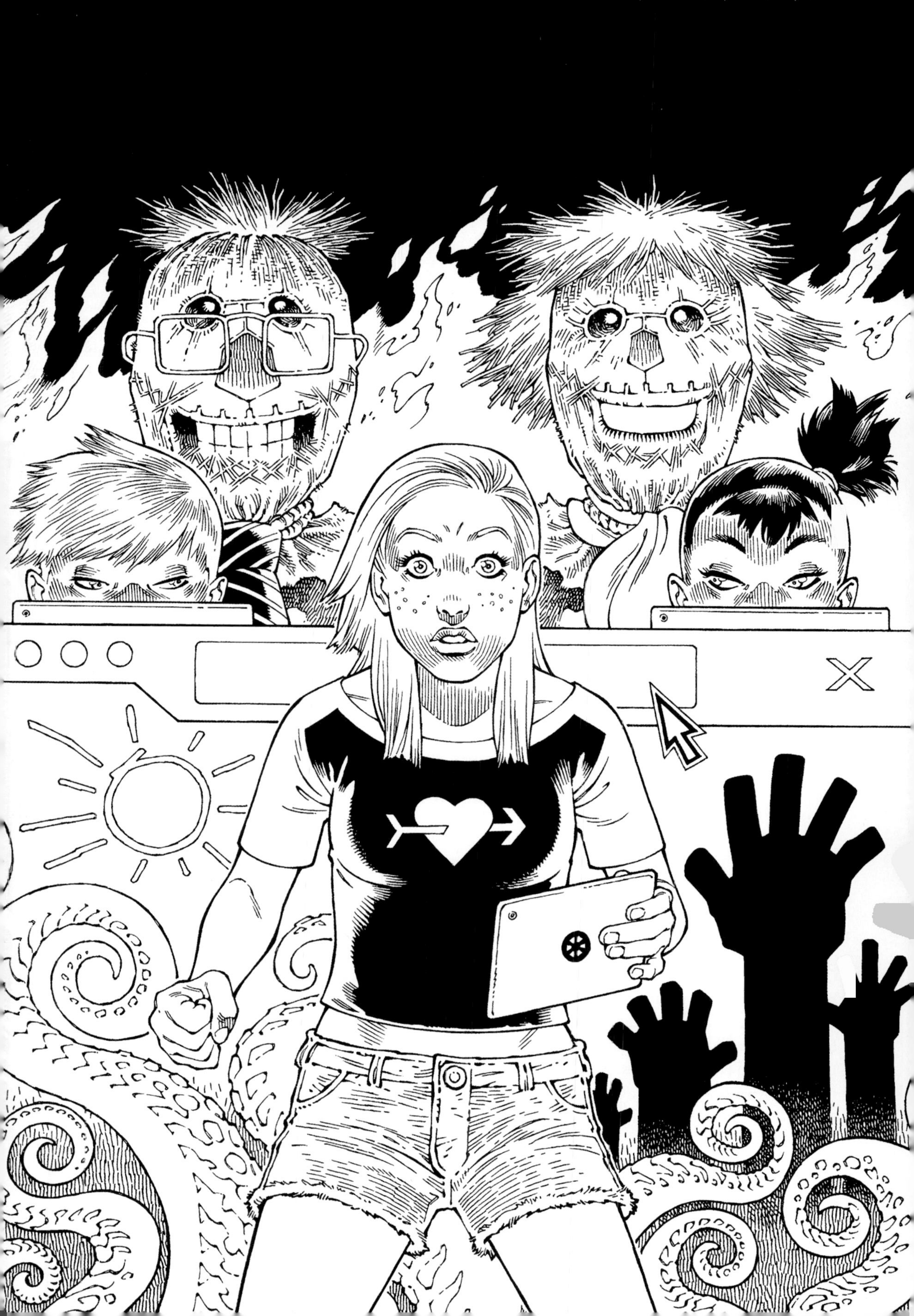

ART BY GABRIEL RODRIGUEZ

MAN LIVES IN THE SUNLIT WORLD OF
WHAT HE BELIEVES TO BE REALITY.
BUT... THERE IS, UNSEEN BY MOST,
AN UNDERWORLD,
A PLACE THAT IS JUST AS REAL,
BUT NOT AS BRIGHTLY LIT... A DARKSIDE.

TELLING TALES: A DARKSIDE CHAT WITH JOE HILL AND GABRIEL RODRíGUEZ
By Brian Truitt

What was special about the original *Tales from the Darkside* for you guys growing up and how does it factor into your take?

Rodríguez: What movies like *Star Wars* or *Close Encounters* did for us in setting standards for science fiction, TV series like *Tales from the Darkside* and *The Twilight Zone* did for our love and fascination for horror, mystery, and dark, twisted fantasy. They were a first glimpse into those wider, weirder universes that challenged everyone's mind and fed more curious and inquisitive imaginations.

That early approach was never matched in any other medium for us until the golden age of Vertigo comics, in titles like *Swamp Thing*, *Sandman* and *Hellblazer*, and on TV probably until the first four seasons of the original *X-Files*. So, with that background, how not to pay them all tribute in a project like this one.

In a way, these "Tales from the Darkside" are a heartfelt tribute to Romero, Zerling, Moore, Wrightson, Gaiman, Totleben and everyone that back then took our hands to lead us into an inwards journey to the human heart, through parallel dimensions' gates into impossible new worlds.

Are the stories contained in the comic all from the bagged TV show or are there new ones you penned just for this medium?

Hill: Yeah—this is the show that could've been. There was a lot more where that came from. *Darkside* was structured to have the scope of *Locke & Key,* but for television instead of comics. It had a vast underlying mythology, and a plan for three solid seasons.

The original *Tales from the Darkside* was a fun, bleak little spin on the *Twilight Zone* style anthology. My idea, because the CW paid me a lot of money, was to give them a little more. Every story was meant to stand alone, but gradually, you would come to see how they all connected, to tell a single larger story. Unfortunately, the comic will only be able to give readers a taste of that—the larger picture only exists as a sketch.

One of the great things about your work together on *Locke & Key* is that it was a horror book but about much more thematically down deep. Is there some of that in these *Darkside* tales or is there more emphasis on the scary stuff?

Rodríguez: The great thing about horror stories, as we explored in *Locke & Key* and will try to do as well here, in the *Darkside*, is the potential to create gripping, thrilling stories while talking about deeply human subjects and concerns. Where *Locke & Key* was fundamentally epic, *Tales from the Darkside* is like an unexpected exploration trip. And for this trip to be interesting and worthy, the key is to be able to build, in a very short space, appealing, flawed, believable characters to relate to and walk along with in this dark, twisted, and fun exploration of the unknown. To be able to stand next to them and feel their struggle and understand their changes, to suffer with their mistakes and cheer in their attempts of heroism in sudden upside down environments of horrible surprises and very, VERY dark humor.

Joe has a unique ability to write such characters, to give them a voice and soul. And for me and everyone else in the team it's a pleasure and a thrilling challenge to give them flesh